Authentic Listening and Discussion for Advanced Students

Instructor's Manual

Jayne Gaunt Leshinsky

 Prentice Hall Regents
Upper Saddle River, New Jersey 07458

VP/Editorial Director: *Arley Gray*
Manager Development Services: *Louisa Hellegers*
Development Editor: *Gino Mastascusa*
Director of Production and Manufacturing: *Aliza Greenblatt*
Editorial Production/Design Manager: *Dominick Mosco*
Editorial/Production Supervision and Interior Design: *Dit Mosco*
Manufacturing Manager: *Ray Keating*

Printed in the United States of America
10 9 8 7 6 5 4 3 2 1

ISBN 0-13-371717-8

Prentice-Hall International (UK) Limited, *London*
Prentice-Hall of Australia Pty. Limited, *Sydney*
Prentice-Hall Canada Inc., *Toronto*
Prentice-Hall Hispanoamericana, S.A., *Mexico*
Prentice-Hall of India Private Limited, *New Delhi*
Prentice-Hall of Japan, Inc., *Tokyo*
Simon & Schuster Asia Pte. Ltd., *Singapore*
Editora Prentice-Hall do Brasil, Ltda., *Rio de Janeiro*

CONTENTS

Answer Key

Audio Transcripts

HOW TO USE THIS BOOK

The Introductory Chapter is the best place to begin to familiarize your students with characteristics of spoken English, such as relaxed speech, stressed words, and fillers. These concepts and others are referred to throughout the chapters, especially in the "Differences between spoken and written English" sections.

The remaining units and chapters can be selected using the following guidelines:

1. PRE-LISTEN

Pre-listen to the selections for the chapter in order to help you choose which selections will challenge your students, and which ones might be too difficult. As you become more familiar with the content of the book and tapes, you'll be able to choose the selections and activities which will suit your students' abilities and level of comprehension. This is <u>not</u> a book that you can walk into class with, turn on the tape, and pull off the perfect lesson without advance preparation.

2. PICK AND CHOOSE

a) Chapters within a unit

The chapters in each unit are arranged by theme. Because the chapters and selections in this text are <u>not</u> arranged in order of difficulty, you can skip around. One option is to choose selections and activities from a variety of chapters which work on a certain skill (notetaking, or understanding the use of analogy). Another option, depending on the length of your course, is to work through one chapter in each unit; if time allows, you can go back at a later point and work through another chapter of a unit which students were particularly interested in. Because classes differ in ability, as you become more familiar with the selections and speakers, you'll find you can choose chapters and selections based on what will challenge the general level of that particular class. Each unit begins with some activities to introduce the vocabulary, the main themes of the unit, and in some units, a short selection to introduce the main speaker so that the students can become familiar with his or her voice. No matter which chapter you first choose from the unit, I recommend you begin with the material at the beginning of the unit to build a framework for the chapter.

If your students are living in the U.S., poll your students as to how many of them own or plan to buy a car, and how many rent (or plan to rent) an apartment during their stay in the U.S. If there's a significant number, Unit 2 "Cars and Driving" and Unit 7 "Renting an Apartment" will be of high interest.

b) Selections within a chapter

The cassette tape icon indicates each time the tape should be rewound to the beginning of the selection; remember to reset the tape counter to 000 when you begin a new selection or make a note in the margin as you begin a new selection. This will make rewinding quick and efficient. Some selections are self-contained; others are excerpts of an interview or conversation which continue through more than one selection. These are noted at the beginning of the selection, and in the tapescripts. Many chapters do build on skills and ideas introduced early in the chapter, especially the "Keys to better comprehension" activities.

c) Activities within a selection

Again, depending on the level of your class, you don't have to do every activity written for a selection. If you have a few students with listening comprehension skills that are significantly lower or higher than the rest of the class, you can have them do one listening activity while others in the class are doing a different one—both groups are listening to the same selection but working on different activities. Use your judgment; once you are familiar with the selections and activities, you'll know if an activity is too hard or too easy for your class.

3. DEALING WITH A WIDE RANGE OF ABILITIES

I have indicated that this book can be used with students with a fairly broad range of listening comprehension, as is typical of intermediate and advanced level courses. At these levels, some students have strong grammar knowledge or reading skills, but are still weak in listening comprehension; conversely, others are strong in listening and weak in reading and writing.

To deal with a class with a wide range, I may have some students do one activity, while others work on another, simultaneously listening to the same selection. Or as in the case of note-taking exercises, you can challenge the more advanced students by telling them to close their books rather than use the outline given in the text.

4. CLASSES WITH HIGH-INTERMEDIATE LISTENING COMPREHENSION

When a class on the whole has a lower range of listening comprehension ability, choose easier, shorter selections or supplement with more reading and discussion material (or a portion of the tapescript copied from the Instructor's Manual) before the listening component of the lesson. While listening (for main ideas, for specific information, etc.), pause the tape more, allowing them to hear the answer or sentence again in their mind before responding, writing, etc.

Keep the tapescript at hand for:

1. quick reference to students' questions or comments:

> Student: "I heard ...?"

> Teacher: "Yes, what he said was..."

2. to help students anticipate information when they are having difficulty:

> "Listen for _____ in this next part..."

3. to identify vocabulary, idioms, occurrences of relaxed pronunciation, grammatical structures, etc. other than those which have been highlighted in the text.

USING DICTATIONS

If you've never used dictations in your teaching, give these a try. You'll find dictations reinforce spelling, punctuation, grammatical structures and vocabulary, especially if you take time to lead the students through an investigation of those structures and uses. Using a dictation which the students have not read or heard before is also a good diagnostic tool for the instructor. It points out pronunciation difficulties (i.e. students who don't pronounce a final -s tend not to hear and write the final -s in dictation) as well as comprehension errors. The listening exercises which call for students to listen and circle one of three word choices in parentheses as they listen were adapted from student answers when those paragraphs were given in dictation. The incorrect words may seem incredible, but students who do not use context well to check their comprehension really do write "horses" when the context has nothing to do with animals!

The process: Assign a dictation for a quiz a few days later, explaining how and why to study the assigned paragraph. For a dictation quiz, read the paragraph in phrases twice, and then once without pauses. Tape yourself reading the dictation and give the tape to a student assigned to be the "dictator" for the next quiz. For a score, divide the number of words spelled correctly by the number of total words (given in parentheses in the dictation exercise). Let students set their own goals for what correctness percentage they want to achieve by the end of the course. For dictations of more than 100 words or if time is limited, I ask the students to prepare the entire dictation, but I only dictate part of it for the quiz.

Another technique used in some of the exercises is to dictate the material only once or twice, perhaps at normal speed, and allow partners and/or small groups time to reconstruct the original.

CLOZE LISTENING EXERCISES

If a student is having difficulty with a cloze/listening exercise, it is usually due more to not being able to read as fast as the speaker talks rather than difficulty with hearing the word to fill in the blank. If this is the case, pause the tape more. Or use copies or an overhead of tapescripts to give students more practice in reading faster, i.e. reading as fast as the speaker talks.

LISTENING JOURNAL

Listening journal assignments give the students opportunity to reflect on what they have listened to, and to tie listening and writing skills together. In addition, students can keep a listening journal similar to the dialogue journals or reading logs popular in current methodology. I require students to listen to 30 minutes of English (TV, radio, video, film, lecture, sermon, etc.) three times a week, and write notes, a summary, and/or reaction in the notebook submitted weekly. I provide a list of recommended programs, movies, etc. with days, channels/stations, times, etc. and point out programs when the content of a TV program or movie is relevant to the theme of a chapter we will be working on. I also mention unsuitable entries (MTV, some game and video contest shows, sports, etc.) Students frequently go to movies or rent videos for a journal entry, even though one movie is four times the amount of required listening for one entry, because they are highly motivated to understand American movies and culture.

Answer Key
Introductory Chapter

RELAXED PRONUNCIATION

REDUCTIONS, P. 1

Dictate the following sentences with the relaxed pronunciation shown:

1. Are they required to show 'im or not?   *(him)*
2. I made several requests to have 'em removed.   *(them)*
3. I said, "I can't believe I was going that fast," 'cause I know I wasn't. *(because)*
4. Some uh this you can't change.   *(of)*
5. There's a couple uh things I'd really like to emphasize.   *(of) (I would)*

MORE REDUCTIONS, P. 2

Dictate the following sentences with the relaxed pronunciation shown:

6. Two adults hafta be working together.   *(have to)*
7. Her mind is on the next thing that hasta be done.   *(has to)*
8. We may wanna talk about it more next time.   *(want to)*
9. You're gonna ask a question that we get asked a lot.   *(You are) (going to)*
10. I was gonna save quite a bit of money.   *(going to)*
11. I gotta tell you something.   *(got to)*

(FORMAL STRUCTURE,) P. 3

I gotta tell you something. → I <u>have to</u> tell you something.
I gotta tell you this and I've said it before... → I <u>have to</u> tell you this and <u>I have</u> said it before...
They've gotta be satisfied. → They <u>have to</u> be satisfied. or They <u>have got to</u> be satisfied.

CONTRACTIONS, P. 4

Dictate the following sentences with the relaxed pronunciation shown:

1. That's the way it <u>should've</u> been in the first place.   *(should have)*
2. It <u>would've</u> been nice if you could've know that earlier.   *(would have)*
3. I wish I <u>would've</u> seen this coming.   *(would have)*
4. <u>I'da</u> gone if I <u>could've</u>.   *(I would have) (could have)*
5. If you have a fuel-injected car, <u>it'll</u> sit on top of that.   *(it will)*
6. <u>That'll</u> invite people to be more honest with you.   *(that will)*
7. Maybe <u>it'd</u> be a good idea to have a book.   *(it would)*

8. They'd throw me out if I'm late. (they would) (I am)

9. It seems unlikely that you'd try to cheat them. (you would)

CONSONANT SUBSTITUTION, P. 5

Dictate the following sentences with the relaxed pronunciation shown:

1. I'll betcha there's not a whole lot you can do about it. (I will), (bet you), (there is)

2. Didja know that marriage was coming? (did you)

3. Couldja tell us who generally takes this program? (could you)

4. Actually he dudn't have to do anything. (doesn't → does not)

5. Romance does make life better, dudn't it? (doesn't → does not)

FILLERS, P. 8

Answers will vary.

1. Also because it's not just the squirrels. ("just" is not a filler here.)

2. Did you sit down and say, "I want to picture my life 15 years from now?"

3. It's similar to many people's experience when they start to buy a new car.

4. You're going to have a beautiful relationship.

5. If he blows you off (→ *disregards you*), you had better find someone to help you, because you are going to have to (→ *need to*) take charge of what you need out of this marriage.

6. If she had wanted to get remarried, she would have gotten married despite what I was doing.

Unit 1
ETHNIC CUISINE

VOCABULARY PREVIEW, P. 16

PART 1:

1. e   2. c   3. a   4. f   5. d   6. b

PART 2:

When the subject of good food and good restaurants comes up, there are so many things we can talk about. My favorite restaurants are <u>ethnic</u> restaurants that are managed by the diverse immigrant populations in our city. For many years, our city has always had a good number of restaurants featuring Southeast Asian, Mexican, German, Italian, Middle Eastern, Greek, and French menus, not to mention various American restaurants that specialize in Creole, barbecue, or soul food. Of course, some of these ethnic restaurants are not really <u>authentic</u> compared with the food you'd find in that country. Instead, they offer dishes that meet an American's expectations or <u>stereotype</u> of what we think is Mexican or German food. In the last 10 years, newer immigrant populations have also introduced more unfamiliar cuisines—Vietnamese, Moroccan, Thai, Ethiopian, Lebanese—as well as restaurants that specialize in the food of a particular <u>region</u> of a country, like Cantonese, northern Italian, Slovenian, Bohemian, and so on. The list can go on and on! What an incredible variety of <u>cuisines</u> the world has to offer, and I can sample them all in my hometown.

DICTATION, P. 16

The paragraph in Vocabulary Preview may be used for a dictation exercise (187 words).

Selection 1   Introduction to the Main Speaker

LISTEN FOR MAIN IDEAS, P. 17

Name of the show: <u>The Restaurant Show</u>
Time of the show: <u>from 2:00</u> to <u>5:00 p.m.</u>
Day: <u>Saturday</u>
Subject: <u>things having to do with restaurants and food; good and bad restaurants</u>

LISTEN FOR SPECIFIC INFORMATION, P. 17

1. <u>because it has a large number of restaurants ("more restaurants than convenience stores.")</u>

2. things having to do with restaurants and food, good and bad restaurants.

))) Chapter 1   What is Ethnic Cuisine?

Selection 2   Introduction to the topic

LISTEN FOR SPECIFIC INFORMATION, P. 18

Refer to transcript for answers.

KEYS TO BETTER COMPREHENSION: RECOGNIZING INCOMPLETE STATEMENTS, P. 19

The incomplete idea:
"Also today what I would <u>like to explore today</u>..."

The completed idea:
"And what I would really like to do today is <u>talk</u> to <u>some</u> of <u>you</u> who <u>know</u> this <u>kind</u> of <u>food</u>..."

Selection 3   Strictly Hungarian

LISTEN FOR SPECIFIC INFORMATION, P. 20

Cuisines	Locations	Restaurants
Hungarian	(none mentioned)	(none mentioned)
Slovenian and Slovak	(none mentioned)	(none mentioned)
Bohemian	Estes Park	Villa Tatra
Bohemian	(none mentioned)	Old Prague Inn
Bohemian	Lookout Mountain	Cody Inn
German	(none mentioned)	(none mentioned)

▶ LISTEN FOR MAIN IDEAS, P. 20

1. Slovenian or Slovak, and Hungarian.
2. No. There was one but it closed, and there are restaurants that serve food from Eastern Europe in general.
3. It closed.
4. A billboard is a large outdoor sign which advertises.
5. The billboard probably brags about what an outstanding restaurant it is (in order to attract tourists driving by).

VOCABULARY AND IDIOMS, P. 20

The underlined phrases indicate vocabulary and idioms to draw attention to. The teacher reads as the students write:

1. That question <u>came up</u> earlier today.
2. I wish there <u>was</u> a good Hungarian restaurant in town.
3. We <u>come close</u>, but we don't have any restaurants that are strictly Hungarian.
4. The food of Bohemia <u>isn't identifiable with</u> one country specifically.
5. Most restaurants that serve food from that part of the world <u>take a</u> pretty <u>broad-brush</u> approach to it.

KEYS TO BETTER COMPREHENSION: RECOGNIZING CONFUSING WORDS, PP. 20-21

1. "I wish there was a good Hungarian restaurant in town. The only one that we had <u>closed</u>. Now we come <u>close</u>—we have restaurants that are...Bohemian."

Point out that the adjective clause "that we had" is separate from the verb "closed."

Students may incorrectly assume the verb is the past perfect form "had closed." "To come close" means "to be similar."

2. come up   <u>happen unexpectedly</u>
   come upon   <u>to find someone or something by accident</u>
   come up with   <u>to find or supply someone or something with information</u>

3. Warren: Well, that question <u>came up</u> earlier today...so I can't <u>come up with</u> anything that is strictly Hungarian for you.

DIFFERENCES BETWEEN SPOKEN AND WRITTEN ENGLISH, P. 21

The correct sentence is: "I wish there <u>were</u> a good Hungarian restaurant in town."

Selection 4   Popular doesn't mean authentic

▶ LISTEN FOR SPECIFIC INFORMATION, P. 22

*Note: The conversation doesn't mention this location; however, students can infer it from Selection 1 or by process of elimination.

Restaurant	Location	Comment
Gasthaus Ridgeview	Denver*	closed
Racquet Club	Vail	recommended
Webers	Breckenridge	not authentic German food
Black Forest Inn	Blackhawk	excellent

⊡ LISTEN FOR MAIN IDEAS, P. 22

1. Tom grew up in a German family; he and his wife lived in Germany for 7 years.
2. Because they have a German chef who cooks absolutely wonderful food.
3. It's always crowded and busy, but it's not authentic German cooking; it's the American concept of German cooking.

⊡ LISTEN AGAIN: INFERENCE, P. 22

You can infer the following:
- A good German restaurant will probably have a German chef (from the comment on the Vail Racquet Club.)
- People who eat at Webers think it has authentic German food, but it doesn't.
- A good German restaurant doesn't have to be strictly German.
- Tom and Warren agree that a great experience is being able to walk into a restaurant and say, "Make me a good dinner," knowing that they'll enjoy anything the chef prepares.

Selection 5   Mexican food

⊡ LISTEN FOR MAIN IDEAS, P. 23

1. He's tired of the Mexican restaurants that serve basically the same type of food (tacos, tamales, burritos, etc.)
2. El Parral goes out of its way to use fresh ingredients.
3. El Parral makes dishes that are not commonly available at other Mexican restaurants.

⊡ LISTEN FOR SPECIFIC INFORMATION, P. 23

1. It's a dish with chicken covered in chocolate sauce.
2. He's crazy about it; it's one of the better Mexican dishes served anywhere.
3. He's tired of that kind of Mexican cuisine because it's the same old thing (nothing new or different).

DIFFERENCES BETWEEN SPOKEN AND WRITTEN ENGLISH, P. 23

Connecting words are underlined:
"As I started to say, I get a little bit tired of some of the Mexican restaurants that all have basically the same type of cuisine, and it's really pleasant to find a place like El Parral where they seem to go out of their way to use fresh ingredients, and make dishes that are not commonly available at other Mexican restaurants, such as their Chicken Molé, which I just absolutely go crazy for over there. If you've never had Chicken Molé, it's a chicken and chocolate sauce, and I think it's one of the better Mexican dishes that's served anywhere in the area, because as I say, I get very tired of burritos and tamales and tacos, and things of that nature."

SUMMARY, P. 24

Stereotypical:	Authentic
burritos	Chicken Molé
tamales	
tacos	

Selection 6   Authentic Mexican vs. Tex-Mex

LISTEN FOR MAIN IDEAS, P. 24

	Tex-Mex	authentic Mexican
ingredients:	ground beef	roast pork marinated pork sauces
dishes:	tacos burritos	seafood

VOCABULARY AND IDIOMS, P. 25

gets away from → offers less

gets into → offers more

check out → try out

Paraphrased sentences will vary. Suggested sentences:
1. I would enjoy a Mexican restaurant that served fewer dishes made with ground beef, and more dishes with roast pork and marinated pork sauces.
2. Why don't you try Las Brisas restaurant?

Chapter 2   Define Your Cuisine

Selection 7   If that's not Polish...

LISTEN FOR MAIN IDEAS, P. 27

pierogi → potato-like dumplings, or cheese dumplings

borscht → red beet soup

golabki → something made with cabbage

LISTEN FOR SPECIFIC INFORMATION, P. 28

The speakers mention these ingredients:
potato   cheese   cabbage   beets   sour cream

VOCABULARY AND IDIOMS, P. 28

Paraphrased answers will vary:
I know Polish food (or restaurants), and I'm very certain that that restaurant is authentically Polish.

Selection 8   What is Bohemian food?

▣ LISTEN FOR SPECIFIC INFORMATION, P. 29

Students should circle these words:

not exotically spiced	peasant	hearty
Central Europe	coarse	

▣ LISTEN FOR MAIN IDEAS, P. 29

1. Chuck wants to know if Warren knows of any good Bohemian or Czech restaurants in this city.
2. roasted dishes featuring pork and duck; a hearty form of home cooking; not spicy
3. It is not Bohemian; it features Ukrainian dishes.
4. Warren recommends the Cody Inn.
5. Warren asks Chuck to call him back after he's been to the Cody Inn to tell Warren whether he considers it Bohemian food.

▣ LISTEN AGAIN, P. 29-30
Part 1:

adverb:	basically	largely	fairly	strictly	essentially
verb phrase:	classify as	oriented toward	built around	based on	
noun:	(none)				
adjective:	distinct				
prepositional phrase:	in my estimation				

Part 2: Answers are underlined in transcript.

LISTENING CHECK, P. 30

Bohemian food	
region:	Central Europe
ingredients:	pork, duck, chicken
method of preparation:	roasted
typical dishes:	roast pork, roast duck, roast chicken, dumplings, brown gravy, red cabbage, sauerkraut, homemade soups, coarse breads
spices:	not exotic, not spicy

VOCABULARY AND IDIOMS, P. 31

Paraphrased sentences will vary. Suggested answers:

1. Bohemian food is influenced by German and Austrian cuisines, but it's not just one or the other.

2. Generally, it features pork and duck in large portions with a home-cooked style.

3. The bread doesn't have a fine texture; it's the kind of food that farmers prepare.

Selection 9 Paella

📼 LISTEN FOR MAIN IDEAS, P. 31

1. She wants suggestions on a restaurant that serves Paella.

2. chicken, seafood, saffron, rice.

📼 LISTEN FOR SPECIFIC INFORMATION, P. 32

1. c. Las Brisas, d. Don Quixote

2. saffron

3. sangría

Selection 10   If you haven't tried Ethiopian...

VOCABULARY PREVIEW, P. 33

---

delectable → delicious

curries → dishes that are flavored with a combination of pungent spices

misnomer → an incorrect name

scoop → use (the bread) as a spoon

condiments → flavorings used to spice a dish

LISTEN FOR MAIN IDEAS, P. 33

📼 Ethiopian Cuisine

I. Main ingredients
   beef lamb chicken vegetables bread (*injera*, a flat bread that's like a yeast bread)

II. Spices and condiments
   curry (but it's not really curry)
   it's a highly seasoned food

III. How it is served
   in a series of little dishes

IV. How it is eaten
   tear off bits of the flat bread to scoop up the food; eaten with the hands

V. How people who have never eaten it before react to it
   they go crazy about it; most of them really love it

VOCABULARY AND IDIOMS, P. 34

The teacher reads:
1. "I've only introduced one or two people to Ethiopian food who didn't go crazy about it." *(answer: c)*
2. "If you're into good food at all, Ethiopian food is great." *(answer: a)*

Selection 11   If you've not had Moroccan food...

📼 LISTEN FOR SPECIFIC INFORMATION, P. 35

Moroccan Cuisine

I. Main ingredients
    lamb   chicken   rabbit

II. Spices and condiments
    olives, lemon

III. How it is served
    you sit on the floor or on low pillows around low tables; there's a ceremonial hand washing with a basin of water (before and after the meal)

IV. How it is eaten
    with the hands, using bread as a utensil to pick up the food

V. What is special about Moroccan restaurants
    entertainment — belly dancers

))) Chapter 3   What Do You Recommend?

Selection 12   Russian cuisine

📼 LISTEN FOR MAIN IDEAS, P. 38

The speaker gives several reasons to recommend Café Tamara, including:
- There is a variety of interesting Russian dishes on the menu.
- There is also a variety of dishes from different European countries on different nights of the week.
- They serve breakfast, lunch, and Sunday brunch, in addition to dinner.
- The restaurant has a quaint atmosphere.
- It's not hard to find something you'll like on the menu.
- The owners are delightful.
- The food is very inexpensive.
- It's not a fancy restaurant, but it's a good restaurant.
- It's different, exciting, and fun.

1. Wednesday, they <u>go Italian</u>.

2. Friday, <u>it's French</u>.

3. So they do all of that; <u>plus,</u> they <u>do</u> breakfast...

4. These <u>folks</u> are <u>just absolutely</u> delightful.

5. The food is very inexpensive; I'm <u>talking like sub</u>-ten dollars.

6. It's the kind of place you can go to <u>three, four</u> nights a week and still not <u>break the budget</u>. *(Note the ambiguity of "to three, four..." which sounds like "two, three, four...")*

7. <u>Check out the</u> Café Tamara, located on East Eighth Avenue.

Selection 13   Italian cuisine

Listen for main ideas, p. 39

1. Jim had a pleasurable experience there.

2. The food was wonderful.

3. It has the best service.

Listen again: Inference, p. 40

1. It's hard to find; it's easy to get lost; three roads form a triangle around the block on which the restaurant is located.

2. He lived in Seattle, where Italian food is very popular, and ate a lot of Italian food.

3. The restaurant wasn't very good before these owners. They had several owners in the last few years.

4. Because you would expect an Italian restaurant which has such good food to have Italian owners and/or an Italian chef. The Olive Oil has neither.

Differences between spoken and written English, p. 40

1. ...and Seattle is <u>big into Italian</u> food.
   Formal: Italian food is popular in Seattle.

2. I just can't <u>go on enough about</u> it.
   Formal: I just can't stop talking about it. I have a lot to say about it.

3. ...and those people, just, y'know, they <u>just bend</u> over <u>backwards</u> to <u>take care</u> of you.
   Formal: They do everything possible to please the customer.

Keys to better comprehension: Recognizing vocabulary in context, pp. 40-41

Part 1: Answers are underlined in the transcript.

Part 2: pleasurable <u>ADJ</u>   northern <u>ADJ</u>   attentive <u>ADJ</u>   ownership <u>N</u>   backwards <u>ADV</u>

Selection 14   Vietnamese cuisine

VOCABULARY PREVIEW, P. 42

The students will hear these words:

cuisine:	Chinese, Vietnamese
dishes:	Dungeness Crab, Black Bean Fish, Moo Shu Pork
description:	semi-spicy
price:	not cheap *(but it's not excessive either)*
other food:	grilled pork, grilled chicken
ingredients:	ginger, vegetables, rice paper, lettuce, sprouts, carrots, fine noodles, rice wrapper

LISTEN FOR GENERAL INFORMATION, P. 42

1. downtown, on 15th and California (streets)
2. Vietnamese and Chinese
3. Vietnamese
4. last night
5. Grilled Pork
6. wonderful, fabulous

LISTEN FOR SPECIFIC INFORMATION, P. 42

1. *There are many answers:* wonderful; out of sight; superb; not the cheapest dish on the menu, but not excessive considering what you get; semi-spicy with a little bit of ginger; when you're finished you get to lick your fingers.
2. It is prepared with different kinds of vegetables and fine noodles, and it's rolled up in rice paper.

VOCABULARY AND IDIOMS, P. 43

1. *stumble* → come upon by accident
2. *chills* → thrills, excitement
3. *out of sight* → indescribably wonderful

synonyms for wonderful: *Consult a thesaurus for synonyms.*

LISTEN AGAIN: TOEFL PRACTICE, P. 44

Tapescript and answers:

1. Man: It's not the cheapest dish on any Chinese restaurant menu...

   Woman: ...but you know, it's not that bad.

   Question: What does the woman mean?

   Answer: c

2. Woman: The price is not excessive at all...

    Man: ...considering what you get!

    Question: What do we learn about the price of the meal?

    Answer: d

3. Man: My favorite restaurant is the Oriental Plate...

    Woman: ...downtown, on 15th and California.

    Question: What does the woman's statement tell us?

    Answer: a

4. Woman: Thank you for calling!

    Man: You bet!

    Question: What does the man's statement mean?

    Answer: b

Selection 15   Salsa

LISTEN FOR MAIN IDEAS, P. 44
1. tomato
2. salsa that is like a paste

KEYS TO BETTER COMPREHENSION: RECOGNIZING VOCABULARY IN CONTEXT, P. 45

Boyd: Tortilla Flats....they have good green chile, and they have a good <u>salsa,</u> probably the best <u>original</u>—I would call it the "tomato salsa"—that I've <u>ever</u> tasted is at Tortilla Flats.

Warren: I think you can tell a lot about a Mexican restaurant by the salsa that arrives at the table, which is usually the first thing that you get at a Mexican restaurant.

Boyd: Yeah, it's not a <u>paste,</u> it's...just like it's a <u>blended</u>-type, <u>tomato</u>-type sauce; and it's very, very good.

Warren: I appreciate your calling.

Selection 16   Arabian cuisine

LISTEN FOR MAIN IDEAS, P. 46
1. Lebanese
2. Syrian
3. Colorado Boulevard and Evans (Street)
4. lamb kabobs and lamb dishes
5. Warren mentions that at Middle Eastern restaurants, there are also many <u>vegetarian</u> dishes on the menu.

6. a lot of variety; intriguing; interestingly spiced, some of it is delicately spiced, and some of it is heavily spiced.

7. served after the meal; it's good; it's very strong; it's like Turkish or Greek coffee; it's a "nice touch."

LISTEN AGAIN: INFERENCE, P. 47

1. Possibly: similar ingredients (lamb), spices, methods of preparation, etc.; vegetarian dishes; strong coffee

2. The spices may be stronger or different from what you are used to, so it catches your attention.

3. It's really strong coffee; this is probably an adaptation of the idiom, "It'll put hair on your chest," suggesting something will make a man out of a boy.

Unit 2
CARS AND DRIVING

VOCABULARY PREVIEW, P. 50

British	American
bonnet	hood
boot	trunk
gear lever	stick shift
a puncture	a flat
tyres	tires
glove box	glove compartment
petrol	gasoline
windscreen	windshield
jump leads	jumper cables
milometer	odometer
indicator	turn signal

Chapter 4 Cars

Selection 1 Buying a used car

LISTEN FOR MAIN IDEAS, P. 51

* Amoco is a service station which sells gasoline.
1. from a dealer
2. two and a half weeks ago
3. ignition problems, electrical
4. She took it to an Amoco station to have it looked at.
5. A thousand dollars
6. She bought it "as is."
7. 1979 Ford Mustang
8. 130,000
9. No. We don't know what he said when Tammy talked to him, but probably he told her she bought it as is, and so he didn't have to fix it.

DIFFERENCES BETWEEN SPOKEN AND WRITTEN ENGLISH, PP. 51-52

1. Answers will vary.
2. We thought that there were ignition problems. So we took it to an Amoco station and had a professional look at it.
3. like

VOCABULARY AND IDIOMS, P. 52

1. *To get taken* means to be a victim of a fraudulent practice.
    Passive.
    Because the subject "you" is the receiver of the action of the verb.
2. The car.
    As is means just the way it exists; no repairs can be made for free after it is purchased.

Selection 2 You bought it; it's yours

LISTEN FOR MAIN IDEAS, P. 53

Suggested answers are underlined. Refer to transcript for more information.
Tom asks Tammy if she realizes that because the car has so many miles on it, she <u>may have problems</u>. Tammy has a question for Tom: Some people have told her that she has <u>30 days</u> to <u>return the car to the dealer</u> if something goes wrong with the car. Tom tells Tammy that what these people told her is <u>wrong</u>, because there is no <u>right to return anything</u>. Tammy has talked to the salesman about <u>taking care of the problems</u>. Tom says there's not much she can do, but hopefully people will learn from her experience that <u>they must get cars checked out before they buy them</u>.

VOCABULARY AND IDIOMS, PP. 53-54

1. *Answers will vary. Suggested answer:*
    <u>Why didn't you get that old car checked out before you bought it?</u>

2. I'll <u>betcha</u> there's...   bet you → *betcha*

3. "There is no right to return anything. <u>Zero</u>! <u>Zip</u>! (these words mean "nothing")
   see thesaurus for other synonyms.

4. "I've talked to him, and he's like giving me the runaround. He says, 'Oh, I'll <u>fix</u> it,' and it's like he's wanting us to <u>pay</u> for the problem."

📼 LISTEN AGAIN, PP. 54-55

Refer to transcript for answers.

SUMMARY, P. 55

Consumer tip #1
There is no <u>right</u> to return anything.

Consumer tip #2
If you buy anything used, you <u>must</u> get it checked out <u>before</u> you buy it.

Selection 3   High-pressure tactics

ANTICIPATE, P. 56

All the answers are false, but don't tell the students the answers yet. Students will learn the correct answers in the "Listening Check" exercise on p. 57.

📼 LISTEN FOR MAIN IDEAS, P. 56

I. What happens to customers at Douglas Toyota
<u>customers are "held captive"</u>
<u>customers have to give their car keys to a salesperson to check out their car (trade-in)</u>
<u>the keys are given to someone else in the dealership</u>
<u>the customer let's them have his registration, too</u>

II. Why Tom is angry with these complaints about Douglas Toyota
<u>He's gotten dozens of calls about the same problem at the same dealership</u>

III. Tom's advice to customers who are going to buy and/or trade in a car at a dealership:
1. Don't let anyone have <u>the keys to your car</u>.
2. Don't let anyone have <u>your license</u>.
3. Don't let anyone have <u>your registration</u>.
4. Don't let anyone take <u>your car</u>.
5. Trade-ins: If they say they have to <u>evaluate</u> your car, <u>go</u> with them.

IV. What customers should do if any of the above happens to them
<u>call the police</u>
<u>make a scene (yell and scream in the dealership) until they give your keys and registration back.</u>

📼 LISTEN FOR SPECIFIC INFORMATION, P. 57

1. Because they really do this, so they'd have to lie to defend themselves.

2. Keeping the customer in the dealership, taking their car keys, car or registration (possible answers not mentioned: passing the customer from one salesperson to another; getting the customer to test drive several cars so the customer will "fall in love" with one; making unbelievable deals to get the customer to buy the car, but the fine print in the contract makes it less than a great deal)

3. They want to keep you in the dealership as long as possible (because it will increase the probability that you will buy a car).

4. Probably not.

5. No, there are now some "classy" dealerships which don't act like this.

6. Because consumers don't like the way many dealerships sell cars, so their demands have forced changes in the industry.

VOCABULARY AND IDIOMS, P. 57

go over the edge → get angry enough to take action

address these concerns → discuss the issues, problems

the bottom line → the sum, the total

cause a scene → to make a public display or disturbance

to be civil → to be polite

a lot of bull → a lot of nonsense, exaggeration

do away with → discontinue

sleazy → contemptible; below accepted norms

classy → high quality, first-rate

LISTENING CHECK, P. 57 (AND ANTICIPATE, P.56)
1. false   2. false   3. false   4. false   5. false
Refer to transcript for reasons why these answers are false.

Selection 4   Value pricing

LISTEN FOR MAIN IDEAS, P. 58
value pricing makes it easy to buy a new car or truck
no more haggling over the price of a vehicle
no hassles
knowledgeable, professional sales people
best price and value for the car you want
saves time
no expensive extras or add-ons to the price of the car

LISTEN FOR SPECIFIC INFORMATION, P. 59
1. The price of the car is set; you don't barter over the price of the car.

2. They won't hassle you or haggle over the price of the vehicle.

3. knowledgeable and professional

4. a full year

5. The customers love it because it saves time and hassle.

6. It gives the customer more time to find the car or truck that fits his or her needs.

7. Because the customers prefer it. They want a hassle-free method of buying cars and trucks.

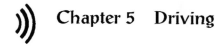 **Chapter 5   Driving**

Selection 5   Can you afford a Ford?

VOCABULARY PREVIEW, PP. 61-62

Refer to the transcript for answers.

LISTEN AGAIN: NEW VOCABULARY IN CONTEXT, P. 62

These words are the same as the ones underlined in the transcript for the Vocabulary Preview exercise on pp. 61-62.

Selection 6   Radar guns

DIFFERENCES BETWEEN SPOKEN AND WRITTEN ENGLISH, P. 63

Suggested answer:
"If I'm driving down the road, and for example, the policeman pulls me over and says I'm driving 90 miles an hour, does he have the right to write me a ticket without showing me the radar gun?"

KEYS TO BETTER LISTENING COMPREHENSION: DISTINGUISHING HOMONYMS, P. 63
The two homonyms in "Differences between spoken and written English" are *right* and *write*.

VOCABULARY PREVIEW, P. 64
   a. *clocked* → to determine the speed by radar *zone* → area which the speed limit pertains to
   b. *cited* → to issue a citation (ticket)
   c. *recalibrate* → to reset to determine speed, etc.
   d. *instrumentation* → the use of, or work done by instruments, such as a radar gun
   e. *lenient* → tolerant, not strict or severe

LISTEN FOR MAIN IDEAS, P. 64

Refer to transcript for details to be used in drawing.
1. True   2. False   3. False   4. False   5. True   6. True   7. True

Selection 7   Error on a Ticket

LISTEN FOR SPECIFIC INFORMATION, P. 65
   1. Brad was driving 68 m.p.h. in a 40 m.p.h. speed zone.

   2. Since the officer made a mistake on the ticket (he wrote down that it was a 35 m.p.h. zone), does that negate the ticket?

   3. No, there would have to be more than one mistake or something really big that would negate the officer's credibility.

   4. If the officer writes something wrong on the ticket, for example, the date, it can be corrected (amended) and doesn't negate or invalidate the ticket.

He *clocked* me <u>at 65 in a 40 zone</u>.   *clocked* → to determine the speed by radar
Does a mistake on a ticket *negate* <u>the entire ticket</u>?   *negate* → invalidate
Is that it *in a nutshell*?   *in a nutshell* → in a few words
That's all...*amendable*.   *amendable* → correctable

Selection 8   Traffic fatalities

DICTATION, P. 66

The instructor reads the following sentences for dictation. Read in phrases.

1. Seven of the victims were not wearing safety belts.

2. Drunk drivers were involved in three of those fatal accidents.

3. With the holiday weekend coming up, highway officials are asking people to buckle up.

4. Five of those seven were thrown from their vehicles, and that was the direct cause of the fatality.

5. Dan Hopkins with the Department of Transportation says eight people died on Colorado roadways last Labor Day weekend.

LISTENING CHECK, P. 66

The correct order of the above sentences is 3, 5, 1, 4, 2.

LISTEN FOR SPECIFIC INFORMATION, P. 66

Refer to the transcript for statistics.

Selection 9   Traffic fatalities decrease

LISTEN FOR SPECIFIC INFORMATION, P. 67

<u>Traffic fatality rate</u>
definition: number of <u>deaths</u> per <u>100,000,000 miles</u> traveled
a barometer of how <u>well</u> we as a <u>nation</u> are doing in <u>highway safety</u>
1992: <u>1.8</u> deaths per 100 million miles <u>traveled</u>
1982: <u>2.8</u> deaths per 100 million miles <u>traveled</u>
difference = <u>22,000</u> lives per year

Selection 10   Who needs auto insurance?

LISTEN FOR SPECIFIC INFORMATION, PP. 68 - 69

1. c   2. d   3. a   4. d   5. d   6. d   7. a   8. d   9. b, c   10. c

KEYS TO BETTER COMPREHENSION: RECOGNIZING EXAMPLES, P. 69

Refer to the transcript for answers.

Selection 11   Auto repair for dummies

ANTICIPATE, PP. 70-71

Don't go over the answers after the Car Care Pre-Test. Students will be asked to check their answers after listening to the selection. Answers are provided in the "Listening Check" exercise.

VOCABULARY PREVIEW, P. 71

1. top off → fill to the very top or maximum capacity

2. dissipate → to scatter or dispel

3. spewed → to pour out violently or in large quantity

4. dispel → disperse, cause to vanish

LISTEN FOR SPECIFIC INFORMATION, PP. 72-73

Basic Car Care

I. Warming up a cold car
   Lengthy warm-ups are bad, for three reasons:
   1. pollute the air
   2. waste fuel
   3. increase wear on your car

II. The oil light
   If the oil light comes on, stop immediately.

III. Changing the air filter
   For every gallon of gas you use, you use enough air to fill a room 10 feet square.
   The air filter is located inside the carburetor.
   How to check the air filter to see if it is dirty:
   1. open the top of the carburetor, take it out
   2. look at the sun or a strong light through the filter

   If you can't see light through it, it's time to change it.
   How to change the air filter:
   1. go to an auto parts store
   2. tell them the year, make and model of your car
   3. change it in the parking lot to make sure it fits

IV. Getting more gas for the same amount of money
   10 gallons of gas will expand by 8/10 of a quart with a temperature increase of 30 degrees.
   You should fill up your tank in the morning /evening when it's cool.

V. Topping off your tank
   When the hose clicks: stop.
   The reason is you lose the extra fuel when you overfill the tank.

VI. Vapor lock
   The car just stops.
   It happens when it's very hot.

   What causes vapor lock:
   the gasoline starts to boil in the metal fuel line
   creating vapor which blocks the line

What to do when the car is in vapor lock:

1.   wrap tin foil around the fuel line or

2.   wrap a wet rag around the fuel line

VII. Overheating

Overheating is caused by:

driving with the air conditioner on

the temperature is 85 degrees (approximately)

Solutions: (Deanna gives two sets of solutions for overheating)

Step one: shut off the air conditioner

Step two: turn on the heater

Step three: open the windows

or

Step one: get to the side of the road

Step two: open the hood, but don't take the radiator cap off

Step three: wait for the car to cool down naturally

VIII. Maintenance

Change the oil often enough.

Change the oil filter at least every other time.

Once a month, you should open the hood and look at:

1.   the hoses

2.   the wiring

3.   the fluid levels

If you do this regularly, you can save about 70% of the reasons why your car might break down.

KEYS TO BETTER COMPREHENSION: RECOGNIZING ANALOGY, P. 74

carburetor is analogous to a cake pan

an air filter is analogous to accordion paper

a quart is analogous to a bottle of milk

four-fifths of a quart is analogous to a bottle of whiskey

oil is analogous to moisturizer

LISTENING CHECK, P. 74 (ANSWERS TO PRE-TEST, PP. 70-71)

1. c	2. a	3. c	4. c	5. a
6. True	7. False	8. True	9. not given*	10. True

* This is true, but this information is not given in the conversation.

))) Unit 3
The Environment

Vocabulary preview, p. 76
<u>c.</u> wildlife
<u>d.</u> roadkill
<u>e.</u> habitat
<u>b.</u> recycle
<u>a.</u> environment

))) Chapter 6   Environmental Awareness

Selection 1   The Green Pages

Listen for specific information, p. 77

Refer to the transcripts for answers.

Selection 2   Transportation alternatives

Listen for specific information, p. 79

1. The RTD (bus system) and the company have agreed to run two new express bus routes especially for the company's employees.
2. The company is subsidizing the cost of bus fares and monthly passes.
3. The company is encouraging carpooling.
4. There's a guaranteed ride-home program.

Selection 3   Eco-conscious construction

Noun phrases with hyphenated words, p. 80
a. south-facing windows
b. a well-lit kitchen
c. a milk-based paint
d. a San Diego-based designer
e. a Taos, New Mexico-based architect
f. an energy-efficient dwelling
g. a uniquely constructed home
h. environmentally beneficial solutions
i. an environmentally sustainable dreamhouse

Prefixed Words, p. 80

eco-conscious   nontoxic   superinsulation

self-sustaining   biodegradable   preconceived

Dictation, p. 81

Dictate words from noun phrases and prefixed words ("Vocabulary Preview" exercise on pp. 79 and 80). Or you can dictate phrases from the tape transcript which use these phrases.

Keys to better comprehension: Understanding connecting words, p. 81

The teacher reads the following sentences. The answers are underlined. Do a couple together to make sure students understand the exercise.

1. Logan has incorporated nearly every aspect of modern eco-conscious design.
2. Every room in this house has a window that faces south, regardless of where it's located.
3. All the rooms in the house have day-lighting, which means that there's ample light coming in high into the room.
4. South-facing glass will provide solar heat. As a result, Logan's house will not have air conditioning.
5. Logan's house will have neither a furnace nor air-conditioning.
6. The so-called superinsulation is required to store the solar heat.
7. Logan is using thermal mass, or dirt, to keep the house both warm in the winter and cool in the summer.
8. He's using milk-based paint, for example, and relatively little of that.
9. Virtually all of the finishes inside this room did not need to be painted.
10. Painting is a fairly un-environmental act in that it is something that involves doing over and over many times in the life of the building.
11. Initially, Logan will get all his water from a well.
12. Logan says he'll eventually install an active system for solar electricity.
13. Weaver says his uniquely-constructed home is helping to solve two ecological problems simultaneously.

Listen for Main Ideas, p. 83

To the instructor: You may only want to play the reporter's comments and turn the tape down while the students are writing during the other speakers' comments.

Selection 4   Providing a habitat for fish

Listen for Specific Information, p. 83

Refer to the tape transcript for information to use in the drawing.

Different people may hear stress slightly differently, but the class can agree on some words (those receiving the strongest stress). Play the selection sentence by sentence and ask the students which word or words have more stress (or sound "higher") in each sentence. This exercise works well with certain speakers whose speech is more characterized by stress. Students who speak languages without much stress or intonation can hear and learn the importance of stressing important words in a sentence to make their speech more communicative and intelligible in English.

Selection 5   Global Youth Forum

LISTEN FOR SPECIFIC INFORMATION, P. 85

1. a. global warming   b. ozone depletion   c. water conservation
2. So that youths from all over the world can share their ideas about protecting the environment.
3. They were chosen from a pool of young people recognized by the United Nations for their efforts to educate their peers about the environment.
4. She and some friends started a recycling program in their school.
5. The leaders (politicians) and the youth.
6. He helped organize environmental clubs in the public schools.
7. The illegal dumping of trash and the destruction of the island's coral reefs.
8. Because if they start there, students will grow up with sound values; they will grow up caring about the environment.
9. Her generation is more aware than her parents' generation.
10. A major goal is to put their awareness into action by crafting a list of environmental priorities which will be written in a declaration and given to the United Nations General Assembly.
11. The goals are huge and it's easy to get discouraged. It's going to take hard work to accomplish their goals.

KEYS TO BETTER COMPREHENSION: RECOGNIZING SYNONYMS, P. 86
teens, youth(s), youngsters, children, students, young people, kids, peers

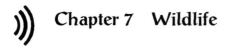

Chapter 7   Wildlife

Selection 6   The impact of a golf course

KEYS TO BETTER COMPREHENSION: RECOGNIZING VOCABULARY IN CONTEXT, P. 89
Answers are underlined in the transcript.

VOCABULARY AND IDIOMS, P. 90

Golf courses	The environment	Wildlife
grooming	conservation	(natural) habitats
excessive water	low impact	killdeer eggs - hatch
greens	grasslands	redtail hawks
fairways	Environmental Steward Award	foxes
construction halted		deer
		great horned owls
		blue herons
		coyotes

Selection 7   Reintroducing river otters

LISTENING CHECK, P. 91

Refer to transcript for correct answers. Remind students that they must rely on their listening skills rather than on their knowledge of grammar or vocabulary. Proper nouns have not been changed. The errors mostly occur in verb tenses, synonyms, word forms and numbers. Be sure to let students count how many errors they corrected, and then let them listen again, challenging them to try to get all 17. Those who get close to 17 will want to listen again and again!

Selection 8   Dolphin captivity

VOCABULARY PREVIEW, PP. 92-93

The teacher reads the sentences below. The underlined form is the words students should hear and write in the appropriate column. The word form as it is used in the sentence is in parentheses at the end of each sentence.

1. Officials are receiving <u>objections</u> over a planned aquatic park. (noun)
2. A planned aquatic park is raising the anger of animal rights <u>activists</u>. (noun)
3. Activists object to a proposal to include a <u>captive</u> dolphins display in the park. (adjective)
4. Bill and Judy Fleming were both animal <u>trainers</u> at Marine World. (noun)
5. Their long-term goal has been to <u>found</u> an educational park in Denver. (verb)
6. That aspect seems too <u>realistic</u> for some dolphin experts. (adjective)
7. Captivity is a form of <u>cruelty</u> to intelligent mammals. (noun)

"Stop. How are you doing?" Check your answers and discuss the word endings and grammatical clues which should help you recognize the word form. Then continue with the rest of the sentences below.

8. There are many reasons the dolphin can't live normal lives in <u>captivity</u>. (noun)
9. Bill is especially <u>critical</u> of his life-expectancy estimates. (adjective)
10. The <u>longevity</u> of a dolphin may reach up to 40 years. (noun)
11. Some animals reject captivity right away, and they're very <u>suicidal</u>. (adjective)

12. These displays are anti-educational because the animals' natural behavior patterns are changed. (adjective)

13. I've observed no dolphins suffering from fractured skulls, fractured ribs, or fractured jaws, as is the case in captivity. (adjective)

14. The Ocean Journey Board will take all factors into consideration before making a final decision. (noun)

KEYS TO BETTER COMPREHENSION: LISTENING FOR SUBJECT-VERB-OBJECT, P. 93

Alan Tu: (1) "A planned aquatic park in Denver is raising the ire of animal rights activists who object to a proposal to include a captive dolphins display. (2) Although officials for Colorado's Ocean Journeys say they have yet to make a final decision on the issue, local and national activists say they have already instigated a "No Dolphins in Denver" campaign. (3) As Colorado Public Radio's Peter Jones reports, the battle lines have been clearly drawn."

Peter Jones: (4) "Colorado's Ocean Journey is the lifelong dream of Bill and Judy Fleming. The couple met in the late 70's when they were both animal trainers at Marine World Africa-USA in southern California. (5) The Flemings went on to co-author *The Tiger on Your Couch*, a book for pet owners. (6) Since then, their long-term goal has been to found an educational aquatic park in Denver, the landlocked hometown of Judy Fleming. (7) If all goes as planned, the $49 million nonprofit facility will open in 1996."

KEYS TO BETTER COMPREHENSION: ORGANIZING INFORMATION, P. 95

A resource which supports some of the statements below and refutes others is National Geographic, 182:3, September 1992, pp. 2-35. For the debate that follows this activity, I copied portions of the article and gave each portion to a different pair of students, asking them to read and identify information that supported one or more of the statements below. They used this further evidence to support their side of the debate and refute the other side.

Issue: Dolphins should be kept in captivity for research and educational purposes.

(Student answers may vary)
Possible PRO statements:

• Aquatic parks are educational.
• The facility will be nonprofit.
• The habitats in the aquatic park will be as lifelike as possible.
• Captivity does not shorten the average life span of dolphins; only a small percentage live 40 years; activists are taking research out of context. Animals can and do live their normal average life span in captivity.
• The aquatic park will use captive-born dolphins, not animals from the wild (so the life expectancy issue is irrelevant).
• There is a surplus of captive-born dolphins.
• The Cousteau family (well-known aquatic research scientists) oppose the captivity industry based on their experience. An "expert opinion."
• Dr. Duffield, a biology professor, found in her research the average life is actually getting longer. (This fact was refuted by the other side in a portion of the interview which was cut from this excerpt because it got too technical. They claimed her research was invalid. It's hard to know who to believe.)
• Educational debate: Captive dolphins play an important role in our basic understanding of the animals; Dr. Duffield claims she cannot learn about their behavior by observing them in the wild.

Possible CON statements:

- Captivity is a form of cruelty to intelligent mammals.
- Captivity shortens the life span of dolphins.
- Separating dolphins from their families adds stress.
- Dolphins in a tank can't swim as much and as far as they are used to in the wild.
- If one aquatic park transfers some captive-born dolphins from one park to another, the first park will just go out and get more from the wild; 50% are caught in the wild.
- Cousteau says some animals reject captivity right away and become suicidal.
- Educational debate: The aquatic park displays are "anti-educational" because the animals' natural behavior patterns are altered by captivity.
- Dolphins don't suffer physically in the wild.

VOCABULARY AND IDIOMS, P. 95

instigate → to provoke to some action

the battle lines have been drawn → the two opposing groups have clearly stated which issues they do not agree on

landlocked → surrounded by land, having no access to water

interactive → acting with one another

sonar → a method for finding and locating objects under water by means of the sound waves they reflect or produce. (SOund NAvigation Ranging)

surplus → an excess, too much

organisms → individual life forms

breeds → to produce offspring

metabolically → pertaining to what is needed to function

altered by → changed by

stranded → left abandoned

Selection 9   Wildlife controversy

 LISTEN FOR SPECIFIC INFORMATION, P. 96

1. c   2. a   3. b   4. a   5. d

))) Chapter 8 Land, Water, and Air

Selection 10 Xeriscape

LISTENING CHECK, P. 99

1. *xeri-* means 'dry'; *-scape* means 'vista' or 'view.'

2. To reduce the amount of water used in a garden, and to provide an attractive lawn or landscape garden area.

3. To counteract some of the problems caused by the droughts in the late 70's; to use less water.

4. Because less water is used, and plants can still grow and look beautiful.

5. To reduce the amount of maintenance.

6. They plant "bluegrass," which is a variety of grass that needs 30-35 inches of water a year to grow.

7. By involving as many people in the profession (of landscaping, gardening) as well as clients who use landscaping.

8. Because it's a big industry ($22 billion was spent in one year on materials and services related to landscaping in the U.S.).

9. The gardening industry is probably opposed to these changes because it will reduce their income!

10. Xeriscape conserves water while still producing a beautiful, useful garden.

Selection 11 Global warming

⟦▭⟧ LISTEN FOR MAIN IDEAS, P. 100

Refer to the transcript for details to fill in this outline.

Unit 4
CUSTOMER SERVICE

VOCABULARY PREVIEW, P. 104

---

warranty → a written guarantee between a customer and a manufacturer

guarantee → an assurance that something is of a specific quality, condition, etc. (can also be written, in which case it is the same as a warranty.)

appliance → a piece of household equipment, usually run by electricity or gas

diagnostic service → a service performed to determine the cause or nature of a problem

consumer → a person who uses a service or product

Selection 1 Introduction to the main speaker

LISTEN FOR MAIN IDEAS, P. 104

Name of the program	The Troubleshooter (Show)
Main phone number	623-8585
Hotline number	629-0402
Purpose of the hotline number	for feedback

VOCABULARY AND IDIOMS, P. 104
  1. e   2. b or f   3. f or b   4. a   5. c   6. d

Chapter 9   What is Customer Service?

Selections 2 through 5

LISTEN FOR SPECIFIC INFORMATION (PAGES 107 THROUGH 109)

Refer to the transcript for answers.

Selection 6   I have a question

LISTEN FOR MAIN IDEAS, P. 110
This conversation illustrates the customer complaint in selection 3.

Selection 7 Press "1" now

🔲 LISTEN FOR MAIN IDEAS, P. 111

This conversation illustrates the customer complaint in selection 4.

Selection 8 Small businesses

VOCABULARY PREVIEW, P. 112

The instructor dictates the following sentences. The underlined phrases are idioms and expressions that should be discussed. Their definitions are given in italics.

1. This business has <u>been there</u> to help me before. *be available*
2. He <u>all but told me</u> I was wasting his time. *said indirectly*
3. The salesperson at the store <u>hung up on</u> me. *ended the phone conversation abruptly*
4. Small companies <u>get ticked off</u> at big ones. *get angry at, are annoyed by*
5. When you buy a mail-order computer, you spend <u>pennies on the dollar</u>. *less money; a percentage of the whole*

🔲 LISTEN FOR MAIN IDEAS, P. 113

1. Dee was having problems with some new fish tank equipment, so she called the Fish Den to ask some questions.
2. Dee's husband.
3. Fish.
4. No.
5. He started getting rude.
6. Dee doesn't understand why the clerk was so rude to her.
7. There are two ways of looking at it. Either the clerk acted unprofessionally and lost a customer, or he doesn't want to help her because she didn't buy the equipment from his store.
8. The real problem is that small businesses are angry at large discount stores which sell equipment but don't sell service. The customers want the lower price, but then when they need service, they go back to the small businesses even though they didn't buy the product there.

🔲 LISTEN AGAIN: INFERENCE, PP. 114-115

There can be several phrases and sentences which infer this information. If this exercise is too difficult, write these sentences on the board out of order, and have students discuss them and/or match them to the sentences in the book.

1. It was a Christmas present.
2. I've bought fish there before.
3. They go to discount stores; then they need help, and then they call us.
4. They have a right to feel the way they want.
5. When you do buy from neighborhood specialty stores, you buy consultation services as well.

DIFFERENCES BETWEEN SPOKEN AND WRITTEN ENGLISH, P. 115

1. There <u>are</u> three ways of looking at it.
2. If he <u>had</u> just talked to me, I probably would have <u>gone</u> down there and <u>looked at</u> what he had.
3. If it <u>were</u> me, I think I probably would have tried to win that customer over.

Selection 9   How to treat a customer

The last paragraph of this selection is a great one to use for discussing intonation. Copy Tom's last comments from the tape transcripts, and have students mark the stressed words.

VOCABULARY PREVIEW, P. 116

1. It sounded kind of like you were defending the Walmarts of the world and <u>cutting down</u> the independent retailers.
2. If it were me, I think I would probably try to <u>win</u> that <u>customer over</u>.
3. These people order computers through the mail, and then <u>cry to</u> their local retailer about problems!
4. And they'll get a new one, (like) <u>without</u> even <u>batting</u> an <u>eye</u>.
5. They have to <u>jack</u> their <u>prices up</u> to take care of all these people.
6. You can <u>tick</u> one person <u>off</u>, and lose thousands and thousands of dollars.
7. There are times to <u>give in</u>.

CONVERSATION STRATEGY: CORRECTING SOMEONE WHO HAS MISUNDERSTOOD YOU, P. 116

1a. *It sounded kind of like* you were defending…
2a. Oh, I *don't think so at all.*
2b. I *said I understand* their feeling.

🔲 LISTEN AGAIN: INFERENCE, P. 117

Refer to the transcript for answers.

Selection 10   Accommodate all the customers

🔲 LISTEN FOR SPECIFIC INFORMATION, PP. 118-119

1. They don't have anything for the kids to do; the kids just run around.
2. McDonald's.
3. They have playgrounds for the kids (inside or outside the restaurant).
4. They could have a play section or just some toys to keep the kids occupied.

🔲 LISTEN AGAIN: INFERENCE, P. 119

1. Kids ask their parents to take them to McDonald's more frequently than parents make the suggestion to their kids.
2. Because it takes a long time for the parents to talk to the salesmen, look at cars, walk around, sign papers, etc. If parents are going to bring their kids in while they're looking at cars, dealerships should be prepared to keep the kids from running around.
3. The unheard caller probably called to complain about parents who let their kids run around while the parents are shopping, or to complain about businesses which don't have a play section, books, or toys for children when it's the kind of business where a family might come in together.

Chapter 10   Principles for Smart Consumers

Selection 11   Send it back

🔲 LISTEN FOR SPECIFIC INFORMATION: TOEFL PRACTICE, P. 122

The instructor plays the selection once; then plays the tape with the following questions.

1. What is the main topic of the conversation?   *Answer:* c
2. Why did the customer complain about the restaurant?   *Answer:* d
3. What do we learn about the customer's steak?   *Answer:* b
4. What do we learn in general about eating in any restaurant
    on a Sunday evening?   *Answer:* d
5. What advice does the man receive?   *Answer:* a

Selection 12   Give it a second chance

VOCABULARY PREVIEW, P. 123

maitre d' → head waiter

botch → ruin something

pick up → pay the bill

make amends → correct something done wrong

incinerated → burned

🔲 LISTEN FOR SPECIFIC INFORMATION, PP. 123 - 124

1. b   2. b   3. a   4. a   5. b and c

Consumer Principle #1
In a restaurant, it's acceptable to send the food back to the kitchen if it is <u>incorrectly</u> prepared, and you haven't eaten more than a bite or two.

Consumer Principle #2
It's okay to complain politely about the food or service to the waiter or waitress, the manager, or the maitre d'. If the restaurant wants you to come back, they'll offer to <u>replace</u> the food or <u>deduct</u> the cost of the dish from your bill.

Consumer Principle #3
If you have a bad experience at a restaurant, give it a <u>second</u> chance. Everyone has a bad night now and then, and there may have been circumstances that night that you could not have known about.

Selection 13   You have to pay for a true estimate

🔲 LISTEN FOR MAIN IDEAS, P. 126

Refer to the transcript for the sentence completions.

Consumer Principle #4
You have to pay for true estimates. If you use someone's time to diagnose your problem, you have to pay for that person's time even if the problem is not fixed.

Selection 14   Save your receipt

🔊 **LISTEN FOR MAIN IDEAS, P. 128**

Refer to the transcript for information.

Consumer Principle #5
Always <u>save</u> your receipt.

Selection 15   Talk to the owner when necessary

🔊 **LISTEN FOR SPECIFIC INFORMATION, P. 129**

1. Because she has electrical problems in her home (and he thinks it will harm his refrigerator).
2. Doyle didn't know that Lynn doesn't have a refrigerator from his store.
3. He'll give her a new refrigerator if she can show him a receipt.
4. She can get a refrigerator with ice and water in the door, or a refrigerator with a one-year exchange privilege, or a refund.
5. Tom thinks Doyle is dealing reasonably with Lynn's problem.

Consumer principle #6
If the salesperson can't solve your problem or complaint quickly and politely, you may need to speak directly to the <u>owner</u> or <u>manager</u> to resolve your problem.

Selection 16   Avoid buying used appliances

🔊 **LISTEN FOR MAIN IDEAS, P. 130**

Refer to the transcript for answers.

Consumer Principle #7
When buying a used appliance, consider buying from <u>individuals</u> and having the appliance <u>checked out</u> before you buy it.

Unit 5
DATING, MARRIAGE, AND DIVORCE

Selection 1   Introduction to the main speaker

VOCABULARY PREVIEW, P. 134

Noun	Verb	Adjective	Adverb
betrayal	betray	betrayed	
ignorance	ignore	ignorant	ignorantly
loyalty	be loyal	loyal	loyally

KEYS TO BETTER COMPREHENSION: RECOGNIZING RELAXED PRONUNCIATION, PP. 134-135

Answers with relaxed pronunciation are underlined.

2.   We're also talking about some of the red flags that people wish they would've saw [sic]. They say, "I wish I would've seen this coming. I wish I would've seen that red flag," and then they make themselves feel worse. I suppose what I'm suggesting to you is, well, yes it would've been nice if you could've known that. It'd kind of be nice if you could know a lot of things, notice a lot of things so that you would never make any mistakes. But sometimes a red flag doesn't look like a red flag when it's happening. It only looks like a red flag after you're smart enough after it's happened. Other times we talk about things, and we say, "Y'know, something went off; my alarm..." —and we talk a lot on this show about the alarm system—so throw one off at me, when it happened...and I knew it was a problem, and I knew I wanted to take care of it except I didn't." Well, that doesn't mean you can't do something about it now. But we'll talk a bit about red flags, and if you even overreact to the red flags.

LISTEN FOR MAIN IDEAS, P. 135

Topics that came up yesterday:

1. friendships
2. love relationships (betrayal/loyalty)
3. people who can't be trusted

Things she'd like to talk about this afternoon:

1. how you might repair a relationship if you want to
2. "red flags" in relationships—things people wish they would have seen

LISTEN FOR SPECIFIC INFORMATION, P. 136

Basic answers are included below. You can add as much detail as your students can come up with.
1. "...A component of loyalty is indeed betrayal."
2. Betrayal means when someone close to you goes behind your back and does things or talks about things that you don't expect them to do or talk about.
3. An example of the ultimate betrayal is when a spouse has an affair with another person.
4. "Some things are worth repairing; other things—life is too short."

5. It's better to <u>over</u>-repair than to <u>under</u>-repair.

6. "Some of the things that might be going <u>wrong</u> ...ought to be <u>red flags</u> for you."

7. We ignore red flags because we <u>want things to work out</u>.

8. It's okay to ignore red flags especially when people are <u>in love</u>.

9. Sometimes a red flag doesn't look like one until <u>after it's happened</u>.

10. Although we didn't take care of a problem at the time it happened, we can still <u>learn from it or maybe we can still do something about it now</u>.

))) Chapter 11   Dating

Selection 2   An age difference

LISTEN FOR MAIN IDEAS, P. 137

1. She's 22 years old. She's dating someone 11 years older than her. The relationship is basically good.

2. "You're so smart for only being 22," or "You're only 22; you wouldn't know."

3. Sherry doesn't like the fact that he's always reminding her of the age difference; he's putting her down.

VOCABULARY PREVIEW, P. 137

Answers are underlined.

...he's somewhat conflicted about the fact that you're a lot <u>younger</u>.

vocabulary: "to be conflicted about" → struggle with, have an inner disagreement

...your first example was kind of a back-handed <u>compliment</u>

idiom: a back-handed compliment → it sounds like a compliment, but

there's a hint of an insult in it also

...he's <u>somewhat</u> demeaning to you

somewhat → to some degree, to some extent

demeaning → treating someone else as lower; not showing respect

Selection 3   Big Daddy

LISTEN FOR SPECIFIC INFORMATION, P. 138

The statements with check marks are referred to by Andrea or Sherry; statements with asterisks can be inferred from their statements:

*1. He appears to be less mature than a typical 33-year-old.

✔2. He's acting like a father to her, because he's treating her like a child.

✔3. He likes to be in control, so he dates women who are much younger.

✔4. Sherry should be tired of hearing about how smart she is for being only 22.

5. Sherry likes to date older men because she didn't have a good father-daughter relationship as she was growing up.

✔6. Sherry should tell him to stop reminding her of their age difference.

7. Sherry should stop dating him.

*8. He should date women who are closer to his own age.

✔9. She should date men who respect her age and intellectual maturity.

10. Sherry should believe that he really does respect her and doesn't mind how young she is, even though he says things that suggest he doesn't.

KEYS TO BETTER COMPREHENSION: DISTINGUISHING HOMONYMS, P. 138

Refer to the transcript for occurrences of "may be" and "maybe." Or you can read from the transcript rather than replaying the tape.

SUMMARY, P. 139

Answers are underlined.

"Let me give you a general rule of thumb. When you're dating someone, and they <u>behave</u> in one way and <u>speak</u> in another, believe <u>behavior</u>. I don't care what he tells you. If his behavior continues to say to you there's a problem with it, believe <u>behavior</u>. And you might care enough about him to do something about it, but when you have two choices, I believe how people <u>behave</u>."

Selection 4   Breaking up

LISTEN FOR MAIN IDEAS, P. 139

Answers are underlined.

who	Sandra and her boyfriend
how long	a year
what happened	decided (together) to break up the relationship
when	3 months ago
how (she feels)	it was a good decision, but she still thinks about him a lot
two questions:	
What	What to do when these feelings come up?
How	How can she get over him faster?

Selection 5   Getting over it

Vocabulary preview, p. 140

1. You feel vulnerable.
2. You reminisce.
3. You get a double dose.
4. They stuff them.
5. You tolerate it.
6. It's a mutual decision.

LISTEN FOR SPECIFIC INFORMATION, PP. 140-141

1. <u>at least 6 months</u>   Why?   <u>That's just how it works.</u>

2. <u>by getting on with your life</u>

3. spend time with people who make her feel good about herself *or* do things she didn't have time for before

4. run away from the pain and the memories

VOCABULARY AND IDIOMS, P. 141

Answers are underlined.

After a year of going together, Sandra and her boyfriend made a mutual decision to break up. Andrea said that the first six months after Sandra broke up with her boyfriend, Sandra would still be vulnerable because she was lonely. A lot of things made her reminisce about the good times they had together. Andrea said she won't get over those feelings quickly. Sandra has to learn to tolerate the sadness for awhile. If she doesn't, and if she just stuffs her feelings inside her and doesn't work through the pain, then the next time she has a break-up, she'll get a double dose of pain.

Dictation: The above paragraph may be used for dictation (107 words).

))) Chapter 12   Marriage

Selection 6   Another expensive wedding

LISTEN FOR MAIN IDEAS, P. 144

Refer to the transcript for information.

CONVERSATION STRATEGY: USING APPROPRIATE WORDING, P. 144

1. Is it a financial issue for you?

2. Why doesn't she provide herself a wedding? At 30, is she not able to do that?

3. No, or at least not all of it.

4. Yes, they can.

5. She doesn't know how to tell her daughter that she doesn't want to pay for another expensive wedding when she already gave the daughter one elaborate wedding.

Selection 7   What to say

LISTEN FOR MAIN IDEAS, P. 145

Refer to transcript for Andrea's advice.

VOCABULARY AND IDIOMS, P. 145

Andrea: "I did a wedding once, and I don't want to do it again."

Joan: "I said I would give half the rehearsal dinner with his folks."

Andrea: "She sounds pretty immature to me at 30..."

Selection 8   The parents' choices

LISTEN FOR MAIN IDEAS, P. 146

1. 18

2. a. Whether they want to pay for their children's college education
   b. Whether they want to pay for their children's weddings.

3. Yes, many do.

4. b and d

5. a and c

6. a and d (b and c are indirectly mentioned)

7. a, b, and d

Selection 9   A new daughter-in-law

LISTEN FOR MAIN IDEAS, P. 147

The new daughter-in-law

- married the son, but she hadn't even met the family

- came out to the town where the daughter's wedding was going to be held, but got so upset that the former daughter-in-law was invited to the wedding that she (and the son) decided not to attend the wedding

- hasn't spoken to her mother-in-law in the 6 months since the wedding; accused her mother-in-law of being a poor parent (after knowing her only 3 days)

The ex-daughter-in-law

- had known the family 4-5 years before she married the son, so she was like family to them (like a godmother to the mother's grandson)

- the daughter and family invited her to the daughter's wedding

The son
- was married for 4-1/2 years; then got divorced (no children)
- 4 days after the divorce, he married someone else
- he's 26 years old
- he and his new wife didn't attend his sister's wedding
- wants to resolve the situation (his new wife being upset)
- he's feeling guilty about his wife's reaction and what he said to her

The daughter

- was getting married

- invited ex-sister-in-law, brother, and new sister-in-law to her wedding

The mother

- wants to resolve the problem with the new daughter-in-law, who hasn't spoken to her in 6 months

Selection 10   Rise to the occasion

VOCABULARY AND IDIOMS, P. 148

> *rise to the occasion* → meet the challenge of an event or difficult task

take the high road → choose the most honorable option

nitwit → a stupid or foolish person

guys (informal) → refers to both the father and the mother

Chapter 13   Divorce

Selection 11   Surviving divorce

VOCABULARY PREVIEW, P. 150

1.

	Noun	Verb	Adjective	Adverb
a.	humility		humble	humbly
b.	femininity		feminine	
c.	contribution, contributor	contribute	contributing	
d.	rage	enrage	enraged	
e.	economics	economize	economical	economically
f.	misery		miserable	miserably
g.	devastation	devastate	devastating	devastatingly
h.	marriage	marry	married or marital	
i.	betrayal	betray	betrayed	

2.   After 24 years of <u>marriage</u>, the woman's husband packed his bags and left her for another man. She still felt <u>enraged</u>, <u>humiliated</u> and <u>miserable</u>. Furthermore, she felt <u>betrayed</u> by her husband's decision; she said her <u>femininity</u> had been destroyed. Harriet agreed that the woman's experience must have been particularly <u>devastating,</u> and advised that she start asking some questions about her future, like how would she support herself <u>economically</u>? She also needs to take an objective look at her <u>contribution</u> to their <u>marital</u> problems so she doesn't just feel like a victim.

DICTATION: THE ABOVE PARAGRAPH MAY BE USED FOR DICTATION (91 WORDS).

KEYS TO BETTER COMPREHENSION: FOCUSING ON CONTENT WORDS, P. 151

DICTATION, P. 152

3.

gvrnmnt	government	abbrvtn*	abbreviation
cnvstn	conversation	cmprhnsn	comprehension
hppnd	happened	prblm	problem
instrctr*	instructor	rltnshp	relationship

The instructor dictates the following sentences:

1. She started to ask her some questions.   *indicates a question*

2. She asked her to take responsibility for what happened.   *indicates a request*

3. She asked her questions about what happened.   *indicates a question*

Selection 12   What's wrong with this picture?

KEYS TO BETTER COMPREHENSION: RECOGNIZING RELAXED PRONUNCIATION, PP. 153-154

This is a good exercise to do on an overhead projector. Listen to a sentence and mark the stresses and rapid speech together. It's not important that everyone agrees; what is important is that students begin to understand that content words (nouns and verbs) are generally stressed in spoken English.

VOCABULARY AND IDIOMS, P. 155

(be) amiss	out of order; wrong
not (be) with it	behind the times; not current; not in step with others
not so hot	not good
(that) old saw	a familiar proverb or saying
fooling around	*(in this context:)* sleeping with someone other than a spouse
a rule of thumb	a rough, practical method or procedure
on the edge	feeling unsure or unsafe
slick	ingenious, clever, glib

Selection 13   An insecure marriage

KEYS TO BETTER COMPREHENSION: RECOGNIZING HOMONYMS, P. 155

a. due (noun)	d. do (main verb)
b. due (adjective)	e. do (helping verb)
c. due to (prepositional phrase)	

The instructor reads several sentences. Students write down the letter of the word and usage of "do" heard in each sentence. Don't let students write the entire sentence. The letter of the answer is in parentheses after the sentence.

1. It's not fun for me to do it. (d)

2. I really want to know what I should do about the situation. (d)

3. It's not fun for me to bowl due to an auto accident, because it hurts my shoulder. (c)

4. Do you know her? (e)

5. This assignment is due on Friday. (b)

Refer to the transcript for main ideas.

Selection 14   An unequal relationship

VOCABULARY PREVIEW, P. 156

The instructor dictates the following sentences from the selection. Meanings of the underlined phrases are given in italics.

1. If you're not primary, then you are <u>at risk</u>.   *in danger*

2. I think you would be <u>better off</u> saying that to him.   *in a better position*

3. That <u>scares me a great deal</u>.   *frightens me a lot*

4. This marriage is not <u>a priority</u> to you.   *most important*

5. You're somebody that's <u>got a long haul</u> ahead of you.   *has many years*

6. ...and if he kind of <u>blows you off</u>...   *doesn't regard you as important*

7. You better find somebody to help you <u>beef up</u> your   *improve; become firm.*
   communication skills and <u>find your spine</u>.

8. The longer you take to do that, the less secure   *shaky*
   and more <u>quivery</u> inside you're going to feel.

LISTEN FOR SPECIFIC INFORMATION, P. 157

Refer to the transcript for questions and answers.

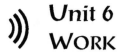 # Unit 6
WORK

Selection 1   Burnout

VOCABULARY PREVIEW, P. 160

> *burn out* → to become tired of doing something, worn out

🔲 LISTEN FOR SPECIFIC INFORMATION, P. 160
1.   Fill-in-the-blank words are underlined.

"Burnout, the need to be <u>needed</u>, an inability to <u>say no</u>—all these are <u>masks</u> of overdoing it that are especially evident in <u>women</u>. Burnout, the need to be in <u>control</u>, an inability to <u>let go</u>—all of these are <u>symptoms</u> of overdoing it that are especially evident in <u>men</u>. But whatever its gender mask, the emotional <u>burnout</u> that comes from obsessive <u>doing</u> and denial of authentic <u>feeling</u> is serious self-abuse."

))) Chapter 14   Overdoing It

Selection 2   Introduction to the topic

🔲 LISTEN FOR MAIN IDEAS, P. 162
1.   Dr. Robinson is one of the most respected authorities in the U.S. on addictive behavior.
2.   *Overdoing It*
3.   *(answers will vary)* being an overachiever, trying to be perfect
4.   *(students may supply their own examples)* Getting straight A's.

Selection 3   Overdoing it

🔲 LISTEN FOR MAIN IDEAS, PP. 164-165

Approximate answers are underlined in the outline. Refer to transcript for more information.

I.   Why is overdoing it such a contemporary problem?
  A.   Because <u>today the boundaries between home and work are becoming so blurred</u>.
  B.   Examples: <u>bringing kids to work; more mothers working in the office; mothers who nurse in the workplace; people going to appointments and running errands during lunch hour</u>

Abstract Concept	Concrete Examples
modern technology:	<u>fax</u> machines

Abstract Concept	Concrete Examples
home being brought to work:	<u>laptop</u> computers <u>cellular</u> telephones <u>bringing kids to work</u> <u>mothers who nurse in the workplace</u>

II. Is working hard a requirement to succeed in today's world?
  A. Answer:
  "I <u>don't think</u> it's a requirement, but I think a lot of people have <u>interpreted</u> that as a requirement."

  B. Example of the woman working on her Ph.D.:
  <u>married, working on Ph.D. full time; her standard was to make an A in her first statistics course.</u>
  <u>She earned an A+ in the first course, so that became her standard for the 2nd and 3rd courses.</u>
  <u>She went into depression when she got an A- on the 3rd course.</u>

  C. The main point of this example:
  "This was her <u>standard</u>, and her own sense of inadequacy...[caused] her to <u>feel</u> as if she <u>failed</u>."

III. Is "overdoing it" taught to us as children?
  A. "Kids tend to look at the world through the eyes of their <u>parents</u>."

  B. Areas where people overdo:

    1. <u>in the workplace</u>

    2. <u>at school (grades); in sports; at home; etc.</u>

  C. About (our) parents:
  <u>Children focus on what the parents focus on; parents expect the best from their kids.</u>

    1. A recent example:
    <u>A teenager won second place in a state essay competition and was very excited, but her</u>
    <u>father was disappointed because she didn't win first place.</u>

    2. The main idea of the example:
    <u>She's still trying to prove to her dad that she can make it (She's now 28 years old.).</u>

IV. How does being an overdoer affect a family?
  A. If I'm "supermom," I hold down a <u>job,</u> bring in <u>money,</u> come home in time to <u>bake cookies</u> and
  <u>listen</u> to my kids and read <u>bedtime</u> stories...don't my kids benefit from this?

  B. Answer:
  <u>It depends. The quality of the time that parents spend with their kids is important.</u>

  C. What are "brownouts"?
  <u>episodes of forgetfulness that occur as a result of being so tired that we can't attend to the</u>
  <u>present</u>

    1. Example:
    <u>A mother doesn't remember her children asking her a question; they have to ask her more</u>
    <u>than once.</u>

    2. Definition:
    <u>(above under "C")</u> also: <u>having your mind on several things but not paying attention to what</u>
    <u>you're doing right now</u>

VOCABULARY PREVIEW, P. 167

guilt	responsibility for doing something wrong
black out	lose consciousness
resent	to feel angry or bitter at
pamper yourself	to treat yourself kindly, make yourself comfortable
go bankrupt	to have nothing left in reserve
deposit	to add to, fill up
withdraw	to take out
nurture	to give care or nourishment to someone else
stereotype	an example of a general type
myth	a false story
telescoping	focusing on the negative or on a flaw

KEYS TO BETTER COMPREHENSION: RECOGNIZING ANALOGY, PP. 167-168

Refer to transcript for answers. The two analogies are the airplane emergency and the bank account.

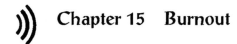 ## LISTEN FOR MAIN IDEAS, P. 168

Refer to transcript for answers.

))) Chapter 15   Burnout

Selection 5   What does an EMT do?

VOCABULARY PREVIEW, P. 171
1. Definitions

paramedic	a person who administers medical attention (especially in an emergency) before a doctor or nurse can tend to the patient
emergency room	in a hospital, an area which treats emergencies and urgent patients
resuscitative equipment	equipment which provides oxygen to a patient to keep him or her alive or breathing
cardiac drugs	medication which is used in treating the heart

an EKG machine	(electrocardiogram) a machine which measures the electric activity of the heart muscles
ambulance	a vehicle which is equipped to help sick people (especially in the case of an emergency) before they can get to a hospital
siren	the prolonged sound on an emergency vehicle to signal its approach

2. Paraphrase *(Answers will vary.)*

    a. Could you describe the details of your job, including what you do as well as what you don't do?

    b. What happened in your life that made you decide to do this kind of work?

    c. What kinds of people begin training (for this job), but then find out that the job isn't suitable for them?

LISTENING CHECK, P. 172

1. What is your day like?

2. Are there days when not much happens?

3. Are there days when lots happens?

4. Can you predict what an average day is like?

LISTEN AGAIN, PP. 172-173

1.
    a. *hands, eyes, ears* → We help a doctor feel, see, and hear (because the doctor isn't there to treat the patient).

    b. *time is of the essence* → It's crucial not to waste time.

    c. *got hooked by* → enthusiastic about something; get taken in

    d. *entails* → involves

    e. *not cut out for it* → not suitable for something

    f. *get out of whack* → out of line, apart from reality

Selection 6   A typical day

LISTEN FOR SPECIFIC INFORMATION, PP. 174-175

Answers are underlined. Refer to transcript for more information.

I. Statistics about emergency room visits:
    A. DGH last year - over <u>45,000</u> emergency room visits
        <u>60</u>% auto accidents
        <u>30</u>% crime-related
        <u>10</u>% other

II. A typical day
    A. Always involves <u>alcohol</u>

    B. Ann works <u>9:00 p.m.</u> until <u>7:00 a.m.</u>

    C. <u>90</u>% of the people she treats are <u>intoxicated</u>.

    D. When EMT's aren't responding to a call, they <u>sit in the ambulance in parks or in parking lots of stores</u>.

E. Their office is in their <u>ambulance,</u> basically.

F. They could have nothing to do for hours, and then <u>it's go, go, go (It suddenly gets very busy.)</u>.

III. How a call comes in

A. With the E911 system, the information comes to them on a <u>computer screen</u>.

B. Kinds of information the paramedics receive:
<u>where a caller is calling from, the address, the phone number</u>

C. Information which the dispatcher can give a caller:
<u>how to do CPR</u>

Selection 7 Coping with burnout

LISTENING CHECK, P. 176

Refer to the transcript for information on why an answer is false.

1. False (not everyone welcomes the sight of an ambulance)

2. True ("He will fight with you physically...")

3. False ("People think we have a cushy job.")

4. True ("The bottom line is we care about people.")

5. False ("My saving grace is to be emotionally distant.")

6. True ("...to realize they can only do so much. We don't walk on water.")

7. True ("late 20's, early 30's")

8. True ("The majority...stay in this field maybe 10 years.")

9. True ("It's not only emotionally taxing; it's very physically draining.")

10. True ("I would say I probably have another good 5 years...")

11. True (same as 6 above)

LISTEN AGAIN, P. 177

Refer to the transcript for answers.

KEYS TO BETTER COMPREHENSION: REVIEW, PP. 177-178

The review list of listening strategies will depend on which chapters and/or units you have completed to this point.

1. wanna
The teacher reads this sentence with relaxed pronunciation of "want to":
"I don't wanna start when I'm burned."

2. Because *like* can be used as a verb, an adverb, an adjective, a preposition, a conjunction, or as a filler word, depending on the context.
The teacher reads this sentence. Students write the sentence down and then discuss the uses of "like."
"It's *like* I really *like* seeing the UPS truck come down the driveway."

3. She compares the ambulance to a UPS (United Parcel Service, a delivery service) truck, because people expect both to bring "good stuff" (i.e. medical assistance; packages or gifts)

4. would've
The teacher reads this sentence with relaxed pronunciation of "would have":
"I guess I would've assumed like everyone else that if you're in trouble and you show up, that's great."

5. Y'know; I mean

))) Chapter 16   Work Force

Selection 8   How do I get into the work force?

🔊 LISTEN FOR SPECIFIC INFORMATION, P. 180

1. How do you get back into the work force if you've been out for quite some time, or what's the best way to get back into the work force.

2. Six years.

3. Taking care of her children.

4. She was a cashier; she did fashion merchandising; she worked in a Payless shoe store.

5. She didn't get any calls from the places where she had applied.

🔊 LISTEN FOR MAIN IDEAS, P. 181

1. You *may* have to be *a little* more <u>aggressive</u> getting information.

2. *Maybe* you need to <u>update</u> your skills.

3. Ask what sorts of skills they look for...in case you need to <u>train</u> yourself to get current for the <u>market</u> now.

4. You got to decide what's <u>important</u> to you right now...you want the <u>flexibility</u>...you *may not* have that <u>luxury</u>.

5. You need something on your <u>resumé</u> and you don't have it.

CONVERSATION STRATEGY: USING APPROPRIATE TONE, P. 181

The words which "soften" the tone are in italics in the above exercise. Suggested answers for a stronger tone are given below.

1. Be more aggressive getting information.

2. You need to update your skills.

3. (no change)

4. ...you don't have that luxury.

5. (no change)

🔊 LISTEN AGAIN, P. 182

Suggested answers are given below.

Advice	Example or supporting statements
1. be more aggressive	Call back and ask what skills they are looking for.
	Go in person again and ask more questions.
2. update your skills	Take a short course in something.
	Find out what has changed in the industry.
	Ask what skills an employer is looking for.
3. get trained for the current market	Find out what skills you are lacking.

Advice	Example or supporting statements
	Get a job in a temporary agency to get into the workforce.
4. decide your priorities	Is it more important to have summer vacation with your kids?
	Is it more important to only work 9 to 3 so you can be home when your kids are home?
	Is it better to work just one day a week and hire a baby sitter?

SUMMARY, P. 182

1. c   2. a   3. d   4. b

Selection 9   Get retrained

KEYS TO BETTER COMPREHENSION: UNDERSTANDING CONNECTING WORDS, P. 183

Kathy uses these transitions: One   Secondly   And then

KEYS TO BETTER COMPREHENSION: RECOGNIZING CONTENT WORDS, PP. 183-184.

If your students need more practice in writing content words in the amount of time it takes to read the sentence, read sentences from the transcript. Or make it a pair exercise, and let the students take turns reading aloud to a partner.

Another optional activity for practice: Copy the transcript for this or another selection from the instructor's manual and analyze the content words in each sentence before listening to the selection. Then have students compare how successfully they took notes compared to the words they underlined.

1.
articles	function	nouns	content
conjunctions	function	adverbs	content
adjectives	content	helping verbs	function
prepositions	function	modal verbs	content and function
		main verbs	content

2. *(suggested answer:)* support - makes - women - comfortable - initial phases - technical & male-dominated field

3. Advantages of WICS program
   1. level of support and help
   2. help with finding a job at the end
   3. mail a resumé book to area employers

Suggested answers. Refer to transcript for more information.

Advantages of WICS program
1. level of support and help
   students don't just come to class, sit in lecture, go home
   support helps women feel more comfortable entering highly technical and male-dominated field

2. help with finding a job at the end
   students have full access to University Career Center, on campus interviewing, and a counselor is assigned to the program because most students work full time during day; counselor comes on lab night to interview, critique resumés, present seminars—seminars on skills analysis, resumé writing, interviewing skills

3. mail a resumé book to area employers
   within 24 hours, employers were calling for interviews; previous graduates call with information on job openings in their companies

Selection 10   People who need retraining

Keys to better comprehension: Recognizing pronoun referents, p. 184

Skip these first two sections if it's too easy for your group, and just listen for the 5 main categories.

1. transition words: still   then   Ø   also   and then

2. pronoun + verb: we have   we have   we get   we get   we get

Listen for main ideas, p. 184

Categories of students who enter the WICS program:
1. the reentry woman
2. people who have dead-end jobs
3. people who have careers and are looking for a transition into another industry
4. people who are seeing their industry dry up and shrink
5. people who need to gain more computer expertise

Listen for specific information, p. 185

1. the reentry woman
   has been at home raising her children
   has decided she needs to or wants to go back to work

2. people who have dead-end jobs
   they're not using their intelligence
   they want a career with more earning potential (money)

3. people who have careers and are looking for a transition into another industry
   they have a career but want to get into another career
   for example: teachers, nurses, med techs

4. people who are seeing their industry dry up and shrink
   in the oil industry: petroleum engineers, geophysicists
   their industry is shrinking, and they don't want to be transferred (or they may lose their job if the company downsizes)

5. people who need to gain more computer expertise
they're happy in their jobs, but computer expertise is needed in order to advance in their job or career.

Selection 11   Interviewing for a job

🔲 LISTEN FOR SPECIFIC INFORMATION, P. 185

If the students need more practice listening for stressed words, copy the entire transcript for this selection. Listen to the selection in small sections, and then discuss each section before continuing. Or play a sentence, and have the students repeat, mimicking Debra's intonation.
2. Debra indicates quotation by <u>pausing</u>.

🔲 LISTENING CHECK, P. 186

1. She wanted to write about the valuable information she learned after being fired from a very good job.

2. "You are born with it and you can relearn it" because we tend to unlearn it.

3. People skills include "chemistry" between two people, impressions that you leave with other people, having a dynamic personality, fitting in with other coworkers, having confidence, projecting your competence, being genuine.

4. Don't be in a hurry, pause until you are noticed, use non-verbal body language and gestures, look a person in the eye, don't give a quick handshake, don't act anxious.

5. Walk in the room in a hurry, put your hands in your lap and look nervous or anxious, give a quick or soft (meaningless) handshake.

6. Business deals are figuratively "closed" with a handshake (before contracts are signed, etc.). It's an important gesture; it sets the tone of an introduction.

7. Listen for it, slow down, take more time, use the name in conversation, write it down after you leave the conversation.

8. They aren't really listening; they are paying more attention to how they are coming across to the other person.

Unit 7
RENTING AN APARTMENT

VOCABULARY PREVIEW, P. 190

1. n	4. l	7. k	10. e	13. a
2. f	5. m	8. b	11. h	14. i
3. o	6. g	9. j	12. c	15. d

VOCABULARY PREVIEW, P. 191

When you decide to <u>rent</u> an apartment, you are entering into a legal agreement, which means you have various rights and responsibilities. You must sign a <u>lease</u> which says that you agree to pay a certain amount of money every month, usually for a minimum of one year. Then you pay a <u>deposit</u>. This money is a form of security for the <u>landlord</u>, who owns the building. As a <u>tenant</u>, you are also responsible for keeping <u>the premises</u> clean and in good condition. If you don't, your deposit will be used to clean and repair the apartment. If you leave it in good condition, your deposit will be returned to you. You agree to pay the <u>rent</u> on or before the first of the month; if you don't, you have to pay a <u>late charge</u>. Occasionally, a landlord will <u>waive</u> this charge if you have a reasonable explanation. If you fail to pay your rent, you can <u>get evicted</u> by the manager, who supervises the building and <u>leases</u> the apartments. Getting an <u>eviction</u> <u>notice</u> is very serious. You will still be held responsible to pay the rent that is due.

On the other hand, if you follow all the <u>provisions</u> of your lease, and the landlord does not follow through on his responsibilities, you can <u>sue</u> him in court for damages.

DICTATION

Some or all of the above paragraph may be used for dictation (225 words total).

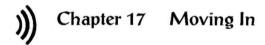

Chapter 17   Moving In

Selection 1   Signing a lease

LISTEN FOR SPECIFIC INFORMATION, P. 193

1. 6 months	4. $625 per month	7. woman
2. about a month	5. two	8. one page
3. three	6. $680	9. no

LISTEN AGAIN, P. 193

1. $208.33
2. Now. Because there are now three people living there instead of two.
3. By $55.
4. He told the landlady to send him a copy, but she hasn't.
5. So they would each be responsible for paying the rent. Probably, yes.
6. The landlord does not have the right to raise the rent until the lease expires.
7. Because he didn't demand a copy of the lease when he signed it.
8. (answers will vary)
9. When the lease expires.
10. Because three people are living there. Originally, there were only supposed to be two.

DIFFERENCES BETWEEN SPOKEN AND WRITTEN ENGLISH, P. 194

Correct: Two of my friends and I moved into this place.

or

Two friends and I moved into this place.

KEYS TO BETTER COMPREHENSION: RECOGNIZING PARAPHRASING, P. 194

1. Greg: "Me and two of my friends... we signed a lease for six months."

   Tom: Now, you <u>all signed the lease, Greg</u>?

2. Greg: "But we all three signed the lease."

   Tom: Okay, now <u>you all signed for all of the lease</u>.

3. Tom: "It wasn't divided in thirds."

   Tom: In other words, <u>you each signed for $625 a month</u>.

4. Greg: "Well no, we're splitting up the rent."

   Tom: I know that. <u>You are splitting up the rent among yourselves</u>.

5. Tom: "Each one of you signed a lease which said $625."

   Tom: You <u>didn't sign one that said a third of that</u>.

CONVERSATION STRATEGIES REVIEW, P. 196

1. Do not just <u>repeat</u> the other speaker's statement exactly. Paraphrase it.
2. Ask a <u>question</u> or use <u>rising</u> intonation.
3. Add <u>reflexive</u> pronouns quantifiers to clarify part of a sentence.
4. Change a <u>positive</u> statement to a negative or a <u>negative</u> statement to a positive.

Tenant responsibilities:

1. Be careful to pay the rent <u>on</u> <u>time</u>.
2. Whenever you sign a lease or any legal document, always, *always*, *ALWAYS* <u>keep</u> <u>a</u> <u>copy</u>.

Landlord responsibility:

1. The landlord must follow the <u>provisions</u> of the lease; they cannot be changed unless the tenants who <u>signed</u> the lease agree to the change.

LISTENING CHECK: TOEFL PRACTICE, P. 197

Tapescript and answers

1. Man: We've been living there a month, and already the landlord wants to raise our rent.
   Woman: How can she do that if you have a lease?

Question: What does the woman mean?

Answer: (c) The landlord can't raise the rent because the man has signed a lease.

2. Woman: How can your landlord raise the rent if you have a lease?
   Man: Yeah! That's what I was wondering.

Question: What does the man's comment mean?

Answer: (d) He also wonders why the landlord raised the rent, because he has a lease.

3. Man: Does it say anything in your lease about the right to raise rent?
   Woman: Not that I remember.

Question: What does the woman mean?

Answer: (d) She doesn't remember what the lease said about the landlord raising the rent.

4. Woman: Do you have a copy of that lease?
   Man: I told the landlord to send me a copy of the lease, but...

Question: What can we infer from the man's comment?

Answer: (c) The man asked for a copy of the lease, but didn't receive one.

5. Man: You signed the lease, and you didn't keep a copy?
   Woman: I know...

Question: What can we infer from the woman's comment?

Answer: (b) She knows she should have kept a copy.

Selection 2   What are the tenant's rights?

LISTEN FOR MAIN IDEAS, PP. 198-199

The answers below begin where the blanks begin in the exercise. Answers are underlined.

Tom: ...The point is this. We all have this idea that when we rent a place, we have <u>certain rights</u>. The only rights we have are the rights set forth in the <u>lease</u>... and an additional right you may not find in the lease, which is <u>peaceful</u> enjoyment of the premises. If there was [sic] a health and safety hazard—let's say there was a health and safety hazard...that still doesn't mean that the landlord <u>has to fix</u> it. All that it means is that you're allowed <u>to move</u>. When it comes to squirrels being just a nuisance, I don't think you could even argue that they're a <u>health</u> and <u>safety</u> hazard.

Brent: Okay, well they have eaten like a hole in the roof...

Tom: What does your lease say about <u>pest</u> control?

Brent: Let me see here...

Tom: ...I don't think you're gonna find anything in the lease that will <u>address</u> this problem. If your landlord doesn't want to fix it, I doubt that you can <u>make</u> him (them) <u>fix</u> it....Is this serious enough, Barrie, that he could say it <u>violates</u> the lease?

Barrie: I think it could be a <u>health hazard</u>. Do you have <u>children</u> in the house with you, Brent?

Brent: No.

Barrie:	Well...
Brent:	Sure don't.
Barrie:	I...even for an adult.
Tom:	Brent,...there are no laws that address <u>habitability</u> in this state.
Brent:	Okay.
Tom:	And I don't think you can make your <u>landlord</u> fix it.
Brent:	Oh yeah, I understand that. I just, it seemed like they're <u>ignoring</u> me all the time.
Tom:	Well, they probably are. Do you have a <u>lease</u>?
Brent:	Yeah.
Barrie:	How long is it?
Brent:	It's a <u>year's</u> lease.
Tom:	Okay, you could probably try asking them to let you <u>out of it</u>, or say that you're going to sue them for a <u>release</u> from the lease, because you can't tolerate it anymore.
Brent:	Well, yeah, I mean, also 'cause it's not just the squirrels. It's, y'know, our house is easily accessible without the use of <u>keys</u>, and I asked—I requested dead bolts, and they says [sic], "Well, you can buy 'em."
Tom:	See, Brent, that's the point...But the bottom line here is there's not a lot of help for tenants when it comes to <u>opinions</u>, like dead bolts...Even though you think it's necessary, <u>they don't</u>. Squirrels being a nuisance, noisy neighborhoods, crime-ridden areas, these are all opinions. There's no habitability that <u>protects</u> you.

KEYS TO BETTER COMPREHENSION: RECOGNIZING RELAXED PRONUNCIATION, P. 199

Relaxed forms include: lemme (let me), gonna, gotta, wanna, yeah,'cause,'em

(You may notice other forms as well.)

Fillers include: y'know, well, like

DIFFERENCES BETWEEN SPOKEN AND WRITTEN ENGLISH, P. 200

Corrected sentences:

If there <u>were</u> a health and safety hazard...that still doesn't mean that the landlord has to fix it.

I requested dead bolts, and they <u>said</u>, "Well, you can buy them."

Selection 3   The cat and the bird cage

VOCABULARY PREVIEW, PP. 200-201

1.	*shorted it out*	to break the path of electricity
2.	*a chain reaction*	a series of events which cause or influence the next event(s)
3.	*negligence*	lack of proper care
4.	*a lineup*	a group of people (or, in this case, cats!) lined up for identification or inspection; used when a witness tries to identify a criminal
5.	*gets framed*	to arrange false evidence so a person (or, in this case, a cat) appears to be guilty

LISTEN FOR MAIN IDEAS, P. 201

> *Refer to transcript.*

KEYS TO BETTER COMPREHENSION: UNDERSTANDING HUMOR, P. 202

Statement "c" is spoken with intonation to indicate humor.

Selection 4   Can she prove it?

LISTEN FOR SPECIFIC INFORMATION, P. 202
1. the animal control officer
2. 40-50 minutes after the "crime" occurred and the woman called the officer.
3. The cat was picked up in the yard.
4. in the neighbor's yard.
5. The cat had nothing to say about it.

KEYS TO BETTER COMPREHENSION: UNDERSTANDING HUMOR, P. 202

The humor lies in Tom's asking whether Susan's cat had anything to say about the situation. Tom also plays with the idea that Susan knows whether her cat is a good cat or not, and can probably guess whether or not the cat would do such a deed. Tom also suggests that Susan take photographs of the neighbor's cats and having a "line-up" for the neighbor to pick the guilty cat from. In a way, he's being facetious, but at the same time, it's also a good idea.

LISTEN FOR SPECIFIC INFORMATION, P. 203
1. True
2. False (40-50 minutes later, in the yard)
3. True
4. False (for damaging property)
5. True
6. True
7. False (The city wants pet owners to be more responsible for their animals.)
8. True
9. False (It's only for dogs.)
10. True

))) Chapter 18 Moving Out

Selection 5 Notify the manager

VOCABULARY AND IDIOMS, P. 205

The instructor dictates the following sentences. Use relaxed pronunciation.
1. Our lease is gonna be up December first.
2. The contract says we have to give 30 days written notice.
3. The manager said this was not a valid letter.
4. The burden of proof is on you.
5. My sister went down there as usual to drop off the rent.
6. She verbally notified the manager that we were moving out.

LISTEN FOR SPECIFIC INFORMATION, P. 206

Refer to transcript for specific information.

SUMMARY, P. 206

The tenants:		Evidence:
1.	They gave 30 days written notice.	photocopy
2.	Her little sister, Stefanie, gave verbal notice.	the woman who gave her a receipt and brochure
3.	Maria's roommate, Sandra, talked to Karen, the manager.	The roommate is a witness.
4.	Stefanie told the leasing agent that Sandra might be staying in the building.	The woman offered to give her keys to look at other apartments.

The manager:		Evidence:
1.	She never received the written notice.	none (How do you prove you don't have it?)
2.	She's never lost anything in 18 years.	Hard to prove!

Selection 6 Write the owner directly

VOCABULARY AND IDIOMS, P. 206

The instructor dictates the following sentences. The focus vocabulary and idioms are underlined. A paraphrase is given in parentheses.
1. I'm going to <u>be out of</u> my deposit, which was 350 bucks.
   (I'm not going to get my deposit of $350 back.)
2. You can <u>sue</u> for <u>triple</u> the <u>amount</u>. (You can take legal action for three times the amount.)
3. It seems unlikely that you'd <u>go through all these lengths</u> to try to cheat them.
   (You probably wouldn't take the time to perform all these actions just to cheat them.)

4. Write the owner that you <u>intend to pursue</u> this. (Notify the owner that you plan to continue seeking action.)

5. That's the <u>bottom line</u>. (That's the most important factor or point.)

KEYS TO BETTER COMPREHENSION: RECOGNIZING INFORMAL ENGLISH, P. 207

I   1.   I'm going to <u>be out of</u> 350 <u>bucks</u>!

I   2.   Now <u>hold on</u> here.

I   3.   You <u>got</u> your sister, you <u>got</u> your roommate, and you <u>got</u> a copy of the letter as proof.

I   4.   It seems unlikely that you'd <u>go through all these lengths</u> to try to cheat them.

I   5.   <u>On top of that</u>, I was speaking with Karen to try to <u>fix</u> the situation <u>up</u>, and the woman <u>hung up</u> on me.

F   6.   <u>Under the terms of the lease</u>, they have a certain amount of time to return the deposit.

F   7.   If you don't hear anything within 60 days, then you can <u>sue</u> for <u>triple</u> the <u>amount of damages</u>.

F   8.   Your <u>ascertation</u>* that I did not send the first letter is ridiculous.

F   9.   I <u>intend</u> to <u>pursue</u> this.

* "Ascertation" is not a word. The speaker meant "assertion" or "ascertainment."

LISTEN FOR MAIN IDEAS, P. 207

Complete answers are given below.

I. What Maria can do
She can sue for triple the amount of the deposit.

II. How Maria can prove her case in court
Her evidence and witnesses include: her sister, her roommate, a copy of the letter

III. Who Marie should write to
the owner of Brooks Towers (the apartment complex)

IV. What Maria should write in this letter
This is going to cost you almost a thousand dollars if I have to take this matter to court.

V. What Maria should write in the follow-up letter when she moves out
This is a follow-up to my original letter dated such-and-such. I expect to get my deposit back within 60 days or I plan on suing for triple the amount of damages. Your ascertainment that I did not send the first letter is ridiculous. I have witnesses, I have a copy of the letter, and I intend to pursue this.

SUMMARY, P. 208

Tenant rights:

1. Don't just tell the landlord or manager that you intend to move out. Give <u>written</u> notice as well as verbal notice.

2. When you give notice to the <u>landlord</u> that you intend to move out, keep a <u>copy</u> of the written notice.

3. If a tenant has followed the conditions of the lease, can provide proof, and the landlord refuses to return the <u>deposit</u> within the required amount of time, the tenant can sue for <u>damages</u>. (This amount will depend on the laws of the state, town, country, etc.)

Landlord responsibilities:

1. The landlord must provide the tenant(s) with copies of the <u>rental</u> (or <u>lease</u>) agreement, the tenant's notice to <u>vacate</u> the premises, or the right to renew the lease (if the tenant wants to stay after the lease is up).

2. The landlord cannot <u>renege on</u> a written contract signed by himself and the tenant.

3. The landlord must return the <u>deposit</u> to the tenant within a specific amount of time which is specified in the lease or by law, if the conditions for its return have been satisfactorily met.

Selection 7   Breaking the lease

VOCABULARY AND IDIOMS, PP. 208-209

a. frail → physically weak

b. affords → provides

c. it's a lost cause → there is no solution

d. likelihood → probability   default → failure to complete

e. say → suppose as a possibility

LISTEN FOR MAIN IDEAS, P. 209

Facts: Nancy's elderly mother needs to move because she needs more care.
- Her mother lives out-of-state in Wisconsin.
- She signed a one-year lease a few months ago.
- The lease says she can give a 90-day termination to move.

The problem:
- Her mother will probably have to lose up to 3 months rent (or at least the deposit) if she wants to move sooner than 90 days.

Possible solutions (*Some of these are mentioned later, in Selection 8.*):
- She could wait to move until the 90 days are up.
- She could ask the landlord to try to rent the apartment sooner, and move out when there is a new tenant.
- She could just move out and lose the deposit, and hope that the landlord doesn't come looking for her to pay the rest of the rent.
- She could try to negotiate with the landlord so she could move sooner and not lose so much rent.
- The mother or the daughter could try to find someone to rent it, or hire a management company to find a tenant.

KEYS TO BETTER COMPREHENSION: RECOGNIZING CONFUSING WORDS, P. 209

Sentences for dictation in Part 2. Students only write a, b, or c.
1. Since I last talked to you, I finally got a copy of her lease. (c)
2. She has lived there since 1990. (a)
3. Since she'll probably lose her deposit, I think it's unlikely they'll come after her for the rest of the money. (b)
4. Since I've gotten a copy of this lease, I've found the answer. (ambiguous; could be either b or c)

5. I've made several requests for repairs since we moved in towards the end of August. (c)

Part 3. See the transcript for answers. The correct words are underlined.

Selection 8   Negotiate a solution

🔊 LISTEN FOR SPECIALIZED VOCABULARY, P. 211

Answers are underlined. Definitions of legal terminology are given in parentheses.
   a.   We're going to give the landlord a 90-day <u>termination</u> when we break the lease. (end of a contract)
   b.   It would make it a lot easier if my mother could move out here in July, so would you do your best to <u>rent the premises</u>? (rent the property)
   c.   If the landlord found a renter during that time, would the mother still be <u>liable</u> (for paying the rent)? (held responsible)
   d.   The landlord is not allowed to collect <u>double damages</u>. (money paid twice as compensation for the same problem)
   e.   My mother wouldn't be liable because notice of termination <u>is specified</u> in the lease. (specifically mentioned)
   f.   They can't collect another month's rent just because you broke the contract. Remember, there has to be more than a <u>breach of contract</u>. (breaking a legal agreement)
   g.   There has to be a <u>loss</u> associated with the breach of contract. (money lost in a transaction)
   h.   If the landlord had to rent it out cheaper because market conditions changed or something like that, he would have to <u>prove damages</u>. (money paid or taken as compensation for a loss)
   i.   Will you declare the lease <u>null and void</u> and free us from the conditions of the lease? (having no legal power)

DICTATION, P. 212

The instructor reads the following sentences for dictation. Meanings of the underlined idioms are given in parentheses.
   1.   You're giving the landlord 90 days' <u>head start</u> to rent it out.
        (give someone an early start or advantage)
   2.   They can't collect another month's rent from you <u>just for grins</u>.
        (just because it will make someone happy to have more money)
   3.   <u>Let's say</u> I had a one-year lease, and I moved out after 2 months. (for example)
   4.   This is not <u>a done deal</u> yet. (a completed or finished transaction)

🔊 LISTEN FOR SPECIFIC INFORMATION, P. 212
   Solution 1: Call the landlord, tell him you're going to do a 90-day termination, and say, "Would you <u>do</u> your <u>best</u> to <u>rent</u> the <u>premises</u>?"

   Solution 2: Ask the landlord if you can <u>help</u> <u>rent</u> it <u>out</u> <u>again</u>.

   Solution 3: Hire a <u>management</u> <u>company</u> to do it.

   Solution 4: Say to the landlord, "We'll give you the <u>month</u> of <u>rent</u> and an extra <u>$200</u> if you <u>rent</u> the <u>apartment</u>."

DISCUSS, P. 212

Tenant responsibilities:
Get all of your <u>leases</u> in <u>writing</u>.

Selection 9   Getting an eviction notice

VOCABULARY AND IDIOMS, P. 213

1. Because she made a deal, she <u>stuck</u> <u>to</u> it.
2. Landlords usually…will <u>work</u> <u>with</u> you to solve the problem.
3. I think you just need to <u>cough up</u> the cash now and <u>make good on</u> the rent.
4. If you can't pay, then I think she's gonna <u>bounce</u> you.
5. And then on my lease agreement, it says nothing about (that) they'd <u>throw</u> me <u>out</u> if I'm late.
6. What he's saying is your rent is due on <u>day one</u>.
7. She's <u>stuck</u> <u>with</u> the terms of the lease.

LISTEN FOR MAIN IDEAS, P. 214

Rick told his landlady that he was going to be late with his <u>rent</u>. The landlady said it was no problem, but he had until Friday to pay it, and there would be a $40 <u>late charge</u>. On Saturday, Rick still hadn't paid the rent, so his landlady put an <u>eviction notice</u> on his door. Rick was surprised; he expected the late charge, but he didn't expect to get <u>evicted</u>. He asked if his landlady had the right to evict him.

Yes, she did. His lease allows a tenant to pay the rent up to <u>three</u> days past due with a penalty. If the tenant doesn't pay in three days, then he's subject to <u>eviction</u>. Rick was too late. Dan encouraged him to pay immediately and not take advantage of his landlady.

Rick also pointed out that his <u>lease</u> says the late charge is only $20, but the landlady told him it was $40. He asked if the landlady has a <u>right</u> to raise this charge. Dan said she doesn't. She must follow the conditions of the lease.

DIFFERENCES BETWEEN SPOKEN AND WRITTEN ENGLISH, PP. 214-215

Suggested answers are given; your answers may be different but equally correct. Words in italics appear in the book but were deleted on the tape.

Dan:	What's going on, Rick?
Rick:	Yes, Dan, I got a question about…I told my landlord that I was going to be late with the rent.
Dan:	Yep.
Rick:	Okay, and she said, "No problem." I could get it in by Friday—that there would be a $20 late charge.
Dan:	Okay, what happened?
Rick:	And come Saturday, she signed a note, "Demand for Payment or Possession of Premises." I'm wondering, "Where do I stand with this?"
Dan:	Well, Rick, she gave you till Friday. Did you give her the rent by Friday?
Rick:	No, but I went down on Friday, and told her I couldn't get the rent. I was waiting for a check, and she says, "Well, there'll be a late charge," and then Saturday she hung this thing on my door. So, am I going to get evicted now?
Dan:	Partner, she's within her rights on this because she made a deal. She stuck to it; by Saturday she was within her rights to do this. Now normally, normally, you can avoid eviction because landlords usually, rather than undergoing the legal expense and trouble

of evicting a tenant, will work with you if you make good on the rent. So number one, I think you just need to cough up the cash now and make good on the rent. If you can't, then yeah, I think she's going to bounce you, and she'll be within her rights.

SUMMARY, P. 216

Landlord rights
- If the rent is not paid when it is due, the landlord has the right to receive a <u>late charge</u> according to the terms of the lease.
- The landlord has the right to give a tenant a notice of <u>eviction</u> if the tenant does not pay by the date which is stated in the lease agreement.

Unit 8
RELATIONSHIPS

Chapter 19   Gender Differences

DICTATION, P. 222

Emphasize the different structures which are used to show comparison and contrast.
a.   Why do women more than men try to change people?
b.   Women are more animated on the outside and men have more going on internally.
c.   There's more space between two men than there is between two women.
d.   Men's traits are self-oriented, if you will, and women's traits are other-oriented.
e.   As far as nagging goes, women get the award for nagging.
f.   Since they have a stronger response to stress, men tend to retreat.

Sentences using "whereas"
a.   Women have a more moderate response to stress whereas men tend to retreat.
b.   Men feel smothered when they are in relationships whereas women need them more.
c.   Respect is as important as power and money for men whereas in the women's world, women worry about disrespect.
d.   Women talk about intimate things whereas men are more discreet.
e.   Men tend to dominate public conversations whereas women tend to retreat.

CONVERSATION STRATEGIES: GIVING EXTENDED ANSWERS, P. 223
1.   Words that introduce a change of topic
Now; let's talk about; wh- questions; well
2.   Phrases to use when agreeing with the other speaker
Yes; Exactly; Yes, that's true; Yes, it is; Oh, absolutely; Right
3.   Answers will vary.

Men	Women	
	✔	are more jealous
✔		have jealous rage
✔		have a stronger response to stress
	✔	try to change people
✔		want to be accepted
✔		don't want to be controlled
	✔	smile more
✔		are more internal
✔		take up more space physically
✔		need more space
✔		are more dominating
✔		tell more jokes and stories
✔		are more self-centered
✔		want to draw attention to self
✔		are reluctant to commit to a relationship
✔		need more physical distance
✔		postpone marriage
	✔	react more
✔		retreat more
	✔	seek outside stimulation
✔		run away from outside stimulation
✔		want to be respected
	✔	worry about not being respected
	✔	have more intimate friendships
	✔	talk about personal things
✔		are more discreet
✔		are more competitive
✔		talk about objects, sports, business, politics
	✔	have more friends
	✔	talk more at home

Men	Women	
✔		talk more in public
✔		show affection physically
✔		feel close by doing things together
✔		brag more
	✔	nag more

LISTEN AGAIN, P. 224

Write your own quiz based on the level of understanding of your students. You may want to give the quiz questions orally rather than in written form to reinforce listening skills. Another type of quiz would be an essay question, such as "Summarize the main characteristics of men."

ANALOGY, P. 225

Refer to the transcript, where Cris compares sports to hunting.

VOCABULARY CHECK, P. 225

1. *animated* → lively, physically active, using more gestures
2. *traits* → characteristics
   if you will → if you will acknowledge this
3. *has to do with* → is related to, concerns
4. *smothered* → to have the life taken out of; stifled
5. *stimuli* → things that produce reactions
   retreating → running away
6. *nag* → to find fault with continually; to remind someone to do something repeatedly

))) Chapter 20   The Science of Romance

Selection 2   Set an objective

KEYS TO BETTER COMPREHENSION: RECOGNIZING PARAPHRASE, P. 228

(Jay)	...my own adventures in singledom... ...you were single for quite a long time...
(Jay)	I set a definite objective. There was something I wanted.
(Jay)	I started to envision what it would be like to be married... and what it would be like to be with this other person.

Suggested answers. Others are possible.
1. That romance can be, or is a science.

2. It makes life a lot more pleasant.

3. The book tells the secrets to successful relationships.

4. That some of the same logical and sensible methods that help to make you a successful person in business or volunteer work can help you in your romantic life.

5. It happened 15 years after he finished college. We don't know exactly when he decided this.

6. Because they discover that they really only liked spending a couple of hours a day with their spouse, not 24 hours a day.

📼 LISTEN FOR SPECIFIC INFORMATION, P. 229

Step 1. Do the things you like to do, and probably you will run across the person you want to spend time with.

Step 2. I made the decision to be married.

Step 3. I figured out what kind of person I wanted in my life and what I wanted my life to be like with that person.

Step 4. I envisioned what it would be like to be married and to be with this other person.

Selection 3   What do you want?

KEYS TO BETTER COMPREHENSION: UNDERSTANDING CONNECTING WORDS, PP. 230-231

Answers to Part 3, p. 230 are underlined in the transcript.

QUESTIONS ON P. 231:
1. and, and so

2. contrast → but   the next step → and so   a conclusion → and so

📼 LISTEN FOR MAIN IDEAS, P. 231

Refer to the transcript for answers.

Selection 4   How to start

DICTATION, P. 232

The instructor reads the following dictation two times (or more if necessary). Read in phrases. Use relaxed pronunciation for "going to." (56 words)
"I can come up with a list of things that I'm interested in and how I imagine things to be from this point forward: who I'm gonna be sharing my life with, how we're gonna be sharing it, what we're gonna be doing on an autumn evening or a summer morning, and what is it like?"

📼 LISTEN FOR MAIN IDEAS, P. 232

Refer to the transcript for answers.

KEYS TO BETTER COMPREHENSION: RECOGNIZING ANALOGY, P. 232

1. what people experience when they decide to start looking for a new car to buy

2. When you decide what kind of car you want to buy, you'll start to notice it on the street a lot. It's the same when you tell your brain what kind of man or woman you're looking for; you'll recognize it when you see it, because you've told your brain what to look for.

Selection 5   Where to meet people

KEYS TO BETTER COMPREHENSION: RECOGNIZING RELAXED PRONUNCIATION, PP. 233-234

1.
a. modal perfect

b. modal perfect

c. future tense, shows intent

d. This sentence contains two homonyms (or nearly so, depending on the speaker) when "they are" is contracted and spoken with relaxed pronunciation.

2. Changes are underlined.
My observation is, you <u>wanna</u> pick things that you love to do, so that number one, <u>you're gonna</u> love being there. If you <u>don't</u> enjoy bars, <u>don't</u> go. I spent a lot of time in bars and I <u>wasn't</u> very happy there. And <u>I'd've</u> been a lot better off doing a lot of other things I was really interested in. <u>Y'know,</u> maybe I liked spending more time in libraries. Maybe I <u>should've</u> spent more time in libraries <u>'cause</u> <u>I'll</u> meet people that are interested in learning things. So I think the key thing is I have people write down a list of 10 or 20 things that they love to do, and then schedule them into their life and go do those things. So, number one, <u>they're</u> <u>gonna</u> enjoy it. <u>They're gonna</u> be having more fun while <u>they're</u> there, and they are more likely to attract people that are similar, have very similar interests to them.

LISTEN FOR SPECIFIC INFORMATION, P. 234

Answers are underlined.
Irene asks where is a good place to <u>meet people</u>. For example, she mentions a bad place to meet people is in <u>bars</u> because people <u>lie to you</u>.

Jay says that you should pick things that you love to do because you're <u>going to love being there</u>. He wasn't happy going to <u>bars</u> but he wishes he had spent more time in <u>libraries</u> because <u>he'd meet people that are interested in learning</u>.

After people make a list of things they love to do, Jay suggests that <u>they schedule them into their life and go do those things</u>.

KEYS TO BETTER COMPREHENSION: RECOGNIZING PARAPHRASE, P. 235

Answers are underlined.
You want to pick things that you love to do, so that number one, you're <u>going to love being there</u>.

I think the key thing is <u>write down a list of 20 things they love to do,</u> and then <u>go do</u> those things.

Number one, they're going to <u>enjoy it</u>. They're going to <u>be having fun while they are there</u> and are more likely to attract people that <u>have similar interests to them</u>.

Selection 6   What it takes to make it work

KEYS TO BETTER COMPREHENSION: RECOGNIZING PARAPHRASE, P. 236

a. ...relationships that require no work, because <u>they just happen</u>, because you are so <u>absolutely compatible (that you might finish each other's sentences.)</u>

b. ...most relationships that are really good, <u>start easy; they work easily</u>.

c. You have to have some conflict negotiation skills, some way to <u>manage that, and you have to be able to deal with those sort of things</u>.

d. Your relationship is going to work, it's <u>going to flow</u>.

e. It's like mentally you're aligned; you're <u>going together</u>.

VOCABULARY AND IDIOMS, P. 236

We're *talking* perfect <u>breakfast</u>. *talking → giving an example*

But *by and large*, your relationship is just <u>going to flow</u>. *by and large → mostly*

They work easily. *I mean* there are still <u>things</u> you have to <u>clear</u> up occasionally...
I mean → a filler, often used to restate

SUMMARY, P. 236

1. Stop focusing all your attention on what you <u>don't</u> want in a relationship.

2. Make a detailed <u>list</u> of what you do want in a relationship. Include details about things that you are <u>interested</u> in doing together.

3. Spend time every day <u>imagining</u> what your future is going to be like.

4. Spend time doing things you <u>enjoy</u> instead of trying to meet people in places you don't enjoy.

 Chapter 21   Getting Love Right

Selection 7   Introduction to the main speaker

LISTEN FOR SPECIFIC INFORMATION, P. 238

1. a nationally and internationally acclaimed speaker who conducts lectures and workshops

2. He give lectures and workshops on relationships.

3. Having bad relationships was often the cause for people to relapse into bad habits that they had had before (drinking, smoking, drugs, etc.).

Selection 8   Healthy relationships: need vs. choice

LISTEN FOR SPECIFIC INFORMATION, PP. 238-239

look like (physical)	personality
social situation	What he'll do for you

LISTEN FOR MAIN IDEAS, P. 239

Answers will vary. Suggested answers below. Refer to transcript.

Terence: Get in touch with your romantic ideal.

Irene: Is there a right answer?

Terence: People in healthy relationships are not bonded together by need but by choice.

Irene: If you're a whole person, you're leading a satisfying life, and you'd like to share it with someone.

Terence: That's a healthy relationship. An unhealthy one is when you look inside of yourself and you don't like what you see.

Irene: Life would be worth living.

Terence: So you go on a quest to find the perfect partner who's going to magically fix you.

KEYS TO BETTER COMPREHENSION: RECOGNIZING EXAMPLES AND INCOMPLETE STATEMENTS, P. 240

1. Refer to transcript for notes.

2. When you're looking at partners, it's important to <u>get in touch with their (your) romantic ideal</u>.

DIFFERENCES BETWEEN SPOKEN AND WRITTEN ENGLISH, P. 240

Connecting words are underlined. For Part 2, the letter of the answer is given in parentheses.
"I was just thinking <u>that</u>, (d) y'know, <u>if</u> (e) you're a whole person, <u>and</u> (b) you're leading a life <u>which</u> (c) is satisfying in all ways <u>except</u> (a) that you'd like to share it with someone, perhaps someone <u>that</u> (c) has your same interests, <u>and</u> (b) you know, you'd like to share your life <u>and</u> (b) do what it is that you like to do <u>when</u> (f) you get someone <u>who</u> (c) is compatible, <u>and</u> (g) it ends up being a nice situation."

DISCUSS, P. 240

1. If you are in a healthy relationship, there is almost <u>nothing</u> that this person can do for you that you <u>can't</u> do for yourself.

2. People who are in healthy relationships are not bonded together by <u>need</u>. They're bonded together by <u>choice</u>.

Selection 9   Helpful/non-helpful ways of communicating

LISTEN FOR SPECIFIC INFORMATION, P. 241

The actual order of the process is not clearly given. What's important is that the students understand who does what, and how the process works.

The initiator:		The responder:	
1.	makes an appointment	2.	both people negotiate for 20-30 minutes
		3.	gets worried
		4.	identifies a time to talk soon
		5.	clears a time to talk about it

Selection 10   How to get a relationship back on track

LISTEN FOR MAIN IDEAS, P. 242

Step 1: Beginning the process

1. You have to start <u>with yourself</u>.

2. I have couples write down a <u>problem list</u> on file cards.

3. Then they <u>classify</u> these problems.

4. We ask what each one is <u>willing</u> to do to <u>address</u> these <u>problems</u>.

Step 2: Communication <u>training</u>

1. You make an <u>appointment</u> to <u>talk</u>.

2. The person with the problem has to <u>introspect</u>.

3. The job of the listener is <u>to only listen</u> and then to give <u>feedback</u>.

4. Then the roles <u>switch</u>.

Keys to better comprehension: Recognizing examples, p. 243

Refer to transcript for examples.

Selection 11   The Law of Neurotic Attraction

Listen for main ideas, p. 243

Refer to transcript for main ideas.

Summary, p. 243

1. Imagine what your ideal partner would <u>look</u> like.

2. Imagine what this person's <u>personality</u> would be like.

3. Imagine how this person would act <u>in public</u>.

4. What would this person be able to <u>do</u> for you that you believe you can't <u>do</u> for yourself?

)) Unit 9
FAMILIES

)) Chapter 22   Parenting

Selection 1 Healthy arguing!

Listen for specific information, p. 247

1. 13 years

2. "healthy arguing"

3. They were arguing; she got frustrated with him and hit him in the face; he pushed her to the bed in retaliation.

4. He was emotionally devastated.

5. The children saw what happened.

6. How do they repair their relationship, and what should they tell the children?

Listen again: Inference, p. 247

1. "Relatively young kids" might imply that they are under 8 or 9 years old.

2. It went over the mark because there was more than just an argument this time; there was a physical element as well.

3. Answers will vary.

Selection 2   The perfect opportunity

KEYS TO BETTER COMPREHENSION: DISTINGUISHING HOMONYMS, P. 248

The teacher reads these sentences for dictation in Part 2:
1. Maybe you need to look at the problem before you talk to them.
2. It may be that your arguing as a couple has been healthy and constructive.
3. It also may be that your marriage has more conflict than you can handle.
4. You need to resolve some of these things so that you argue, but maybe not quite so much.

VOCABULARY PREVIEW, P. 249

1. trigger → the catalyst; something that initiates or precipitates a response or action
2. constructive → helping to improve
3. resolve → settle or solve

LISTEN FOR SPECIFIC INFORMATION, P. 249

Refer to the transcript for answers.

Selection 3   Conflicting roles

KEYS TO BETTER COMPREHENSION: ANTICIPATING INFORMATION, PP. 250-251
1. People who have to choose between a job and a family have <u>more</u> problems than those who don't have to make this choice.
2. <u>Some</u> people are able to have both a career and a family; they're able to do both well.
3. A woman who has a husband, children, and a job outside the home may feel <u>torn in different directions</u>.
4. People who feel they aren't doing anything well because they are doing too many things may need to <u>learn to manage them</u> (or <u>get out of one of those roles</u>).

Selection 4   Working mothers: another perspective

LISTEN FOR MAIN IDEAS, P. 251

Don't go over the main ideas with students. Let them listen more than once if needed, but in "Listening check," they will find out if their notes (and listening skills) are adequate.

LISTENING CHECK, PP. 251-252

Some answers may vary. Complete answers are given below.
1. Motherhood is a big challenge today because mothers often believe <u>they have to work or have children; they think they can't do both</u>.
2. Beth believes that women find a balance; they can have children and also work without trying to be <u>superwomen</u>.
3. Beth says that it's important in the early years of your child's life to <u>build a solid foundation (of love) with the child</u>.
4. Some recent research says that it's important for a child to be with his/her mother until the child is nearly <u>4</u> years old.

5. Beth thinks a mother <u>doesn't have to</u> stay home with a child full time until the child is 4.

6. Research is also showing that the bonding process lasts <u>longer</u> than we had thought previously.

7. Some children <u>go into shock</u> if they are separated too early from their parents.

8. Parents are trying to establish laws for "parental leave," which allows <u>both mother and father to have time (away from jobs) with their children within the first 2 years, not just the first few months.</u>

9. People need the concrete support of their community because <u>we often don't have the support of parents, brothers and sisters who live nearby; they frequently live in another state or even in another country; a new mother needs a group to help her combat the isolation and loneliness of the first few months or years of motherhood.</u>

10. A wonderful trait that mothers develop is <u>"peripheral vision"—the ability to attend to multiple demands and to think about more than one thing at a time.</u>

Selection 5   A Dad on the road

LISTEN FOR MAIN IDEAS, P. 253

Refer to the transcript for main ideas.

Selection 6   A Dad in the air

LISTEN FOR MAIN IDEAS AND SUMMARY, P. 254

Refer to the transcript for main ideas.

 Chapter 23   Stepfamilies

VOCABULARY PREVIEW, PP. 256-257

Possible sentences for Part 1:
> Herbert is Donald and Mary's stepfather.
> Mina is Trudy and Robert's stepmother.
> Donald and Mary are Herbert's stepchildren.
> Trudy and Robert are Mina's stepchildren.
> Trudy and Robert are stepsiblings of Donald and Mary.
> Harvey and Larry are half brothers of Mary and Donald (because they have the same mother).
> Harvey and Larry are half brothers of Trudy and Robert (because they have the same father).

Part 2. Answers are underlined.
> When a man and woman marry and have children, they are called a <u>nuclear family.</u> Each parent is a <u>biological parent</u> of their children. A family undergoes many changes when the parents divorce. One's husband or wife is now known as an <u>ex-spouse.</u> The terms of the divorce are worked out in court or in custody mediation, depending on the relationship of each parent to the children. The term "<u>joint custody</u>" refers to families in which children are allowed to live with either parent at any time; a child may spend weekdays with Mom, and weekends with Dad, or two weeks living at one parent's house, and the rest of the month at the home of the other <u>single parent.</u> If a judge decides one parent is not suitable, the <u>non-custodial parent</u> may have only restricted visitation rights to see the children. When a <u>spouse</u> decides to divorce his/her <u>mate</u> and remarry, many new relationships are also

created. A child not only has a biological mother or father, but now gains a <u>stepfather</u> or <u>stepmother</u> as a third parent. This stepparent must adjust quickly, not only to having a new husband or wife, but also to having one or more <u>stepchildren</u>. This new family is known as a <u>stepfamily</u> or a <u>blended family</u>. To make relationships even more complicated, if both parents are divorced and bring kids into the new family, the children in each family must adjust to having <u>stepsiblings</u>.

Selection 7   Stepfamilies

LISTEN FOR MAIN IDEAS, PP. 257-258

1. Judith Bond is a licensed clinical social worker.

2. "The Stepfamily Challenge"

3. There will be more stepfamilies than any other kind of family.

4. In children's literature, the stepmothers were always bad or wicked, the stepfathers were abusive, and the stepchildren were abused.

5. "blended family"

Selection 8   Yours, mine, and ours

LISTEN FOR SPECIFIC INFORMATION, PP. 258-260

Stepfamilies

I. Seminar for stepfamilies
   Q: What kind of <u>education</u> should people have before they enter a stepfamily situation?

   A: Our seminar talks about the <u>differences</u> between <u>nuclear</u> families.

II. Stages of a nuclear family
   A. Two people <u>come together</u>.
   B. They have a <u>honeymoon</u>.
   C. They <u>spend time</u> together.
   D. They learn how to <u>interact</u> together.
   E. They decide to have a <u>child</u>.
   F. They have nine months to <u>prepare</u> for that child.
   G. They start developing their <u>parenting</u> skills with that child.
   H. The children come one by <u>one</u>.

III. Stages of a stepfamily
   A. Stepfamilies start with a <u>fantasy</u>.
   B. The stepparent thinks the biological parent is already a <u>wonderful person</u>.
   C. The biological parent is looking for someone to <u>replace</u> (<u>the previous parent</u>).
   D. In their own fantasy, they are <u>recreating</u> the <u>nuclear</u> family.
   E. If a former <u>spouse</u> dies, the issues are:
      the children have <u>glorified</u> the dead parent.

IV. A personal anecdote (Irene)
   A. Irene was <u>6 (years old)</u> when her dad died.
   B. Her mother went <u>on dates</u>.
   C. Irene reacted by <u>bringing out pictures of her father</u>.

D.   Years later, Irene felt <u>guilty</u> because her mother never <u>remarried</u>.

E.   Irene wonders how many kids put <u>obstacles</u> in their parent's way when the parent is looking for a new <u>relationship</u>.

V. The children's perspective

A.   Most children want their parents to be <u>reunited</u>.

B.   When a parent starts to date, it starts to <u>destroy</u> their fantasy.

C.   Problems will come because the children lose their <u>status</u> when the parent <u>remarries</u>.

D.   When a parent remarries, the child becomes part of:

---

1.   The first family → the <u>nuclear</u> <u>parent</u> family.

2.   The second family → the two <u>single</u> <u>parent</u> families.

3.   The third family → when a parent <u>remarries</u>.

VI. Problems

A.   Single-custody families:
The non-custodial parent tends to <u>spoil</u> the children.
Examples:
spending a little more time with the children
spending a little more money (on gifts) on the children
taking the children on more exotic vacations

B.   Joint-custody families:
There can be some subtle <u>rivalry</u> about who's the better <u>parent</u> or who the kids <u>care</u> more about.

C.   Children lose status—for example:
Usually one of the children sat <u>in the front seat of the car</u>.
After the remarriage, the children have to go <u>to the back seat</u>.
The effect on the children: <u>it's hard on them</u>.

Selection 9   Communication issues

LISTEN FOR MAIN IDEAS, P. 261

Question: How do you keep the child from feeling <u>resentful</u>?

Answer: The most important thing in any marriage, but especially in stepfamilies, is <u>communication</u>.

Question: How much time does it take for a stepfamily to be successfully integrated?

Answer: <u>Five</u> to <u>seven</u> years. What's sad is that the majority of stepfamilies fail within <u>4</u> to <u>5</u> years because of <u>the kids</u> (or <u>resentment</u>). Families get stuck in the <u>first</u>, <u>second</u>, or <u>third</u> phase. The <u>stepparent</u> feels most uncomfortable, so they [he/she] need to realize something is <u>wrong</u> and to start bringing up the <u>issues</u>.

Selection 10   The phases of a stepfamily

LISTENING CHECK, PP. 261-262

Suggested answers. Refer to the transcript for more information.

I. The phases of stepfamilies
1. The first stage is fantasy (they think they'll be the "Brady" family, i.e. the perfect stepfamily.
2. A stepparent thinks there is something wrong with them; they aren't fitting in.
3. A stepparent will talk to a professional or other parents about what's wrong and what is going on.
4. The stepparent starts talking to their spouse; they feel they have a right to ask for what they want.
5. The stepparent and biological parent start working as a team.

The results of the fifth phase:
   a. the parents become a cohesive family unit.
   b. the bond between the biological parent and children becomes weaker.

II. Question: What if both parents have children of their own?
Answer: It's just more complicated.
1. You still have the same <u>stages</u>.
2. The two adults have to <u>work together</u>.
3. The added complications:
   a. children dealing with <u>stepsiblings</u>
   b. children who live at home <u>full time</u> vs. children who <u>are coming and going on weekends</u>

III. Conclusion:
"Stepfamilies are very <u>complicated</u>, and I do believe you can <u>survive</u> stepfamily life, and it can be very <u>enriching</u>. And children and adults all alike can become more <u>flexible</u>; they can develop incredible <u>coping</u> skills that the children will take with them into <u>adult</u> life."

 Chapter 24   Adoption

VOCABULARY PREVIEW, P. 264

Dictation. The paragraph may be used for dictation (85 words).

Verb	Noun	Adjective
give birth	(fertility*)	infertile
adopt	fertilization	adoptive
	(birth*)	adopted
	adoption	birth*
	abortion	fertility*
*Students may recognize these words as nouns by suffix and common usage; in the context, they are actually used as adjectives		

Selection 11   Facts and figures

🔊 LISTEN FOR SPECIFIC INFORMATION, P. 265

teenage pregnancies	(no information given)
abortions	so many million in the U.S. (no specific number)
infertile couples	4.9 million (couples) in the U.S.
fertility services	one billion (dollars) spent this year
Barbara's children	2 adopted daughters
Lynne's children	1 adopted son (Kenny - age 4) and 6-month-old son born as a result of in vitro fertilization

🔊 LISTEN AGAIN, P. 265

Answers may vary.
1. to tell their story of what it was like to want to be a mother, and not be able to.

2. The book is a compilation of letters that Barbara and Lynne wrote to each other while they were waiting and trying to become mothers.

Selection 12   Is it worth the cost?

SUMMARY, P. 266

The information in this paragraph is taken from a part of the interview which is not on tape. Answers may vary.

Barbara and her husband had tried / tried to get pregnant for many years, but without success. By 1985, they had begun / began using fertility drugs and the latest technology recommended by their doctors, but it wasn't going well. One lonely night, while her husband was out of town, Barbara decided to write a letter. She couldn't tolerate the loneliness and despair over being told that once again she was not pregnant. That night, she wrote to Resolve, a national organization for infertile couples. Her letter was published in the organization's newsletter, which contained articles and letters by women struggling with infertility.

A short time later in another part of the country, Lynne was sitting in her doctor's office, waiting for her next infertility treatment. She picked up the Resolve newsletter and happened to read Barbara's letter. Lynne was amazed to find someone else who was feeling the same pain and anguish as she was, so she wrote back to Barbara. This was the beginning of their three-year correspondence, which is compiled in their book, *Dear Barbara, Dear Lynne.*

🔊 LISTEN FOR MAIN IDEAS: TOEFL PRACTICE, P. 266

The instructor reads the following questions. Allow 12 seconds for students to read and select an answer. You might want to allow students to read the answers before you begin reading the questions.

1. Lynne's first child was adopted. When she and her husband decided they wanted another child, why didn't they adopt a second child?   Answer: d

2. According to Lynne, why did she want to have more than one child?   Answer: a

3. Do insurance companies pay for infertility treatments?   Answer: c

4. How much did Lynne have to pay for the infertility treatments (the "Gift" procedure)? Answer: a

5. How much did Barbara's adoptions each cost? Answer: d

Selection 13 The emotional impact

🔲 LISTEN FOR SPECIFIC INFORMATION, P. 267

Refer to the transcript for more complete information.

Barbara
  had a child <u>for 5 days through adoption</u>
  birth mother <u>changed her mind</u>
  infertility treatments <u>for 3 years</u>
  waited to adopt <u>for almost 2 years before they found their first daughter</u>

Lynne
  tried to get pregnant <u>since her early 20's</u> — <u>for many, many years</u>

🔲 LISTEN AGAIN, P. 267

The effect on themselves
  Barbara <u>far worse than any physical pain, felt enormous stress, anxiety, depression for a long time</u>

The effect on their husbands and their marriages
  For both husbands <u>just wanted to solve the problem, but difficult to solve, so there was miscommunication</u>
  Women help each other go through it by <u>talking about their feelings, but men can't.</u>
  It was a problem that their husbands <u>didn't know how to support their wives</u>.

How Barbara felt when Lynne got pregnant
  Barbara felt <u>no jealousy; she was thrilled</u>.
  Before that, Barbara used to <u>not be able to look at pregnant women, or people with children</u>.

CONVERSATION STRATEGY: INCLUDING OTHERS IN THE CONVERSATION, P. 268

Parts 2 & 3:

Part 2 Phrases in the conversation:	Part 3 Purpose:
Selection 11:	
a. Why don't we talk with you first?	[identifies who should speak first]
b. And you?	[brings Lynne into the conversation]
Selection 12:	
c. Let me ask you, Barbara...	[directs the question to a specific person, brings Barbara back into the conversation]
d. But you both feel...	[summarizes; allows for clarification]
Selection 13:	
e. And you, Lynne?	[brings Lynne into the conversation again]
f. How did you feel, Barbara, when...	[directs the question to a specific person]

Selection 14   Child-free living vs. motherhood

VOCABULARY AND IDIOMS, P. 269

> 1. "I have many friends who have <u>opted</u> for a child-free life."
>   opted: I have a great deal of respect for their <u>choice</u>.
>
> 2. "What was that that made you so <u>obsessed</u> and <u>compelled</u> and <u>driven</u>?"
>   obsessed, compelled, driven: You <u>had to have</u> children. Nothing would stop you.

LISTEN FOR MAIN IDEAS, P. 269

Refer to transcript for main ideas.

Selection 15   Advice for couples

LISTEN FOR SPECIFIC INFORMATION, P. 269

1. Note to instructor: for students with lower comprehension, provide the first word or phrase of each answer before the students listen.

    a. Get your feelings out to someone.

    b. Find some support.

    c. It's okay to be jealous of women who are pregnant or who have babies.

    d. Take care of yourself.

    e. Take charge of your life as much as it is possible to do.

    f. Decide if you want to have children or (also) you want to experience being pregnant.

    g. Consider child-free living.

    h. Go to a therapist.

    other possible answers: Take a break.
                                  Consider adoption.

2. More than one answer is correct.

    b   1. Where can I find a support group?

    h, f   2. How can I decide if adoption is the answer for me?

    e, g   3. What is a specific way I can take charge of my life?

    c, h   4. Why do I feel jealous of others who are pregnant or have babies?

    a, b, h   5. Why is it important to have support?

KEYS TO BETTER COMPREHENSION: LISTENING FOR SUPPORTING FACTS, P. 270

1. Find a support group.
    "It's important to get your feelings out to someone, and to find some support."

2. It is important to have support.
    "I think support is essential...that's the key to getting through it."

3. It's okay to feel jealous of others who are pregnant or have babies.
    "When you're trying to become pregnant, every second woman on the street probably seems to be pregnant."

4. Take charge of your life.

   "There's always one more procedure that you could try...it's okay to say, 'If such and such a technique doesn't work, then I'm going to stop for awhile, or consider child-free living, or go to a therapist, or take a break, or start working on adoption.'"

5. Decide if adoption is the answer for you.

   "Barbara and I both had to decide, do we both want to be mothers or do we want to be pregnant?...When you can answer that question...then you're able to move on to the next step."

Selection 16   Adopting a friend's child

KEYS TO BETTER COMPREHENSION: LISTENING FOR SUPPORTING FACTS, P. 271

Tom's opinion:

   It's a bad idea to adopt a baby from a friend or when you already know the parents.

Support for his opinion:

   Tom and his wife tried to adopt children, so they know the process.

   In his job, he has heard sad stories of parents coming back to their friend years later and then wanting to be parents to the child they gave up for adoption. (Other family members also interfere.)

VOCABULARY AND IDIOMS, P. 272

1. a. And we have just <u>got the runaround</u> (through adoption agencies and stuff.)

    b. It may be <u>hunky-dory</u> now, because she needs someone.

    c. If the child wants to <u>go and search (his) roots later</u>, that's different.

    d. It could be an ethical or a moral challenge to <u>your upbringing</u> of that child.

    e. Having said all that about the <u>hassles</u> of knowing the parents...

    f. It <u>muddies</u> the situation.

    g. It really does <u>stand in your way</u> of (being) a parent.

2. (Dictionaries may not agree:)

    a. slang expressions: hunky-dory, hassles

    b. informal: got the runaround

Selection 17   Legal process of adoption

LISTEN FOR MAIN IDEAS, P. 273

1. The adoptive couple should consult <u>an attorney who is an expert on adoptions to ask questions about their situation, and get legal advice</u>.
2. The couple has to pay <u>for a home study conducted by Social Services</u>.
3. Social Services decides <u>if the couple will provide a good home for the child</u>.
4. The birth mother <u>has to give signed consent to have the child adopted, but she has a certain time period after the birth in which she can change her mind</u>.

LISTEN FOR SPECIFIC INFORMATION, P. 273

1. Have a "home study" done by Social Services.

2. Anywhere from $900 to $5000.

3. Yes. Social Services has to be satisfied that you will provide a good home for the child.

4. To get correct legal advice from an expert, who answers their questions before they spend a lot of money.

5. Yes. Dan doesn't know (or say) how long after the birth she can change her mind. (We know from Selection 13 that the birth mother changed her mind 5 days after the adoption.)

6. (We can infer:) $150.

7. It won't matter.

8. She already has one child.

9. Parents who want to adopt have to go through years of investigations, background checks, and home studies, but anybody else who becomes a parent naturally doesn't have to do anything, or be approved by anybody.

KEYS TO BETTER COMPREHENSION: RECOGNIZING INFORMAL LANGUAGE, P. 273

Dan uses the following informal language: info, gonna, hey, (big) bucks, kid, kill the deal, gotta

AUDIO TRANSCRIPTS

As a teacher, I rarely provide the students with an entire tapescript, except to provide further development of recognition of stressed words, content words, grammatical structures, etc. Listening and reading simultaneously may push the students to accelerate their reading speed, but it can also frustrate them if they cannot read fast enough to keep up with the speaker.

Relaxed pronunciations for the most part have been retained in the tapescripts, i.e. contractions, reduced forms *gonna, wanna*, filler words *y'know, I mean*, etc. The innumerable occurrences of *uh* and *um* were deleted for the most part from the transcripts. Ellipses in the transcript usually indicated pauses or hesitations by the speaker. Local references have been deleted from the tapes and the transcripts except when they were relevant to the topic, or could not be deleted without significantly altering the phrasing of the sentence. Portions of the transcripts are included in various activities throughout the textbook.

LIST OF SPEAKERS; LIST OF FORMATS

The following chart indicates the main speaker and format for each selection.

Selection	Title of Selection	Main Speaker	Format
⟩⟩ Unit 1 ETHNIC CUISINE			
1	Introduction to the main speaker	Warren Byrne	introduction
⟩⟩ Chapter 1 What is Ethnic Cuisine?			
2	Introduction to the topic	Warren Byrne	comment
3	Strictly Hungarian	Warren Byrne	conversation
4	Popular doesn't mean authentic	Warren Byrne	conversation
5	Mexican food	Warren Byrne	comment
6	Authentic Mexican vs. Tex-Mex	Warren Byrne	conversation
⟩⟩ Chapter 2 Define Your Cuisine			
7	If that's not Polish…	Warren Byrne	conversation
8	What is Bohemian food?	Warren Byrne	conversation
9	Paella	Warren Byrne	conversation
10	If you haven't tried Ethiopian…	Warren Byrne	conversation
11	If you've not had Moroccan food…	Warren Byrne	conversation
⟩⟩ Chapter 3 What Do You Recommend?			
12	Russian cuisine	Warren Byrne	commercial
13	Italian cuisine	Warren Byrne	conversation
14	Vietnamese cuisine	Warren Byrne	conversation
comment = 1 speaker conversation = 2 speakers discussion = 3 + speakers			

Selection	Title of Selection	Main Speaker	Format
15	Salsa	Warren Byrne	conversation
16	Arabian cuisine	Warren Byrne	conversation

)) Unit 2   CARS AND DRIVING

)) Chapter 4   Cars

1	Buying a used car	Tom Martino	conversation
2	You bought it; it's yours	Tom Martino	conversation
3	High-pressure tactics	Tom Martino	comment
4	Value pricing		commercial

)) Chapter 5   Driving

5	Can you afford a Ford?	Elliot Abrams	weather report
6	Radar guns	Tom Martino	conversation
7	Error on a ticket	Tom Martino	conversation
8	Traffic fatalities		news report
9	Traffic fatalities decrease		news report
10	Who needs auto insurance?	Tom Martino	conversation
11	Auto repair for dummies	Irene Rawlings	interview

)) Unit 3   THE ENVIRONMENT

)) Chapter 6   Environmental Awareness

1	The Green Pages	Steve Chavis	news item
2	Transportation alternatives	Steve Chavis	news item
3	Eco-conscious construction	Colorado Public Radio	news/interviews
4	Providing a habitat for fish	Steve Chavis	news item
5	Global Youth Forum	Colorado Public Radio	news/interviews

)) Chapter 7   Wildlife

6	The impact of a golf course	Steve Chavis	news item
7	Reintroducing river otters	Steve Chavis	news item

comment = 1 speaker   conversation = 2 speakers   discussion = 3 + speakers

Selection	Title of Selection	Main Speaker	Format
8	Dolphin captivity	Colorado Public Radio	news/interviews
9	Wildlife controversy	Steve Chavis	news item
))) Chapter 8 Land, Water, and Air			
10	Xeriscape	Irene Rawlings	interview
11	Global warming	Irene Rawlings	interview
))) Unit 4 CUSTOMER SERVICE			
1	Introduction to the main speaker	Tom Martino	program intro
))) Chapter 9 What is Customer Service?			
2	Red tape		commercial
3	The runaround		commercial
4	Recorded messages		commercial
5	Distant headquarters		commercial
6	I have a question		commercial
7	Press "1" now		commercial
8	Small businesses	Tom Martino	conversation
9	How to treat a customer	Tom Martino	conversation
10	Accommodate all the customers	Tom Martino	comment
))) Chapter 10 Principles for Smart Consumers			
11	Send it back	Warren Byrne	conversation
12	Give it a second chance	Warren Byrne	conversation
13	You have to pay for a true estimate	Tom Martino	comment
14	Save your receipt	Tom Martino	conversation
15	Talk to the owner when necessary	Tom Martino	discussion
16	Avoid buying used appliances	Tom Martino	comment
))) Unit 5 DATING, MARRIAGE, AND DIVORCE			
1	Introduction to the main speaker	Andrea Van Steenhouse	comment

comment = 1 speaker   conversation = 2 speakers   discussion = 3 + speakers

Selection	Title of Selection	Main Speaker	Format
))) Chapter 11	Dating		
2	An age difference	Andrea Van Steenhouse	conversation
3	Big Daddy	Andrea Van Steenhouse	conversation
4	Breaking up	Andrea Van Steenhouse	conversation
5	Getting over it	Andrea Van Steenhouse	conversation
))) Chapter 12	Marriage		
6	Another expensive wedding	Andrea Van Steenhouse	conversation
7	What to say	Andrea Van Steenhouse	conversation
8	The parents' choices	Andrea Van Steenhouse	
9	A new daughter-in-law	Andrea Van Steenhouse	conversation
10	Rise to the occasion	Andrea Van Steenhouse	conversation
))) Chapter 13	Divorce		
11	Surviving divorce	Andrea Van Steenhouse	comment
12	What's wrong with this picture?	Andrea Van Steenhouse	comment
13	An insecure marriage	Andrea Van Steenhouse	conversation
14	An unequal relationship	Andrea Van Steenhouse	conversation

comment = 1 speaker   conversation = 2 speakers   discussion = 3+ speakers

Selection	Title of Selection	Main Speaker	Format
))) Unit 6　WORK			
1	Burnout	Irene Rawlings	quotation
))) Chapter 14　Overdoing it			
2	Introduction to the topic	Irene Rawlings	introduction
3	Overdoing it	Irene Rawlings	interview
4	What should overdoers do to change?	Irene Rawlings	interview
))) Chapter 15　Burnout			
5	What does an EMT do?	Andrea Van Steenhouse	interview
6	A typical day	Andrea Van Steenhouse	interview
7	Coping with burnout	Andrea Van Steenhouse	interview
))) Chapter 16　The Work Force			
8	How do I get into the work force?	Andrea Van Steenhouse	conversation
9	Get retrained	Irene Rawlings	interview
10	People who need retraining	Irene Rawlings	interview
11	Interviewing for a job	Irene Rawlings	interview
))) Unit 7　RENTING AN APARTMENT			
))) Chapter 17　Moving In			
1	Signing a lease	Tom Martino	discussion
2	What are the tenant's rights?	Tom Martino	discussion
3	The cat and the bird cage	Tom Martino	discussion
4	Can she prove it?	Tom Martino	discussion
))) Chapter 18 Moving Out			
5	Notify the manager	Tom Martino	conversation

comment = 1 speaker　　　conversation = 2 speakers　　　discussion = 3 + speakers

comment = 1 speaker   conversation = 2 speakers   discussion = 3 + speakers

Selection	Title of Selection	Main Speaker	Format
3	Conflicting roles	Andrea Van Steenhouse	comment
4	Working mothers: another perspective	Irene Rawlings	interview
5	A Dad on the road	Andrea Van Steenhouse	comment
6	A Dad in the air	Andrea Van Steenhouse	conversation
))) Chapter 23 Stepfamilies			
7	Stepfamilies	Irene Rawlings	interview
8	Yours, mine, and ours	Irene Rawlings	interview
9	Communication issues	Irene Rawlings	interview
10	The phases of a stepfamily	Irene Rawlings	interview
))) Chapter 24 Adoption			
11	Facts and figures	Irene Rawlings	discussion
12	Is it worth the cost?	Irene Rawlings	discussion
13	The emotional impact	Irene Rawlings	discussion
14	Child-free living vs. motherhood	Irene Rawlings	discussion
15	Advice for couples	Irene Rawlings	discussion
16	Adopting a friend's child	Tom Martino	conversation
17	Legal process of adoption	Tom Martino	discussion

comment = 1 speaker   conversation = 2 speakers   discussion = 3 + speakers

Unit 1
ETHNIC CUISINE

Selection 1   Introduction to the main speaker

Announcer: From the city that has more restaurants than convenience stores, it's the Restaurant Show on news radio 85 KOA. Here's Warren Byrne.

Warren: Good afternoon. Five minutes after two. It's Saturday afternoon, and time once again for our regular Saturday edition of the Restaurant Show. I'm glad you could join us today. Hopefully you'll stay with us from now until the end, which is 5:00, three hours from now. And we're going to be talking about lots of things having to do with restaurants and food, and good places, bad places. I have been into several places this week...

Chapter 1   What is Ethnic Cuisine?

Selection 2   Introduction to the topic

Warren: Also today what I would like to explore today—and I think this can be fun. We have so many restaurants. We were talking this week about this and somehow the subject came up of ethnic restaurants. And my goodness! It's a...it's incredible. There are so many different types of ethnic food, from all the Southeast Asian foods, Mexican food, Italian food, the list goes on and on—Ethiopian food. What I would really like to do today is talk to some of you who know this kind of food, who are of this particular ethnic background, whatever it is, and can speak to what constitutes good Mexican food, what really constitutes good Italian food, what did you grow up with, what kind of food did you have when you were growing up? What evokes positive memories for you? Where do you go to get that authentic kind of food? So we'll talk about that as we go along too at 623-8585.

Selection 3   Strictly Hungarian

Sharon: Hi, Warren. I was also interested in Slovenian or Slovak cuisines. I know I've seen a restaurant up along the back road to Estes Park, and I'm not sure if any of your listeners have ever eaten there, and if it lives up to the billboard out in front?

Warren: You're talking about the Villa Tatra again?

Sharon: Yes, and then...also if there were any good Hungarian restaurants in town?

Warren: Well, that question came up earlier today. It seems like everybody wants to...I mentioned ethnic, and everyone wants to talk about Hungarian, which I wish there was. I wish there was a good Hungarian restaurant in town. The only one that we had closed. Now we come close, we come...we have restaurants that are I guess classified it as Bohemian, it's the food of that area, but it isn't identified with one country specifically: places like the Old Prague Inn, and you mentioned the Villa Tatra which is on the way up to Estes Park. The Cody Inn on top of Lookout Mountain is a wonderful place to go.

We do have some German restaurants around that are strictly German, but most of the restaurants that serve food from that part of the world take a pretty broad-brush approach to it. So I can't come up with anything that is strictly Slovak or certainly nothing that is strictly Hungarian for you.

Sharon: Okay, thank you.

Selection 4   Popular doesn't mean authentic

Tom: Yeah, Warren, you were asking for ethnic food recommendations, and I grew up in a very ethnic German family; my mother did some wonderful cooking. And my wife and I lived in Germany for 7 years. So...and we have not found a good German restaurant since the Gasthaus Ridgeview closed.

Warren: What constitutes good German food?

Tom: Well, I would say the kind of food you get when you go to the corner Gasthaus. It's...it's basic cooking; they have some...oh, there are some Swiss specialties like zuricher geshneltes, where you have cut up veal in a cream sauce, a good—very good wiener schnitzel. Things like that.

Warren: Okay. Do you feel...

Tom: But I do have a couple of—I have one recommendation, and one place in the mountains that I would not recommend.

Warren: Okay.

Tom: And the recommendation would be the Vail Racquet Club.

Warren: For...for specifically for German food?

Tom: For German food.

Warren: Really?

Tom: They have a German chef...

Warren: Okay.

Tom: ...and it's absolutely wonderful.

Warren: And where's the place you wouldn't recommend?

Tom: Webers in Breckenridge.

Warren: Really! That's interesting. We were in Breckenridge yesterday, and almost...or we considered going into Webers, and did not, but I've heard some good things about Webers.

Tom: Well, it's always packed.

Warren: Yes.

Tom: They do a tremendous business. But I did not...and I suppose it's the American conception [sic] of German cooking. But if you lived in Germany, it's not German cooking.

Warren: Okay, and again that comes back to how you define German cooking.

Tom: That's right, and I don't know how I could define it. But Vail Racquet Club, we went there on a recommendation from a friend who said that if you want good German cooking—and of course, they've got a continental menu—it's not just German...

Warren: Right...

Tom: ...go there. And we told our waiter our background—that we had lived in Germany for seven years, and that we thought the food was absolutely wonderful, and the chef started sending out little tidbits of everything that they had.

Warren: Oh, how wonderful!

Tom: So we were very impressed.

Warren: That sounds like the kind of place where if you feel comfortable doing it, you just walk in and tell the chef, "Make me a good German dinner."

Tom: We did that years ago at the Black Forest Inn...

Warren: Uh-huh, in Blackhawk.

Tom: ...in Blackhawk, and I haven't been there for many years. Is that still good?

Warren: I was up there about 2, 3 weeks ago. It was excellent. Okay? I do have to move along, and I appreciate your calling.

Tom: Okay.

Selection 5   Mexican food

Warren: As I started to say, I...I get a little bit tired of some of the Mexican restaurants that all have basically the same type of cuisine, and it's really pleasant to find a place like El Parral where they seem to go out of their way to use fresh ingredients, and make dishes that are not commonly available at other Mexican restaurants, such as their Chicken Molé, which I just absolutely go crazy for over there. If you've never had Chicken Molé, it's a chicken and chocolate sauce, and I think it's one of the better Mexican dishes that's served anywhere in the area, because as I say, I get very tired of burritos and tamales and tacos, and things of that nature.

Selection 6   Authentic Mexican vs. Tex-Mex

Eric: Hi, I'm fairly new to the area, and I was wondering if you had any recommendations on some good, authentic Mexican restaurants around town.

Warren: Well, now we're coming back to the question I asked earlier, which is, "What is authentic Mexican food?"

Eric: Well, what I'd like to see is a restaurant that gets away so much from the ground beef, and gets into the roast pork, some good marinated pork sauces, that kind of thing.

Warren: Mm-hmm. Right, something other than the standard Tex-Mex fare. And I agree with you. I would suggest if you've not been there yet, and I've mentioned these two restaurants before, I would suggest you check out a restaurant called Las Brisas, which is down at Arapahoe and I-25. And they have a lot of seafood dishes down there, dishes of that nature that are not your ordinary Tex-Mex stuff. They have some of the Tex-Mex stuff as well, but it goes way beyond that. And the other restaurant I would recommend you is a restaurant called Pasquarros out on West 38th. And he...what they do out there is the regional cuisine of Mexico, because Mexican food is so much more than tacos and burritos and things like that. When you consider how much coastline Mexico has, they have a tremendous amount of seafood.

Eric: Okay.

Warren: So those are two places that I would recommend to you.

Eric: Great.

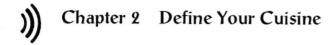 **Chapter 2   Define Your Cuisine**

Selection 7   If that's not Polish…

Elizabeth: My family and I have been getting up to Villa Tatra once or twice a year for about the last 10 years. So I would like to offer first of all, they don't accept (I don't believe) reservations, but in any case they are not necessary. But secondly, I am Polish and if that restaurant is not Polish, I don't know what is. They have…I mean the foods that we've enjoyed there are very, very Polish. Whether or not these foods are typical of other countries, I don't know.

Warren: How do you…let's define Polish food.

Elizabeth: Well, pierogi…

Warren: Okay, which are the little potato-like dumplings…

Elizabeth: Right, or cheese or whatever, the…cabbage, what we call golabki…[or galumpki]

Warren: Okay.

Elizabeth: The borscht I understand is—you know, many nations have the red beet soup. I know that.

Warren: Right, it crosses many borders.

Elizabeth: Right, but I mean these two dishes particularly in the way they are served, like with sour cream and so forth are very Polish as far as I know.

Warren: I agree with you. That's the way…that to me is Polish food.

Selection 8   What is Bohemian food?

Underlined words refer to the exercise, "Listen again."

Chuck: Hi, Warren, I enjoy your show very much when I can catch it. I travel a whole lot. I'm originally from Chicago, and I was very pleased to hear your comments earlier about Chicago food, but one thing I was used to in Chicago that I cannot seem to find here at all, and that's a good Bohemian restaurant or a good Czech restaurant.

Warren: Alright, let's talk about…what…how do you define Bohemian food?

Chuck: Bohemian food, I <u>classify</u> from the region as <u>largely</u> dishes like roast pork, roast duck, roast chicken, dumplings made in a way where they're…they can be individually made, but generally it's a large loaf that they slice. Brown gravy, sauerkraut, red cabbage, homemade soups. It's <u>largely</u> a hearty form of home cooking <u>based on</u> not exotic spices, but <u>basically</u> a good home-cooking format <u>built around</u> pork and duck…

Warren: It's <u>essentially</u> a peasant food, I guess.

Chuck: Pretty much so, yeah.

Warren: Yeah…and there are some places around…

Chuck: I've been to Little Moscow, and it—for Ukrainian style food—is marvelous.

Warren: Yeah, but it's not Bohemian.

Chuck: …but it's not Bohemian.

Warren: No. I would suggest, if you want to try some Bohemian food in the area, I think one of the best representations <u>in my estimation</u> is the Cody Inn on top of Lookout Mountain.

Chuck: Oh, okay.

Warren: Yeah, I don't know if you've been there yet or not.

Chuck: No, I never had.

Warren: Why don't you try that, and I'd like to hear back from you whether you consider that Bohemian food. Bohemian food to me is the kind of the food from central Europe there, it's…it is rather the…

[Chuck: Definitely, yeah.]…the peasant food. It has <u>distinctly</u> German/Austrian overtones, although it is not strictly German or <u>strictly</u> Austrian.

Chuck: Very much so. And it's a little less <u>oriented toward</u> the spicy sausage or elements like the rouladen in Germany.

Warren: Right.

Chuck: But it's good <u>basic</u> home cooking.

Warren: Right.

Chuck: It's <u>fairly</u> coarse peasant food, coarse breads.

Selection 9   Paella

Alita: Yes, hi, I'm just wondering if you have any suggestions for a place to find paella? We enjoyed La Petite Spain when it was still going, but now that it's no longer there, do you have any other suggestions?

Warren: Yeah, and the Mallorca went away, of course; they were doing paella. The only place I…you might try Las Brisas—they might be doing it—I think they did it at one point in time. I know Don Quixote is doing paella. And for those who don't know, you want to tell people what paella is?

Alita: Well, it's…you can have it with chicken, or just with seafood. And it's over saffroned rice, and it's just wonderful. We were just…I was lucky enough to be able to be in New York, and found a wonderful restaurant where we had paella. It's just a wonderful way to eat seafood. When it's great, it's wonderful and they…the sangria usually goes with it.

Warren: Oh, it's wonderful. Gosh, you're making me hungry again. Yeah, that sangria and paella.

Alita: Okay, I'll try your suggestions on that.

Warren: Okay, do that.

Selection 10   If you haven't tried Ethiopian…

Mike: I don't know how authentic this is, and I haven't been to this place, but it's an Ethiopian restaurant and it's in south Boulder at Eldorado Springs Road on 92: Ras Kassa's.

Warren: It's called Ras Kassa's. Right.

Mike: Every time I drive by there it smells delectable.

Warren: Have you been in there?

Mike: No, I haven't. But I've heard so many good things about it. Have you?

Warren: Yeah, let me tell you what it's all about. Of all the cuisines of the world, I think Ethiopian's one of my absolute favorites. Ethiopian food is…there's a lot of beef, a lot of lamb, chicken, many vegetarian dishes…

Mike: …a lot of curry…

Warren: It's not really curry.

Mike:	Oh.
Warren:	Curry is a misnomer anyway, because curry can be any combination of spices. There are many different curries in the world. But what it is is it's a very highly seasoned food. And when you order it, they bring them out in little dishes, about, oh maybe 4 inches across, and you'll get a series of these dishes. The more people you have at an Ethiopian restaurant, the more fun you'll have. And then they bring out this bread that is called "injera," and it's kind of like a thick spongy pancake almost; it's a flat bread, but it's like a yeast bread—it's got a lot of bubbles in it, okay. And they lay that out on a plate, and then you pour this other food over it. And then you tear off bits of this bread, and you use it to scoop up the food, so you're eating with your hands. Kids love this kind of stuff.
Mike:	Sounds like fun!
Warren:	Oh, it is wonderful fun. I've only introduced one or two people to Ethiopian food who didn't go crazy about it.
Mike:	Well, I was just concerned about that particular place.
Warren:	Go for it; try it. I think you'll really like it. Certainly Ethiopian food does fit into the category of ethnic cuisine, and it's a good one. If you haven't tried Ethiopian cuisine, you simply must. If you're into good food at all, it's great.

Selection 11   If you've not had Moroccan food…

Eric:	I've seen an ad for—I believe it's the Moroccan food at a place called Mataam Fez? [mispronounced]
Warren:	[correcting pronunciation:] Mataam Fez, yes.
Eric:	Can you tell me a little bit about that?
Warren:	Well, that's another interesting type of cuisine. The thing about Moroccan food is again, we were discussing Ethiopian food earlier, and there is some kinship there. And this is another type of food that is eaten with the hands, using bread as a utensil to pick it up. And there's a lot of lamb in the Moroccan diet, lamb, chicken, rabbit, and it's prepared in a different fashion than you're used to. A lot of olives, lemon, that type of condiment around the dish. Because it's eaten with the hands, it's usually pretty well cooked. It kind of falls apart.
	And when you go to an Ethiopian restaurant…not Ethiopian; when you go to a Moroccan restaurant, they usually—you sit on the floor or on low pillows around very low tables. And you cross your legs, and when you go to get up, you discover just how old you are anymore! But they put like a bath towel on your lap, and then they…they begin the meal with a ceremonial washing of the hands, they have a thing called a "tass," and you hold your hands out over a basin, and they pour water, and you wash your hands, because you're going to be eating with your hands. And then you enjoy the meal, and then when the meal is over, they come around and once again wash your hands in this little ceremonial thing. A lot of the Moroccan restaurants including the Mataam Fez have belly dancers and entertainment of that nature, so it's quite an experience. If you've not had Moroccan food, I would suggest that the Mataam Fez is a good place to discover it.
Eric:	Okay, great.
Warren:	You bet. Bye.

Chapter 3   What Do You Recommend?

Selection 12   Russian cuisine

Warren: I don't know if you've ever had Russian cuisine or not, but if you've not, and you would like to try it, check out a little restaurant called the Café Tamara, which is located over on East 8th Avenue just east of Colorado Boulevard. Isaak and Tamara are from Russia, and they have quite a few really interesting Russian dishes on the menu. But that's in addition to their regular menu, which is an American menu and features all kinds of seafood and chicken and beef dishes; plus, every night of the week they also have a variety of dishes from a selected European country, such as Yugoslavia on Monday night, Poland on Tuesday night, Wednesday, they go Italian, Thursday, it's Hungarian, Friday, it's French, and Saturday, it's German.

And so they have all of that; plus, they do breakfast, they do lunch, they do brunch on Sunday, and a very quaint little setting, and I guarantee if you can't find something on the menu to like at the Café Tamara, you're not trying. These folks are just absolutely delightful. The food is very inexpensive; I'm talking like sub-ten dollars. It's not a fancy "Cliff Young's" type restaurant. But it's a good restaurant, and it's the kind of place you can go to three, four nights a week and still not break the budget. So when you're looking for something really different, exciting, fun, check out the Café Tamara located on east Eighth Avenue, just east of Colorado Boulevard. Phone number 322-9343. Café Tamara.

Selection 13   Italian cuisine

Underlined words refer to the exercise, "Keys to better comprehension: recognize vocabulary in context."

Jim: I just wanted to let you and your listeners know about a pleasurable experience that I had recently at the Olive Oil on Parker Road.

Warren: Sure.

Jim: And it's kind of in a...if you're not familiar with this part of town, it's kind of a Bermuda Triangle. I live near that area, and I tried it out, and I had some of the best <u>northern</u> Italian food I've ever had.

Warren: I agree.

Jim: I've eaten a lot of Italian food because I moved here a <u>couple</u> of years ago from Seattle, and Seattle is big into Italian food.

Warren: Yes, it is.

Jim: So I've had a little bit to <u>compare</u> it to. But the best <u>service</u> I've ever had: very, very <u>attentive</u>, and excellent appetizers—sautéed calamari; I had a salmon with smoked mussels and sauce over pasta; excellent bread with a dipping sauce, and I just can't go on enough about it. It's really, really a <u>pleasurable</u> experience for me.

Warren: Well, I've commented before on the Olive Oil and the fact that this is, I believe, the third <u>ownership</u> there in the last two or three years, and it is absolutely the best it has <u>ever</u> been.

Jim: Yes, I agree. I met the owner, Amir, and his brother is the <u>chef</u>, who is also an <u>owner</u> of it. And those people, just, y'know, they just bend over backwards to take care of you, anything that you want.

Warren: It's interesting too that they are from Afghanistan.

Jim: They are Afghans...

Warren: Yeah, they are not Italian at all, and yet they've got one of the best Italian restaurants in Denver.

Selection 14   Vietnamese cuisine

Wendy: I had to call you. I felt compelled to call you about my favorite restaurant...

Warren: Okay.

Wendy: ...and that is the Oriental Plate.

Warren: ...downtown, 15th and California.

Wendy: Yes. This is wonderful. Well, I guess when I was living down there, I stumbled upon it. But this is food that will give you pleasure chills. I mean, it's really good Vietnamese and Chinese, I think.

Warren: Yes, it is both Vietnamese and Chinese.

Wendy: I always eat the Vietnamese though 'cause I love it. But the Dungeness Crab, have you tried that?

Warren: Well, I was gonna ask you if you'd had his crab.

Wendy: Oh yes! Last night, it was wonderful!

Warren: Yes, that crab is out of sight. Good.

Wendy: Oh, yeah.

Warren: It's not the cheapest dish on any Chinese restaurant menu.

Wendy: ...but you know, it's not that bad! Really, it's not excessive at all.

Warren: Considering what you get...

Wendy: Oh, yes!

Warren: ...which is the entire dungeness crab, in just a superb...it's kind of semi-spicy...

Wendy: With a little bit of ginger in there, I think...

Warren: The best part is when you're all done eating the crab, you can sit there and lick your fingers.

Wendy: We've tried the Black Bean Fish, and that was...I think that's delicious down there, and (excuse me) the Grilled Pork, which is one of my favorites. And you can kind of make it— it's sort of like a Vietnamese burrito, sort of...

Warren: Uh-huh.

Wendy: ...y'know, with all the vegetables and...I hope I'm not offending anybody by saying that.

Warren: No, is that like Moo Shu Pork?

Wendy: Well, it's a grilled pork, or I believe you can get grilled chicken, and then they have just different kinds of vegetables you put in the rice paper. And then you roll it all up. It has...there's lettuce, and some sprouts, and carrots, and let's see, what else? Gee... and then the grilled pork and the fine noodles.

Warren: Right, so that's the real thin, the very fragile rice wrapper you put that in.

Wendy: Right.

Warren: Yeah, that's Vietnamese, and that is very, very good.

Wendy: Oh, it's just...this restaurant is fabulous, and that's my favorite place for dinner.

Warren: Okay. Wendy, thanks for calling.

Wendy: You betcha!

Selection 15   Salsa

Boyd: Tortilla Flats...they have good green chili, and they have a good salsa, probably the best original—(well) I would call it the "tomato salsa"—that I've ever tasted is at Tortilla Flats.

Warren: I think you can tell a lot about a Mexican restaurant by the salsa that arrives at the table, which is usually the first thing you get at a Mexican restaurant.

Boyd: Yeah, it's not a paste; it's...just like it's a blended-type, tomato-type sauce; and it's very, very good.

Warren: I appreciate your calling.

Selection 16   Arabian cuisine

Lisa: Hi, Warren, how are you?

Warren: Doing great.

Lisa: Great. I heard you talking earlier with someone about Arabian restaurants?

Warren: Right.

Lisa: And...I know a few like Lebanese restaurants, she was speaking about Cedars restaurant.

Warren: Right...

Lisa: And...there is another restaurant that I've been to a little while back and it is called The Damascus Restaurant and it's like—they specialize like in Syrian-type foods.

Warren: Right.

Lisa: And...they have like...kabobs, and they have like different types of salads and things like that, and it's really wonderful.

Warren: Yeah.

Lisa: I'm not exactly sure of the location. I know it's like around Colorado Boulevard and Evans, but like the street number, I don't know where it is.

Warren: And I don't know either; I haven't been there, but I know it's right in the vicinity of Colorado and Evans...

Lisa: Right.

Warren: ...and it is called The Damascus. The food from that part of the world, when she said Arabian food, all that food has certain similarities from the Middle East, and maybe that's what she meant when she said Arabian. But, I think that food is wonderful; it's one of my favorites. What do you enjoy at the Damascus?

Lisa: Well, they serve a lot of lamb, which I'm a big lamb lover. And they have like lamb kabobs, and they have a lot of lamb dishes...I think that's probably my favorite for like those "lamb lovers" out there.

Warren: There are also at a lot of Mid-Eastern restaurants, you will find many vegetarian dishes as well. And for those people who...

Lisa: Yeah, I went in just a while back and I had a look at the menu, and they have a lot of like dishes that don't have meat, and it's pretty good.

Warren: Yeah. It's nice if you're a vegetarian. It's good to know that those middle Eastern restaurants serve a variety of food, and it's not boring salads or anything. This is really intriguing food, interestingly spiced, some of it very delicate, some of it will wake you up, but it's all good food.

Lisa:	Right.
Warren:	Okay.
Lisa:	Then just one more thing: to top it off, they have like the Arabic coffee, I guess it's like Turkish coffee or something?
Warren:	Yeah.
Lisa:	...and like at the end of the meal, they offer like a cup of coffee, and it's kind of a nice touch. It was really good.
Warren:	It's good, but it's strong.
Lisa:	Yeah, it's a lot stronger.
Warren:	Yeah.
Lisa:	But it was great.
Warren:	That stuff will put hair on your tongue if you're not careful. Thanks for calling.
Lisa:	Alright, bye-bye.
Warren:	Alright, talking about Middle-Eastern food, and Arabian coffee, or Turkish coffee, Greek coffee, it's all pretty much the same; really strong coffee and you drink about three-quarters of the way down, and then you run into the grounds at the bottom. Boy, they are there; it's good stuff though, if you've never had that kind of coffee. The restaurant she's talking about is called Damascus, and it's located on South Colorado Boulevard right in the vicinity of Evans.

))) Unit 2
CARS AND DRIVING

))) Chapter 4   Cars

Selection 1   Buying a used car

[main speaker: Tom Martino]
(music intro)

Tom:	Hello. This is Tom Martino, the Troubleshooter, talking about consumer problems, questions, and complaints, Tammy. How are you doing, Tammy, and you want to talk about what?
Tammy:	A used car that I had bought from a dealer.
Tom:	Ah. When did you buy that used car, Tammy?
Tammy:	About two and a half weeks ago.
Tom:	Okay, what's the problem?
Tammy:	We thought that there was [sic] ignition problems, because it's electrical as far as the lights and the blinkers and all. So we had taken it to an Amoco station, had a professional to [sic] look at it.

Tom: This is before you bought it?

Tammy: No, it was after we had bought it.

Tom: You didn't have anyone check it before you bought it? Oh, Tammy…

Tammy: No.

Tom: Okay, all right, so what happened?

Tammy: So when we had taken it to the Amoco station, and they had looked at it and said that there was [sic] major problems with it and it was gonna cost like a thousand dollars to have everything fixed to be able to even drive it safely.

Tom: So you got taken.

Tammy: So, yeah, we went back to the dealer, I talked to him and he…

Tom: You bought it "as is," didn't you, Tammy?

Tammy: Yeah.

Tom: What year is this?

Tammy: It's a '79.

Tom: '79. What kind?

Tammy: Ford Mustang.

Tom: A Ford Mustang…and how many miles on it?

Tammy: I think like a 130,000.

Selection 2   You bought it; it's yours

[The conversation from Selection 1 between Tom Martino and Tammy continues:]

Answers to "Listen again" exercise are underlined.

Tom: Did it ever occur to you, with 130,000 miles on a car, that you should check it out?

Tammy: Yeah, and we asked the guy…We told him that we wanted to go check it. Well, he wanted to go with us every time, you know? And I was like…

Tom: So? So? So? I mean, Tammy, did it really, did it ever occur to you that with a car with this many miles, you may have problems?

Tammy: Right. Yes, it did.

Tom: Okay. I'm really sorry about it. But I'll betcha there's not a lot you can do about it.

Tammy: Okay, well one question I had to ask is I've had a few people tell me that even with an "as is" on it, that you have like 30 days if something goes wrong buying it at a used car lot, that you can take it back to them and they…

Tom: Who would tell you something so stupid?

Tammy: I just had a couple people that told me that.

Tom: Well that's too bad, because—and I don't mean to make fun of them—but…it's the prob—the reason I say that so strongly is because so many people get into trouble because they believe this garbage. You know, they believe they have a three-day right, or they have 72 hours (same thing), or they have a week, or they have 30 days. There is no right to return anything. Zero! Zip! Not even in a regular store. That's it! You buy it; it's yours.

Tammy: Right. Well, I wasn't even as much, you know, wanting to return it, just if he could take care of it, you know, or…

Tom: Well, did you call the guy just to ask him?

Tammy: Yeah. I've talked to him, and he's like giving me the runaround, he says, "Oh, I'll fix it," and it's like he's wanting us to pay for the problem...

Tom: Technically, he <u>doesn't</u> [pronunciation: dudn't] have to do anything—period. Tammy, I'm really sorry to have to tell you that. But there's <u>not</u> much you can do. And at least y'know, maybe people listening will finally learn you <u>must, you must, you must</u> get things checked out. You <u>cannot</u> depend on someone to tell you what a car is...y'know, someone who's selling it to say it's <u>all right</u>. And if you <u>don't</u> get it checked out, <u>don't</u> expect anything. Zero. You have <u>no right</u> to return it.

Selection 3 High-pressure tactics

[Tom Martino comments on high pressure sales tactics at some auto dealerships:]

Tom: Let me say something here. We heard a story of captivity, I call it, from Douglas Toyota—about Douglas Toyota. Somebody went there and say that they were held captive. And what they said was they surrendered their keys so someone could check out a used car—his car as a trade-in. And what the salesperson did was disappeared [sic] with the keys, someone else got the keys, he let them have his registration.

And as I said, if I had gotten just one complaint, I would say, "That's tough," because y'know, you gave your keys to the guy and he was probably checking it out. However, as it turns out, we've gotten dozens of calls before that. And it was on my mind, and this one just was the one that made me go over the edge. I said, "Y'know, this is way too much." And I get a lot of them particularly about Douglas Toyota. And we wanted Douglas Toyota to come on to address these concerns. Of course, they have yet...they have not found someone to come on the air yet. And in fact, today their public relations person said that they doubt they would get someone—they're trying. I don't know what that means.

But the bottom line is I've gotten a lot of complaints. And here's...and particularly about Douglas Toyota, and I have to tell you something. If you're going to buy a car, and you're thinking about trading your car in, do not ever let anyone have the keys to your car. If they say they have to evaluate it, go with them. Do not let them take the car, do not let them have the keys, do not let them have your registration, do not, do not, do not. Because I've gotten too many calls from people for it to be a coincidence.

And they do a sleazy, sleazy thing. They want to keep you in the dealership as long as possible, and in order to do that, to break you down, they will make it difficult for you to leave. Now people do not want to cause a scene. They don't want to say, "I WANT TO GET OUT OF HERE!" They want to be civil about it. So consequently they end up staying, and saying, "Oh, by the way, where's my car? Please, I want to leave." And they say, "Oh, I don't know, ba ba ba," they change the subject, and then you end up staying. They actually move your car, too, so you don't know where it is. Now as I said, if I had gotten one or two complaints, I'd say those are consumers who are just complaining because they're mad. But when I get this many over months and years, it's a real problem.

So folks, my advice to you, especially if you're dealing with Douglas Toyota is not to let them have the keys to your car—not! Do not let them go near your car without you so they cannot move it; they cannot keep you there. Do not let them have your license; do not let them have your registration. They can do a credit check without your license. They can do a check on your car without your registration. All they have to do is look at it and copy some numbers down. So folks, they give you a lot of bull when they tell you they need the keys.

I don't think they do anything illegal as far as the car transaction, no. This is high pressure sales, and people end up feeling bad about buying a car as opposed to feeling good.

And here's what I advise. If you still—if you want to go to Douglas Toyota and you want to do business with them, just don't give 'em your keys, okay? Don't give 'em your registration; don't give 'em your license.

Now is Douglas Toyota the only dealership doing this? No, it's not. There are some others I've gotten complaints in the past, not as many as I have had about Douglas Toyota.

Now if you want to call about this, you can do it too, because I want to hear about your captivity experiences, because I make a pledge to you that I want to do away with this practice. I think it's sleazy to have to keep consumers in your shop captive, and not tell them where their car is.

I suggest if it ever happens to you that you call the police, and that you make a scene; you yell and scream in the dealership. But what you do is make a scene until they give you your keys back, and your registration back. Now, you know why we don't hear from Douglas Toyota? Cause it's true; you see, they do it. They do it! This is one of their practices. This used to be a common practice in the auto business, but most dealerships—and I'm happy to say this, I'm serious. We have some good dealers! And I think part of it's because consumers demanded it. And I think we have a new breed of car dealers, and a lot of them, they're really classy operations. Sure they have an errant salesman here or there, but you see, Douglas—aah, scum, sleaze right now—that's what they are in my opinion of course. Heh heh. What's my opinion? Not much, I guess, not to them. But I tell you this: if you come across a dealer that tries to do sleazy things like that, why don't you let me know? We'll put an end to it.

Selection 4   Value pricing

[Commercial for Phil Long Ford:]

Dave: Hi, everybody. This is Dave Logan, and I'm here with Dan Jeneska, the general manager of Phil Long Ford. If there's anybody out there who is even thinking about a new car or truck and who hasn't heard about Phil Long's exclusive value pricing, believe me, you're missing out. Dan, why don't you tell us about it?

Dan: Dave, value pricing is Phil Long Ford's commitment to making it easy to buy a new car or truck. At Phil Long, you won't find the typical haggling and hassling over the price of a vehicle. You'll find the most knowledgeable, professional sales people able to give you Phil Long's best price, the value price on the vehicle you've selected.

Dave: That sounds like a real time saver. That's the way I'd like to buy a car.

Dan: It is, Dave. It's great. We've had value pricing now at Phil Long for a full year. Our customers love it. It saves time and hassle, and you won't find any extras or expensive add-on sticker with Phil Long's value pricing. It gives you more quality time to find the car or truck that fits your needs. Buying a new car or truck should be easy, fun and hassle-free, and that's why we've created value pricing.

Dave: Value pricing from the value store. Think Phil Long Ford first at Hampden and Kipling, or give them a call: 988-FORD.

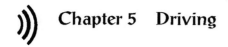 **Chapter 5   Driving**

Selection 5   Can you afford a Ford?

[An idiomatic and conversational weather forecast. David is the talk show host; Elliot is the meteorologist. Words and idioms related to cars are underlined for the exercise "Preview Vocabulary."]

*NHRA stands for National Hot Rod Association

David: Yes, Elliot and I had a disagreement. I felt…I just, I don't know why, I had this feeling that it was just going to be a cloudy old day today. You said, "Nope, clear as a bell." You got a bell there anywhere?

Elliot: I probably do. [sound effect: bell]

David: Yeah, and…

Elliot: Meanwhile this weekend though, the NHRA* U.S. Nationals are held.

David: You're absolutely right. [Sound effect: car starting] Oh boy.

Elliot: And in the temperature department, the <u>mercury</u> will be <u>hitting the brakes</u> at night. But today and tomorrow, temperatures will be <u>revved up</u> from <u>Dodge</u> City, Kansas to <u>Pontiac</u>, Michigan.

David: <u>Cranking</u> up a forecast here…

Elliot: And this'll af<u>ford</u> an opportunity to enjoy sunshine.

David: You said "A <u>Ford</u>."

Elliot: This isn't <u>universal</u>, but some people are real <u>crank cases</u> when it gets cloudy like it was. Oh, and if that applies to you, and your name is Rod, I have one piece of news for you: It's…well, it's not going to be <u>hot, Rod</u>. Actually the temperature'll be in the 80s this weekend, and it'll be quite a while before the dry air is <u>exhausted</u>. I don't think the temperature's going into <u>reverse</u> any time soon. Outdoor levels will get so much <u>mileage</u> out of sunshine today, tomorrow, and Sunday, but a fast moving <u>battery</u> of thunderstorms could <u>race</u> through tomorrow night or Sunday morning before the temperature <u>downshifts</u>. Of course, we don't know when the storms will hit, but we'll be there in the <u>clutch</u>.

David: Okay!

Elliot: Now behind the cold front that could cause the brief thundershowers across our area, it looks like the <u>fan belt</u> in the upper atmosphere will be coming through and making it a little bit cooler early next week; we may have an <u>alternator</u> between sunshine and thunderstorms. But here we are, home stretch of August, and you have the <u>green light</u> for sunshine today and tomorrow. The weekend'll be great, and it'll even be good when you go home this afternoon to <u>crash</u>.

David: Okay. I was going to take in a <u>Chevy</u> Chase movie, but it's too nice of weather, so…I won't; I'll <u>dodge</u> that and go to a Chiefs game instead.

Selection 6   Radar guns

[Chuck has a question for Tom Martino and Barrie Sullivan, a lawyer, about radar guns used by police officers to ticket speeding drivers.]

Tom: Right now, Chuck wants to talk about…uh-oh…a speeding ticket. Chuck…

Chuck: Yes.

Tom:	What's going on?
Chuck:	Well, I have a question about the speeding ticket. I was stopped over here at highway 79 going south out by Bennett. And the officer—actually, he was going north and I was going south. He turned around, followed us for 2 miles, stopped us in Bennett, pulled me over and said, "I clocked you at 68 miles per hour in a 55 zone. I need to see your driver's license, registration and insurance," which I gave to him. And he says, "I'm gonna cite you for this," and said, "Stay in the car, I'll be back to give you everything," and I said, "Fine."
Tom:	So what's...so far, sounds pretty normal.
Chuck:	Okay.
Tom:	What's the...hook here?
Chuck:	Then, when he came back, I said to him, "Y'know"—in between, well, I asked him, I said, "I can't believe I was going that fast, 'cause I know I wasn't."
Tom:	Yeah, no one ever does, I mean, y'know...
Chuck:	Well, I know that's really true.
Tom:	I know, I'm just kidding. But go ahead.
Chuck:	I said, "I would like to see the speed I was clocked at." And he says, "I'm not required to show you that, and I've already recalibrated it."
Tom:	Barrie, are they required to show him or not? I don't know.
Barrie:	No, they're not.
Tom:	Okay.
Barrie:	He has the right to have already recalibrated it without showing it to him.
Tom:	Okay, so Chuck, did you think that would negate your ticket?
Chuck:	Well, no, I didn't think it was right. I mean—could they—I mean, if I'm going down the road, and say he pulls him over and says I'm going 90 miles an hour, he has the right to write me a ticket without showing me that?
Tom:	Yeah. Yeah, they don't even have to have that to show you. In fact, they can give you a speeding ticket without any instrumentation whatsoever, just based on their judgment. You didn't know that?
Chuck:	Well, I guess that's the power of the law, I suppose.
Tom:	Yeah, that's the way traf-...y'know, technically, I don't think they have to have an instrument to begin with, so then I'd guess...
Barrie:	That's right. They do <u>not</u> have to.
Tom:	Right, so then I'd guess that basically not showing you doesn't really hurt the case at all. But, what would happen is if you do a pre-trial conference with an attorney, most likely, I think what you would find is they'd probably be lenient on you if you haven't had a lot of tickets, and especially if you relay, y'know...
Chuck:	I haven't had any tickets since 1970.
Tom:	Well, then that would be good. And then if you ask or tell them that he could not show you that, then I would say basically they may reduce it.
Chuck:	Uh-huh.
Tom:	Now, have you tried that?
Chuck:	I just got the ticket and I didn't, y'know—then he said that they set the date for April for the trial.
Tom:	Okay.

Barrie: You do have a right, though, to call the courthouse, give them the number of your ticket and citation, and say, "I'd like to come in sooner than that so I can get rid of this thing if I can."

Chuck: Okay.

Barrie: And ask to speak to the prosecuting attorney.

Tom: Actually the more time that goes by, the better.

Barrie: The better, sure, but if it's bothering you...I'd be delighted...

Tom: First of all, you know it doesn't count against you until it's adjudicated, so the fact that it's pending doesn't mean a thing to anybody, including your insurance company.

Chuck: Right.

Tom: It doesn't even show up. Now, what about the officer? Barrie, in court, what records do they have to show the 68?

Barrie: He has the calibration records to show when he calibrated it that morning, and when he recorded it, and what his normal procedure is, where he was parked or stopped, or when he saw this fellow.

Tom: But he doesn't have to show him the gun?

Barrie: No, he doesn't have to show him the gun, because he reuses it again.

Tom: Okay.

Selection 7 Error on a ticket

[Brad calls Tom Martino about a speeding ticket he received—with an error on the ticket.]

Tom: Hi, Brad, what's going on?

Brad: Well, I just had a question. Two months ago, I got a speeding ticket; I was doing 68, which he said he clocked me at in a 40 zone. And on the ticket he wrote down that I was in a 35 zone.

Tom: He made a mistake, hunh?

Brad: Yep.

Tom: Okay, he can adjust that.

Brad: He can adjust it?

Tom: Yeah. In other words, you're gonna ask a question that we get asked a lot: "Does a mistake on a ticket negate the entire ticket?"

Barrie: Yeah.

Tom: In a nutshell, no.

Barrie: No.

Tom: Not unless it is such a mistake that it would...it would actually damage his credibility. And even then, it would have to be more than one mistake. Barrie, is that in a nutshell basically?

Barrie: You carried it—covered it.

Tom: A lot of people though really get that impression, and it's not so.

Barrie: The date on the ticket's wrong, stuff like that, that's all correctable, amendable.

Selection 8　Traffic fatalities

[A brief news report on the latest holiday traffic fatalities]

News announcer:

With the holiday weekend coming up, highway officials are asking people to buckle up. Dan Hopkins with the Department of Transportation says eight people died on Colorado roadways last Labor Day weekend.

Dan:　　Seven of the victims were <u>not</u> wearing safety belts. Five of those seven were thrown from their vehicles, and that was the direct cause of the fatality.

News announcer:

Drunk drivers were involved in three of those fatal accidents.

Selection 9　Traffic fatalities decrease

[A brief news report on national statistics for traffic fatalities]

News reporter:

Good news today on the nation's highways announced by Transportation Secretary, Andrew Card:

Andrew Card:

The traffic fatality rate, expressed as number of deaths per 100 million miles of travel, is the commonly accepted barometer of how well we as a nation are doing in highway safety. We are now projecting, that the traffic fatality rate for 1992 will be 1.8 deaths, the lowest in history.

News reporter:

That's 1.8 per 100 million miles traveled. That's down from 2.8 just ten years ago. The difference is about 22,000 lives a year.

Selection 10　Who needs auto insurance?

[Mary has a question for Tom Martino about a problem with her auto insurance policy. Tom discusses the dangers of not having auto insurance:]

Tom:　　Mary, how are you doing and what do you want to talk about?

Mary:　　Hi!

Tom:　　Hi!

Mary:　　Thanks for taking my call.

Tom:　　No problem. What's going on?

Mary:　　I may be calling prematurely, but maybe you can give me an answer.

Tom:　　Okay.

Mary:　　I switched auto insurance companies in November, and I...

Tom:　　So did I.

Mary:　　Oh didja? [→ did you]

Tom:　　Just coincidently, in November, yes.

Mary:　　Okay. I was gonna save quite a bit of money.

Tom:　　So was I.

Mary:	It was this new company...
Tom:	Yeah.
Mary:	...and I paid them a quarter of the premiums for six months...
Tom:	Right.
Mary:	...on November 19. Then the new insurance I scheduled to go into effect on December 10 and consequently I cancelled my old insurance.
Tom:	Well, didn't they do that for you?
Mary:	No, they didn't.
Tom:	Okay. So December 10: new coverage.
Mary:	Right.
Tom:	Theoretically.
Mary:	Right.
Tom:	Okay, now what's your question?
Mary:	Well, I didn't receive any paperwork from them...proof of insurance or anything...
Tom:	Well, when I did it, I got a temporary card immediately.
Mary:	Well, my agent told me that my application would—the copy of my application would serve as proof of insurance.
Tom:	No, it doesn't.
Mary:	Oh?
Tom:	Is it signed by him?
Mary:	I think so, yeah.
Tom:	Well, it could depending on what it says, but...
Mary:	Okay.
Tom:	Basically, they have temporary cards. Is your question, do you have insurance?
Mary:	Well, my question is—I called them—the home office of this new car insurance place this morning to find out what was going on since I hadn't received anything. And they told me that the underwriter had declined to cover me.
Tom:	WHAT?
Mary:	Yeah.
Tom:	Well, hold on a second. Well, you were definitely bound over if you could prove it, but now what do you do? You cancelled your old one!
Mary:	Well, that's just it. And they told me on the phone that they have returned my premium, and that they wrote me a letter of explanation on December 21, but I haven't received anything yet.
Tom:	Well, you know the mail now— it's only...really, it hasn't been that long.
Mary:	Right, it hasn't.
Tom:	What's the name of this company?
Mary:	The insurance company is Metropolitan Life.
Tom:	Okay, so it's a pretty respectable company...
Mary:	Well, I think so.
Tom:	So, I guess now, can you get your old insurance back?
Mary:	I don't know. I haven't talked to my old agent yet.

Barrie:	I don't know if…
Mary:	I guess my question is—my new agent told me that they've got like 21 days—that I am covered for 21 days after I received cancellation.
Tom:	I don't know, I really don't know. I would definitely want to check before you took that for granted…
Mary:	Yeah…
Barrie:	…Because you haven't been cancelled. One you terminated, the other—you didn't get accepted.
Mary:	Well, yeah.
Barrie:	So there's a big difference, you haven't been cancelled.
Tom:	…and it's very, very, very important that you not be caught without insurance for one day because then they're going to put you in a high risk pool, because they're going to say to you—whenever anyone goes without insurance for even a day, they call you a "high risk" and then when you try to get insurance…y'know. I had a company car one time, and I was covered by the company. Therefore—this was years ago—therefore, when I tried to get insurance on my own, when I got another job, I was considered a high risk even though I had been driving and my record wasn't bad!
Mary:	Yeah?
Tom:	Yeah, so you need to take, you need to take action before that expires—immediately, today! You need to call some agents, get some prices, say "Look, here's what happened, I applied and was rejected." Now why were you rejected? I'm cur-, I'm curious.
Mary:	They told me that it was because of claims that I had put in—three claims over the past two years…
Tom:	Uh-oh, man, you may—you're gonna have a tough time maybe even getting back to your old company.
Mary:	That's what I'm afraid of. They were, the claims weren't traffic accidents, they were hail damage and two broken windshields…
Tom:	Yeah, I know, but still, I'll tell you what. For some reason, insurance companies want you to pay, but they don't want you to use it.
Mary:	Yeah! [laughs]
Tom:	And you know, I can see, if they were traffic accidents, dropping you like a hot potato.
Mary:	Sure.
Tom:	I'm gonna tell you something, when it comes to comprehensive claims, how can they possibly blame people, Barrie, for—for—for windshields, and…
Barrie:	Owning a car when a hailstorm occurred! How can they blame you for that!
Tom:	I don't know. I'm serious, but they do. They do.
Mary:	Yeah?
Tom:	And your homeowners', if you have a roof destroyed by hail two times—maybe they think God's mad at you or something, I don't know, but they don't, they don't have you. Mary, please, today, start immediately.

Selection 11   Auto repair for dummies

[A long interview between Irene Rawlings and Deanna Sclar, author of <u>Auto Repair for Dummies</u>.]

Irene: Starting the car is what we're gonna talk about in the morning. You say that you should start your car but not to warm it up.

Deanna: True.

Irene: You say that lengthy warm-ups just pollute the air, they waste fuel, and they increase wear on your car.

Deanna: Yes. Anytime you are sitting still with the engine running, you are getting zero miles to the gallon. This is seriously affecting fuel economy. It's also noisy; it also pollutes the air. Every car should be able to be started and to go. If your car needs a lengthy warm-up, you need to take it in and have it adjusted. It's probably nothing very expensive.

Irene: In case you've just joined us, we're talking with Deanna Sclar. Deanna Sclar has just written a glove-compartment-sized book called the *Auto Repair for Dummies* and she several years ago, I think in the 70's, wrote a big book, sort of a spiral-bound book called *Auto Repair for Dummies*, and that has a lot more information in it. This little one is just something you put in your glovebox because it has information on things that might happen to you as you're zooming down the highway. And the other involves, the bigger one involves things like, y'know, changing your oil, and a variety of things like that. You can change your own oil.

Deanna: Yes. There's also a lot more how-to stuff, there's also a lot of...

Irene: Right, but you're not going to change your oil in the middle of the highway presumably, unless you need to. But then you're really in trouble.

Deanna: Don't need to...

Irene: When your oil light comes on...

Deanna: Stop—immediately. At the side of the road. Yes.

Irene: Air filters. The air filter is inside the carburetor, which is that sort of round thing that looks like a cake pan with a lid, sitting in the middle.

Deanna: Right. It actually sits on top of the carburetor.

Irene: Okay.

Deanna: Or if you have a fuel-injected car, it'll sit on top of that. It's the place where the air comes in. People don't realize that cars run more on air than they do on gasoline. For every gallon of gas, you use enough air to fill a room 10 feet square. All that air comes in through the air filter. If the air filter is dirty, your car is asthmatic.

Irene: How can we tell if the air filter is dirty? I mean it just—everything in the engine looks kind of a little bit dirty.

Deanna: True. The idea is to simply open the top of that round pot you were describing, lift out the air filter, which is kind of accordion paper, look at the sun through it, or any strong light. If you can't see through—see the light coming through it—it is time to change it. They cost very little. It is very simple to simply drive to an auto parts store, give them the year, make and model of your car, bring out the new air filter right there in the parking lot, change it because they may've given you the wrong one, you'll tell right away in the parking lot if it's the wrong size.

Irene: If it doesn't fit, if it doesn't fit in the thing, then you know. You know, one thing in your book that really intrigued me, and you're gonna tell us about it...how can we fill up, we can get more gasoline at less cost? You had some sugges-...a suggestion in there that really just kinda made me giggle.

Deanna: One way is simply to fill up in the morning when it's cool.

Irene: You said that gas expands…

Deanna: Yes, it does, mm-hmm.

Irene: …at a certain rate, and that you could—I wish I could find it in the book. I bet you don't remember quite really what you said. I'm sure you do, but not in terms of the— in terms of the exact numbers, it was one of these things where the gas expands, so you actually get as much as a, y'know, like a quart milk bottle almost more…of gas for the same price if you fill up first thing in the morning when the gas in the tanks and the pumps is cool.

Deanna: That's true.

Irene: I love it.

Deanna: The actual figures were that 10 gallons of gas will expand by eight tenths of a quart, which is the same as four fifths, like whiskey fifths.

Irene: Like a bottle of whiskey.

Deanna: With a temperature increase of 30 degrees. So if it's gonna be hot during the day, fill up in the morning or in the evening, when the air is cooler.

Irene: So you get that much more gas for the same price.

Deanna: Exactly.

Irene: Oh, I love it!

Deanna: Now, another thing related to that is don't top off your tank. When that hose clicks, you're done. The reason for that is, if you keep inching a little bit more gas in, you'll overfill the tank. When you drive away, as soon as the area around the tank is hotter, that gas will expand and it will go right out the overflow pipe. Not only will you just lose it onto the road, but it also creates air pollution. So don't top it off; you just want it till the hose clicks.

Irene: Vapor lock. Y'know, it's…I've heard a lot about vapor lock. And it seems to happen when it's hot.

Deanna: Yes.

Irene: How do we know if the car is in vapor lock, and what do we do about it?

Deanna: Vapor lock is one of the few situations where the car will just stop.

Irene: It'll just sort of seize up?

Deanna: Yeah, most of the time, your car is gonna lose power and so forth. What it is, basically, and it only happens when it's very hot…is that the gasoline will start to boil right in that metal fuel line, because the air is so hot. And when it does, it creates vapor, and that creates a block in the line. People who live in very hot areas, very often will wrap tin foil around the metal fuel line that leads to the carburetor or to the fuel injectors, and that helps to dissipate that heat. If it happens to you, and you don't have any tin foil handy, but you do have your handy jug of water in the car—for drinking, it's okay to wet a rag and wrap it around the metal fuel line.

Irene: And that will just cool it down enough for this vapor lock to kind of take care of itself.

Deanna: It'll dissipate immediately, yeah. There are some cars that are prone to it, because the fuel line runs very close to the top of the engine, which is very hot, and that's just poor design.

Irene: Yeah, that does happen. Now, we're driving along the freeway, we have the air conditioner on, it's 85 degrees, and the sun is unrelenting, and suddenly the car starts heating up. What do we do?

Deanna: The first thing you do is shut off the air conditioner, because it's placing a load on the engine. The second thing you do, and this is not good news, is you turn on the heater.

Irene: Ooh!

Deanna: Okay, you open the windows—yes, you're going to be hotter, but it will help to dispel the heat around the engine, and might just keep you from overheating to the point where you have to stop.

Irene: Now, if the car is overheating, and I've seen this happen in the mountains, people who come from flatter areas, the plains, come to the mountains and their cars are overheating like mad.

Deanna: Mm-hmm.

Irene: ...and just a couple weeks ago, oh, a middle-aged man—well y'know, middle-aged meaning a lot older than I am, right—who should know better, his car was overheating, and he opened up the radiator, and it spewed water all over him, hot water all over him.

Deanna: Oh, yes...

Irene: Well, I was probably 20 feet away and I got wet, and I looked over, and I thought, one of the first things I learned was not to do this. What do you do in terms of cooling down the radiator if your car is overheating, and how long do you have to wait before you do open it?

Deanna: The first thing to do if the car is overheating that badly is to get to the side of the road. You open the hood, but you don't open the radiator cap. And you wait. You exercise patience; you read your book; you look at the mountains.

Irene: Maybe it'd be a good idea to have a book, or some knitting or needlepoint...

Deanna: Right. You want the car to cool down naturally. How fast it does will depend on how hot it got, and how hot it is out, but it'll take its time. The one thing that you absolutely do not want to do is to add water to a hot engine. So even if you...there are radiator caps that have a little lever, you open the lever and it dispels the pressure, and that makes it slightly safer to open. You want to open it with a rag in your hand, and you want to tilt it away from you, even if you're pretty sure it's cool. It should just become habit.

Irene: This is common sense. What other...if you want to leave us with something about what we should do to keep our cars running for a long time?

Deanna: Right.

Irene: What do we commonly not do that you've noticed should be done?

Deanna: I think most people don't change their oil long enough...often enough. And don't think that they remember to change the oil filter or have it changed at least every other time, if not every time. And every other time, to take the car somewhere and have it lubricated. If you can keep...it's like moisturizer...okay, if you can keep the moving parts of the engine in a nice cushion of oil and grease, your car will last a heck of a lot longer. Also, I suggest that people get in the habit of opening the hoods once a month, and looking at the hoses, and looking at the wiring. It doesn't take a professional to see when rubber has had it.

Irene: ...or when something is hanging off.

Deanna: Yes. And to look at the fluid levels. If you can do those things, you'll save about 70% of the reasons why the car might break down on the highway. Do yourself a big favor. Only takes a few minutes.

Irene: Well, thank you very much. We appreciate your taking the time to talk to us. Cars have changed, but the newest book is just this cute little thing that is a [sic] <u>Auto Repair for Dummies</u> to put in your glove compartment so that when common things go wrong with your car, you will know how to fix them, and you'll have a reference guide with you. Thanks an awful lot, Deanna.

Deanna: Thank you. This has been fun.

))) Unit 3
The Environment

))) Chapter 6   Environmental Awareness

Selection 1   The Green Pages

[News reporter: Steve Chavis]

Steve: This is the KBCO Environ-minute. I'm Steve Chavis. A new local directory for the environmentally-aware is now available, called the "Boulder County Green Pages." The Rotary Clubs in Boulder County got together with local recycling and environmental specialists to put together this first-ever directory. It includes quick reference to green products and services for recycling, xeriscaping, energy conservation, and more. The $5 cost helps raise funds for the sponsoring groups, and the local Boy Scouts and YMCA. You'll find the new "Boulder County Green Pages" printed on recycled paper, of course, and available at Ecology House on the Mall, Planetary Solutions on 28th Street, Eco-Products on 55th, and Ecocyle in Boulder and Longmont. Also, through Boulder Valley Rotary Clubs. That's the Environ-minute on 97.3 FM, KBCO.

Selection 2   Transportation alternatives

[News reporter: Steve Chavis]

Steve: I'm Steve Chavis with this KBCO "Environ-minute." High pollution season's got us watching our driving pretty closely. But workers at Martin Marietta are getting really practical help. Through 1993, RTD and Martin Marietta will run two new express routes especially for Martin Marietta employees. With eight morning arrivals and eight afternoon departures, the company is even subsidizing bus fare books and monthly passes as an added incentive to use mass transit. Carpooling is encouraged. And to solve a major concern for people using alternate transportation, there's a guaranteed ride-home program. The company's goal is to double the number of workers using alternate modes to the single occupant vehicle by the end of the year. The program will be studied by the State Health Department. The State Legislature also wants to find out which are the most effective ways to cut vehicle miles traveled and help clear the air. That's today's "Environ-minute" on 97.3 FM, KBCO.

Selection 3   Eco-conscious construction

SPEAKERS:

Alan Tu:	announcer for Colorado Public Radio
Peter Jones:	reporter for Colorado Public Radio
Jim Logan:	architect, building an eco-conscious house
Adamson:	works at Planetary Solutions store

Jim Bell: designer and consultant

Dennis Weaver: an actor, now building an "Earth Ship" solar mass home

Michael Reynolds: architect, developer of "Earth Ship" concept

Public Service is the company that provides electrical power to the city.

Alan: Many environmentalists and energy experts say that the wave of the future won't be any one miracle cure, but rather overall conservation of available resources. The approach is being spearheaded by a quiet revolution in the eco-conscious construction business. Colorado Public Radio's Peter Jones recently visited a building site near Boulder and brings us this report:

[construction noises]

Jones: Architect Jim Logan is building his environmentally-sustainable dreamhouse at the site of a former commune a few miles north of Boulder. Logan has incorporated nearly every aspect of modern eco-conscious design. As you drive onto the small farm property, you're immediately struck by a series of large south-facing windows. Walk through the well-lit kitchen, and you'll see that even the north side of the building has a passive solar component.

Logan: Every room in this house has a window that faces south, regardless of where it's located, so all the rooms in the house have both daylighting, which means that there's ample light coming in high into the room so that we don't need to use electric lights during the day, and also have south-facing glass that provide solar heat.

Jones: As a result, Logan's house will have neither a furnace nor air-conditioning. For hot water, he'll use an active solar heater. But efficient use of the sun is only one of the building's many eco-conscious features.

Logan: The outside walls—if you include a foot of adobe, a foot of insulation, and another foot of adobe—are three feet thick.

Jones: The so-called super-insulation is required to store the solar heat, but Logan is also using thermal mass, or dirt, to keep the house both warm in the winter and cool in the summer.

Logan: Okay, this is…this is a dirt wall, and it's nothing more than common dirt from outside, and we've packed it down to make it hard, and it is the structural wall. And I'm gonna pound a nail into it, so you can…[sound of hammering] see how hard it is. It's like pounding a nail into a piece of wood.

Jones: In all facets of construction, Logan is emphasizing both biodegradable building products and nontoxic materials. He's using milk-based paint, for example, and relatively little of that.

Logan: This room and the inside of this room—virtually all the finishes did not need to be painted. The ceiling is made out of galvanized metal and the walls are plaster. Painting is a fairly un-environmental act in that it is something that involves chemistry, it involves doing it over and over many times in the lifetime of the building.

Jones: And don't look for any carpeting in Logan's house.

Logan: Well even if carpet is made from recycled material, it still can't be recycled the second time currently, so carpet virtually always gets thrown away. Also most carpet gives off volatile organic compounds.

Jones: Initially, Logan will get all his water from a well. The house won't be connected to a city water system. But he says the roof has gutters and will eventually collect rainwater for general use. Logan is paying $75 a square foot to build his house, and estimates environmental features added 10-15% to the up-front costs. But he says he'll save money in the long run.

Logan: In many cases, many environmentally-beneficial solutions pay for themselves in as little as 6 or 7 or 8 months. A low-flow showerhead in most situations will pay for itself in a month.

Jones: Many of Logan's eco-products were purchased at Planetary Solutions, a Boulder store specializing in environment-friendly building supplies. Compact fluorescent light bulbs are among the stores most popular items. Marketing director David Adamson says the products last 10 times as long and are 4 times more efficient than your average light bulbs, but they cost between 15 and 40 dollars.

Adamson: When you buy one of those little 75 cent light bulbs, you're committing to Public Service* that you want them to supply you with a bunch of electricity over the life of that bulb. So really, what you're doing when you're buying compact fluorescents is you're buying a lot less energy.

Jones: Still, there's no perfect solution. When the bulbs burn out, they can't yet be recycled. Other store items include ceramic tile made from recycled windshields, low-flow toilets, cotton insulation, and so-called "plastic wood" made from recycled bottles. Adamson thinks consumers are slowly beginning to realize the personal benefit of these eco-conscious products.

Adamson: American buildings essentially are a lot like American cars were in the 1950's, y'know; they use a lot more resources than they need to. They're unsafe in many respects.

Jones: San Diego-based designer and consultant Jim Bell says ecological lessons for the future can best be learned from the past, but he goes back much further than the 1950's.

Bell: The fossil fuels kind of played a trick on us, and we thought, "Oh, do we have all this energy that we can do all these things?" But we lost track of what wealth was, and when people didn't have the fossil fuels, of course they made their dwelling energy-efficient, and utilized sunlight where it made sense.

Jones: Actor Dennis Weaver takes the history lesson a step further. He compares his so-called "Earth Ship" solar mass home in Ridgway, Colorado to man's earliest form of housing.

Weaver: It's just like a cave. A cave in the wintertime is warm; a cave in the summertime is cool, relative to the outside temperature.

Jones: Weaver says his uniquely constructed home is helping to solve two ecological problems simultaneously: conserving resources and recycling used tires.

Weaver: We pound 'em full of dirt—ram the dirt in until it's packed very tight; we call them "tire bricks" and we use 'em just as you would ordinary bricks so that every living space in the house is surrounded by this tremendous amount of mass.

Jones: Weaver's house is called an "Earth Ship" because like a water vessel, the building is self-sustaining and independent of traditional power grids.

Weaver: We take photovoltaic cells and we capture the sun's energy. The cells convert that energy into electricity and we store the electricity in batteries, and then all of the appliances in the house are powered off of that energy source: the refrigerator and the freezer, dryer, washing machine, dishwasher, shaver, hair drier, everything.

Jones: The Earth Ship concept was developed by Taos, New Mexico-based architect Michael Reynolds:

Reynolds: We wanted a name for these buildings that wasn't housing, because the word "house" has preconceived ideas, because it's hooked up to life support-systems like a house is a box, basically, that has power piped to it and gas piped to it, and sewage piped out of it, and water piped to it. It's like a person being on a life-support system in a hospital.

Jones: Some are critical of Reynold's Earth Ship concept. Because it's now possible to break tires back down to their original components, Logan sees little ecological benefit in using them for building construction.

Logan: So in my ideal world, tires would be recycled into tires, pop cans would be recycled into pop cans, and I see actually no structural or any other need for putting the tires in the wall—that earth buildings have been made for thousands of years without tires.

Jones: And there are other disagreements: According to Logan and Bell, the first step in eco-construction is recognizing that any building project is anti-environmental. Therefore, Weaver's 10,000 square foot Earth Ship at a hundred dollars a square foot is not exactly their idea of an eco-conscious dream home. Reynolds says yes and no.

Reynolds: See, there are still a lot of wealthy people out there that are gonna build large houses. Dennis wanted to be an example to those kind of people. We have people building homes—the lowest one now is $11 a square foot.

Jones: Regardless of their differences, all environmental designers hold some values in common. Logan and Bell both say Weaver's house is far more eco-conscious than most being built today. And according to Bell, environmentalism is really a personal choice, and the process is easier than most people think.

Bell: There's this big deal about consciousness, where people say, "Y'know, well, consciousness is this sort of magical, mystical thing." And to me, consciousness is just the process of becoming less of a jerk. It's just being more sensitive to each other and to our surroundings.

Jones: For Colorado Public Radio, I'm Peter Jones in Boulder.

[more construction sounds to fade]

Selection 4   Providing a habitat for fish

[News reporter: Steve Chavis]
Steve: I'm Steve Chavis with this edition of the KBCO "Environ-minute." The State Division of Wildlife has come up with a new way to use recycled Christmas trees. This weekend, the largest fish habitat the state has ever built goes in at Chatfield Reservoir using 3,000 donated trees. Volunteers from fishing clubs and the Division will tie trees to cinder blocks and arrange them into tree groves directly on the ice. When the ice melts, the blocks and trees will sink, providing excellent cover for a variety of fish—hopefully, walleyes, black bass, crappies, and perch. Wildlife officials say building tree cover for fish is lots harder in the summer when the structures have to be built on shore, then loaded onto boats. The frozen cover at Chatfield makes the operation naturally easy and fish can prosper. That's the Environ-minute on 97.3 FM, KBCO.

Selection 5   Global Youth Forum

[background voices]
Lesley: They have traveled from as far as Japan and Russia to exchange ideas and propose solutions to the environmental problems facing their countries: global warming, ozone depletion, water conservation. For 17-year-old Borja Celebi of Turkey, this is a rare opportunity to talk to lots of other teens and find out that they have many of the same problems.

Borja: It's important that it's [sic] gathers the youths from all over the world here, and we will share our ideas about the environment—protection of the environment—and we'll help us in many ways. We'll make friendships; we'll share our everything.

Lesley: Celebi, like the others attending this conference, was chosen from a pool of youngsters recognized by the United Nations for their efforts to educate their peers about the environment. She and some friends started a recycling program in their school in Turkey. Dulce DeMontanac coordinated the United Nations Global Youth Forum.

Dulce: We are going to have a compilation of the success stories that the children have brought in because the criterion for being here is that you have been involved in a success story. What has emerged is the very, very important partnership role that is being created now. The elders, meaning the politicians, the leaders passing on to youth the baton as we move into the 21st century, because they are going to be the decision makers and leaders.

Lesley: One success story comes from 17-year-old Nicolas Scotts of densely-populated Barbados. He helped organize environmental clubs in the public schools that developed into a network of youth tackling such problems as the illegal dumping of trash, and the destruction of the island's coral reefs.

Nicolas: We have participated in several beach cleanups. We have a newsletter published by our organization, which is circulated to students. We basically aim at students, because we think if we start there, they will grow up with these values.

Lesley: Many of the young people attending this conference think they're a step ahead of their parents and grandparents on complex issues such as global warming and the depleting ozone layer. Fourteen-year-old Kenyon Whitehead of Boulder:

Kenyon: I think we're definitely more aware than our parents were, because of all the stuff that's going on in the world today, and how everybody's all freaked about how the ice caps might be melting and all this other stuff. But we're actually more aware than anybody else that I think has ever been alive just about.

Lesley: A major goal of this conference is to put that awareness into action. Kids not only get the opportunity to learn from their peers, but to craft a list of environmental priorities:

[Male voice, speaking at conference:] One of the things that we've been asked to help you do today is to form a declaration that will be given to the United Nations General Assembly. If you can start coming up with your impressions of these presentations.

Lesley: They break off into smaller groups and begin brainstorming. Later the youngsters present their ideas to the larger group.

[Student at conference:] We also believe like that group over there that education is where we have to start, and so we need to affect the curriculums, and we need to get in the schools; we need to get into the communities.

Lesley: The declaration they are drafting is an effort by the United Nations to give them a say in decisions that will affect their future. And while the environmental problems seem at times overwhelming, 18-year-old Jeff Goins of Racine, Wisconsin says he tries to remain upbeat.

Jeff: It's huge. I mean it just hangs over your head. It's easy to get pessimistic about it; I didn't know any of these people before today, y'know, and they're not even from the same country or the same state that I am, and they all wanna do the same things. So I think it's inevitable that something good is going to happen, y'know. It's probably gonna be hard; it's gonna be a pain to get there.

Lesley: For Colorado Public Radio, I'm Lesley Dahlkemper in Boulder.

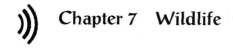 **Chapter 7 Wildlife**

Selection 6   The impact of a golf course

[News reporter: Steve Chavis]

The underlined words refer to answers in the exercise, "Keys to better comprehension: recognize vocabulary in context."

Steve: This is the KBCO Environ-minute. I'm Steve Chavis. Golf courses and the environment have historically been at <u>odds</u>. It's hard to reconcile the careful <u>grooming</u> and excessive water needed for <u>greens</u> and fairways with conservation and <u>natural</u> habitats. One case in point, Lakewood's Fox Hollow Golf Course had its construction temporarily <u>halted</u> so some killdeer eggs could <u>hatch</u>. A pair of redtail hawks were also born during the construction of Fox Hollow. However, the golf course has recently won <u>an award</u> for its relatively low <u>impact</u> and sustained wildlife. The Golf Course Superintendents of America say Lakewood's 27-hole Fox Hollow course <u>blends</u> well with Bear Creek Lake's grasslands, and the land still <u>hosts</u> foxes, deer, great horned owls, blue herons, coyotes and other wildlife. Only three Environmental <u>Steward</u> awards are given out each year, so Lakewood <u>officials</u> are pretty excited about helping set the <u>standard</u> for golf courses with a soft <u>touch</u>. That's the Environ-minute on 97.3 FM, KBCO.

Selection 7   Reintroducing river otters

[News reporter: Steve Chavis]

For the "Listening check" exercise, the corrected errors are underlined in this transcription. There are actually more than 17 corrections.

Steve: It's time for the KBCO Environ-minute. The State Division of Wildlife has sent <u>us</u> word about the <u>success</u> of the river otter reintroduction program in Colorado. River otters used to be <u>plenteous</u> in the Rocky Mountain <u>west</u> but trapping, pollution, and habitat destruction <u>depleted</u> their numbers. The last evidence of <u>wild</u> otters in Colorado is a photo of <u>two</u> otters trapped on the Yampa River in 19<u>06</u>. But the reintroduction <u>of</u> river otters begun <u>17</u> years ago has proved successful, and these sleek, <u>brown</u> swimmers can now be found around Cheesman Reservoir, the Gunnison, Cache La Poudre, and Piedra Rivers, also the Colorado and Dolores Rivers. Wildlife rangers suggest you look for otters at <u>dusk</u> along river banks using ice over rivers as pull-out spots. Otters are <u>longer</u> than beavers or muskrats, with short legs and long whiskers, and they're active <u>all</u> year. One particularly good <u>spot</u> to see otters [<u>is</u>] north of <u>Lake Granby</u> at Shadow Mountain Reservoir. [<u>It</u>] might be a <u>good</u> side trip after skiing at Winter Park. I'm Steve Chavis with the Environ-minute on 97.<u>3</u>, KBCO.

Selection 8   Dolphin captivity

[Alan Tu is an announcer for Colorado Public Radio; Peter Jones is a reporter for Colorado Public Radio. The other speakers are identified in the report.]

Alan Tu: A planned aquatic park in Denver is raising the ire of animal rights activists who object to a proposal to include a captive dolphin display. Although officials for Colorado's Ocean Journeys say they have yet to make a final decision on the issue, local and national activists have already instigated a "No Dolphins in Denver" campaign. As Colorado Public Radio's Peter Jones reports, the battle lines have been clearly drawn.

Peter Jones:	Colorado's Ocean Journey is the lifelong dream of Bill and Judy Fleming. The couple met in the late 70's when they were both animal trainers at Marine World Africa–USA in southern California. The Flemings went on to co-author *The Tiger on Your Couch*, a book for pet owners. Since then, their long-term goal has been to found an educational aquatic park in Denver, the landlocked hometown of Judy Fleming. If all goes as planned, the $49 million nonprofit facility will open in 1996.
Judy Fleming:	The whole essence is interactive, so what we want you to do is if you are walking through Indonesia, we want you to feel like you're there—you're gonna be walking through fog. Or as you're walking along the Kona coast, you will be seeing the different tropical fish of the Kona coast, or maybe some captive-born dolphins that live there.
Peter Jones:	That aspect is a little too realistic for some dolphin experts who see captivity as a form of cruelty to intelligent mammals. Rick Troud, a former navy dolphin trainer based in Florida, is taking an active role in the "No Dolphins" campaign.
Rick Troud:	Average age in the wild ranges anywhere in some of the studies between 30 and 40 years of age. In captivity, you can expect a dolphin to live maybe 5.13 years, and every 7 years in captivity, the dolphin population is dead.
Peter Jones:	According to Troud, there are many reasons why dolphins can't live full lives in captivity.
Rick Troud:	If you take a look at where the real dolphin is in the real ocean, you find the dolphin who swims 40 miles a day, is very family-oriented. These animals are separated from their mothers; that's a stress. You put them in a concrete tank where their sonar bounces off of walls, they can't swim in the same amount of time and direction that they can in the wild.
Peter Jones:	Ocean Journey disputes much of Troud's data. Bill Fleming is especially critical of his life-expectancy estimates:
Bill Fleming:	If someone said a dolphin lives up to 40 years, that is a small percentage of animals that would reach actually 40 years. So in context, if a person is stating longevity of an animal, they should say the average, which is in the teens.
Peter Jones:	Fleming says animal rights activists are also taking research out of its proper context by confusing longevity with an animal's total stay in a given park:
Bill Fleming:	The same study that stated a 5.13 years—there were animals at Marine World Africa–USA that were in that study. For the whole 12 years, those animals were alive and are still alive.
Peter Jones:	Judy Fleming says the life-expectancy issue is largely irrelevant because Ocean Journey wouldn't be taking dolphins from the wild but from other aquatic parks.
Judy Fleming:	We're not gonna go out and collect a dolphin; we don't believe in that. There is a surplus of these animals; they are not going to be released. This is a captive-born situation.
Jean Michel Cousteau:	So what!
Peter Jones:	Environmentalist and explorer, Jean Michel Cousteau:

Jean Michel Cousteau:	Sea World will go and get some other ones out of the wild; 50% of the ones they have there are caught in the wild.
Peter Jones:	The son of Jacques Cousteau has had personal experience with captive marine mammals. He was caretaker for dolphins his father trapped in the late 50's. Cousteau says a series of dramatic experiences led his family to oppose the captivity industry.
Jean Michel Cousteau:	There are some animals which reject captivity right away, and they're very suicidal. I've had one of those in my own arms for many days. The next morning when I came to take care of him, he was dead. And what he'd done was to swim as fast as he could from one end of the pool on [sic] to the other side and destroyed his head by hitting the wall. They have a very sophisticated brain. I don't think we have any rights to play with the lives of these animals.
Peter Jones:	Cousteau's anti-captivity position is challenged by Dr. Deborah Duffield, a biology professor at Portland State College in Oregon. Her 1990 study compared captive dolphins to the wild population of Sarasota Bay, Florida. Among other findings, the study showed little if any difference in the average age of death. And Duffield says life is generally getting better for captive dolphins.
Deborah Duffield:	The census data say that every time I do a census, I've got older and older animals in it as well as this normal age distribution that we've been looking at. So my feeling is that the trend in captivity has been that the group of animals that we're following are [sic] getting older, and if they continue to do that over the next five years, they will then indeed be older than the wild population.
Peter Jones:	There is also a debate over the educational benefits of keeping marine mammals in captivity. According to Duffield, captive dolphins play an important role in our basic understanding of the animals.
Deborah Duffield:	I firmly believe that we cannot learn anything about organisms that we share this world with if we do not understand how they live in an environment, and what they do, and that watching them go by in the wild will not do it. I cannot tell what an animal needs, unless I know how it operates, how it breeds, what it needs metabolically, and I can't learn that from animals in the wild.
Peter Jones:	But Troud says the dolphin displays are anti-educational because the animals' natural behavior patterns are altered by captivity.
Rick Troud:	In the wild, you don't have dolphins who beat each other to death. There are no dolphins that I've ever seen stranded on the beach, who are suffering from fractured skulls, fractured ribs or fractured jaws, as is the case in captivity.
Peter Jones:	The Flemings say the Ocean Journey board will take all factors into consideration before making a final decision on whether to include dolphins in the park. There's some discrepancy as to when a final announcement will be made on the issue. Estimates range from late May to late this year. Depending on the eventual decision, the battle could be long and hard. The Flemings aren't giving up the fight, and animal rights activists won't rest until they're assured dolphins will be staying at sea-level, not the Mile High City. For Colorado Public Radio, I'm Peter Jones.

[dolphin sounds and music to fade]

Selection 9   Wildlife controversy

[News reporter: Steve Chavis]

Steve: Ranger Brian Peck says the numbers of deer may be down. One indicator is the drop in deer kill within the city of Boulder.

Brian: We were having almost 200 roadkills per year; it's dropped substantially back towards what I'd say the historical average is, which is closer to about 120 or 130. And of course the other thing we suspect we're getting is increased predation from mountain lions.

Steve: This aerial deer count may help city planners deal with the controversy over urban wildlife: deer on the roads, deer in the backyards, deer grazing at flower beds and ornamental shrubs. Early indications are that the deer count is around 400, and that number is easily within the county's capacity. This is the Environ-minute on 97.3 FM, KBCO.

Chapter 8   Land, Water, and Air

Selection 10   Xeriscape

[Interview: Irene Rawlings with Tom Stephens]

Irene: We're talking today with Tom Stephens; he is a landscape architect here in Colorado. And we're gonna be talking with him about his new book which has to do with xeriscape gardening. It's really kind of a really—well, not kind of—it is a very, very pretty book, published by MacMillan. He, Connie Ellefson, Tom Stephens, and Doug Welsh are the authors of the book. And it has to do, as we said earlier, with xeriscape gardening. Tom, thanks for joining us, and why don't we ask you right off, what is xeriscape gar—spell it for us first...

Tom: Well, xeriscape is X-E-R-I-S-C-A-P-E, as opposed to Z-E-R-O, which a lot of people call it.

Irene: Mm-hmm, yeah, "zero-" like zeroscape.

Irene: We should probably note that since 1981, more than 40 states have adopted xeriscape programs which promote landscaping that's both easy on water consumption and also easy to grow, and Colorado is one of the pioneers—was one of the pioneers back in the very early 80's. Why don't you tell us about that?

Tom: Yes, it started at the Water Department. And there was an effort to try to counteract some of the problems that had been caused by droughts in the late 70's, and to use less water. And the Water Department had a task force of people including some people from the university extension offices and other places, and they sat around trying to come up with a program, and in the process, a name for what they were trying to develop. And some lady in the office—and I frankly don't remember her name now, but I've read the story many times—came up with a name "xeri-"... "xeri-" being 'dry' in Greek, and "scape" being 'vista or view,' and put the two together to make "xeriscape," which goes along with "landscape."

What we're trying to do with xeriscape gardening is to reduce the amount of water that's used but also provide an attractive—and I like a useful—lawn or landscape garden area. In our area out here, we call it landscaping; in the East, they call it gardening, but it's using less water to make plants grow and to look beautiful; that's really what we're trying to do.

Irene: You said useful—you said beautiful and useful. Now, what do you mean by useful?

Tom: Well I like to use plants that have fruit, because I like to eat...

Irene: [laughing] Well everyone eats—I mean—we do all eat.

Tom: ...and they can be beautiful in the landscape.

Irene: As we did say earlier, picture-perfect lawns are expensive; they require a lot of work and also a lot of water.

Tom: Yes, I find that when I teach classes in home landscaping, I have 7 basic reasons that people landscape. And the one that probably gets the most attention, and I get requests most from is to reduce the amount of maintenance. And once you have a xeriscape installation in, and it's taken over and become situated, you can reduce the amount of maintenance considerably.

Irene: Americans did sow and mow last year to the tune of $22 billion. $22 billion—that's a lot of fertilizer and a lot of weed killer, isn't it?

Tom: Yes, it is, and it's a big industry. And that's...the xeriscape is a small portion of that industry, and it's one...an industry when it gets that large becomes difficult to change its direction, so we're in the process of trying to push and pull and tug the industry to change its direction to some degree. And that's by involving as many people both on the professional side as well as on the client side to be interested as well as educated about what xeriscape's all about. And that's really what the book does.

Irene: Let me ask you, what are some of the most common ways in which homeowners waste water while caring for their lawns?

Tom: Well, having bluegrass, you have to keep it moist, and it takes 30 to 35 inches of moisture a year to do that. And so we turn on that what's called an "automatic system." Yesterday's paper was excellent, a cartoon, and I'm an avid cartoon fan, so...

Irene: I like 'em too.

Tom: It was a cartoon about watering grass, and the irrigation system was on, and it said, "Automatic Irrigation" and it was raining like crazy, and here's this sprinkler system. Well we see a lot of that.

Selection 11   Global Warming

[Interview: Irene Rawlings with Dr. Robert Balling, director of climatology at Arizona State University, and Eugene Trisco, attorney at law, leading energy economist.]

Irene: Okay, so let's start first with Dr. Robert Balling. Robert, let me ask you, what do scientists know about the greenhouse effect? I mean, is it a lot of press that's jumping in there and saying that we should or should not be doing certain things? What concrete information do we have?

Robert: We absolutely know that the greenhouse gases are increasing in concentration. There's no doubt that we're putting out carbon dioxide and methane and chlorofluorocarbons. We all agree on that. We also agree that these gases have the ability to warm the earth, and so virtually everyone in my field agrees that by putting more greenhouse gases in the atmosphere, we will see some warming.

Irene: Okay, you're the director of the office of climatology at Arizona State University. What actually is your field, I mean, let's talk...

Robert: I'm a climatologist.

Irene: ...and there's a degree in climatology. And that's...that's...

Robert: Yes, absolutely.

Irene: Oh, I didn't know that. I just wondered.

Robert: Yes, I have a Ph.D. from the University of Oklahoma.

Irene: ...in climatology.

Robert: ...and the...

Irene: So it's important enough, I mean in this country, important enough that degrees are issued so that we can study clima-...climatic changes, right? Good.

Robert: Yes, when I did my Ph.D. back in '79, the big threat was global cooling. And so we thought it was very important to get people trained to understand why the world was getting cool. And so the debate clearly has changed quite a bit in the last 12 years.

Irene: Well, that sounds like 180 degrees almost, hunh?

Robert: It's 180 degrees in certain respects.

Irene: Maybe not temperature degrees—but nevertheless, 180 compass degrees.

Robert: You have to remember, we thought back in the late 70's that human interference with the climate system could cause cooling; today we think that human activities could cause some warming. So in a way, the story line has remained the same: that humans have the ability to affect climate. Today we're faced with a problem though of deciding how much climate change can we expect, given the fact that we're going to double the greenhouse gases someplace in the middle of the next century?

Irene: And what does that actually mean? We do hear this a lot in the press. What does it mean that we're gonna double the greenhouse gases? What does that mean in terms of my breathing, my getting skin cancer, my sitting out in the sun, the tomato plants I'm growing—what does it mean in terms of day to day?

Robert: That's the debate. There are people who argue that we are going to see massive changes in climate. People say we're going to see four degrees of warming, and ice caps melting, and drought on the American plains and super-sized hurricanes and Yellowstone Park will burn down more frequently. There are people who still believe in this apocalyptic view of the greenhouse effect. There are still other people who argue that there are very few reasons to expect this catastrophe. Some people even go so far as to suggest there are great benefits of having more carbon dioxide in the atmosphere.

Irene: What would be...okay, what would be the benefits then? I mean, we've all heard about the bad things; what would be the benefits?

Robert: Well, for example, the models all say we'll probably get about a 10% increase in rainfall, and in the western U.S. that's not altogether bad news, to think that we might have a 10% increase...

Irene: But it wouldn't be acid rain or something bad like that, hunh?

Robert: No, not at all.

Irene: Just regular rain.

Robert: Regular good old rain.

Irene: Wa-, wa-, wait. Gene Triscoe needs to say something here.

Gene: Yeah, Irene, I think it's important to point out also that the temperature analysis of the temperature records over the last hundred years or so indicates that the very minor warming that has occurred has tended to occur in the winter months and at night. And that trend also would be expected to continue. Consequently, to the degree we do have some modest temperature change, and Bob Balling will talk further to that, in essence, it might give us slightly warmer winter months, and that's simply not...that scenario is not associated with any of the apocalyptic visions of glacial melting in Hawaii.

Irene: I was just gonna ask, is that good or bad? I mean I'd like to be warm in the night in the winter.

Robert: It doesn't necessarily have to be good or bad. There are some organisms probably that dwell on having more frost evenings. But overall I think...

Irene: Lobsters, they like it cold.

Robert: ...if you reduce the stress on plants from cold conditions, you probably have some benefit. More importantly, plants intake carbon dioxide, and more carbon dioxide would mean more plant growth. And there've been literally hundreds of studies done around the world showing that more carbon dioxide in the atmosphere would probably stimulate plant growth. So I think we've all been trained to think about carbon dioxide as some evil gas in the atmosphere. And in fact there are some benefits. In the long run, we'll have to weigh what are the costs and what are the benefits. But I'm suggesting to you and to anyone else that so far we've been told over and over about the horrible consequences of having these greenhouse gases.

Irene: And your point is that we just—we don't know; there are benefits to either side.

Robert: The fundamental point I make in the book is that we've already gone halfway to doubling the greenhouse gases in the atmosphere.

Irene: You've mentioned the book a couple times. Why don't you give us the title of your book?

Robert: The book is called *The Heated Debate*. It's available in the bookstores everywhere, and I tried my best to be unbiased and sit back and say here are two sides of this greenhouse story, and try to show that one of the elements of the debate is that we should have seen many more climate changes than we have observed. We've gone halfway to doubling the greenhouse gases and basically we have not seen very many things happen that are all that unusual.

It's very likely in the next century that we will see a very modest increase in temperature. As Gene mentioned, most of the temperature rise will occur at night in the winter months. We're going to see more precipitation; we'll see more clouds. So I don't see any great threat. I see no reason whatsoever to lose sleep over the greenhouse effect. If you want to act now and do something, that's fine. If folks want to cut back on wood burning and coal burning and quit driving their cars so much, that's their decision. But be fully alert to the fact that countries like China have fully intents—enormous intentions to burn fantastic amounts of coal in the next 50 years, that absolutely dwarf our ability to cut back on the emission.

Irene: Well, what influence do the people in China burning coal—and China is a very smoggy country. If you've traveled in China, you know that in the winter when you walk around, your eyes burn because of the coal and various other fuels that are being burned to keep these people warm. What effects do...does this have on people in Washington DC, people in Arizona, wherever?

Robert: Well, clearly the greenhouse gases get into the atmosphere and they stay there for up to a hundred years. So this morning when someone in China burns coal, the carbon dioxide from that coal will be with us for 100 years or more in the atmosphere. So if we do have this great greenhouse effect that is going to be revealed sometime in the next century, the Chinese have somehow affected the climate. So we are all interconnected in this. I mean, an emission of carbon dioxide today in the southern hemisphere eventually has the potential of affecting the climate here, and the key is there are many countries around the world that have no intention of cutting back and in fact have every intention of burning far more coal in the future. So we can sit around here all day and talk about the U.S. cutting back 10 or 15% of our carbon dioxide emission, but it really has no effect whatsoever on the global concentration of the greenhouse gases.

Unit 4
CUSTOMER SERVICE

Selection 1   Introduction to the main speaker

[Introduction begins with music]

Tom Martino: Hey, how ya doin'? I hope, I really hope things are going well. If not, do me a favor: stick around and listen and call. We'll help. And even if things are going well, I think you'll have fun anyway.

Announcer: Get ready. It's time for "The Troubleshooter," Tom Martino, fighting for you on news radio 85 KOA.

Tom: Hey, what ticks you off? What makes you angry? What gets under your skin? You know what? There's a whole bunch of things and you will hear about them if you listen to this show. But we do more than just listen to these gripes. We try to solve the problems, and I think that is the important thing. We're never going to tickle your ears. We'll tell you where you went wrong, and that's important, too, so give us a call at 623-8585 whenever there's a line open. And I will let you know when a line is open, or when you hear someone end a conversation, please call.

We also have a "hotline" on this show. Remember, this show alone: 629-0402. What is it for? For feedback—I need feedback, because we don't do it alone. It's a big family, and I need help, so when you hear something you could help with, call 629-0402.

Chapter 9   What is Customer Service?

Selection 2   Red tape

Answers to "Listen for specific information" exercise are underlined.

Announcer: Getting through the red <u>tape</u> at some managed care companies can be almost <u>impossible</u>. Well, at TakeCare Colorado, we want to know what you <u>think</u>. When you call us with a <u>question</u>, a <u>suggestion</u>, and yes—even a <u>complaint</u>, you'll talk to a real <u>person</u>. Together, we can find a <u>solution</u> and make our service even <u>better</u>. So if you belong to a company of <u>ten</u> or more, call your broker or call TakeCare at 1-800-<u>255-1139</u>. You'll see that we're the <u>cure</u> for the common health plan.

Selection 3   The runaround

Answers to "Listen for specific information" exercise are underlined.

Announcer: Ever get the feeling your managed care company doesn't really want to <u>help</u> you? Well, at TakeCare Colorado, we won't give you the <u>runaround</u>. We'll answer your questions <u>quickly</u>, <u>completely</u> and <u>honestly</u> the first time you call. So if you belong to a <u>company</u> of 10 or more, call your broker or call TakeCare at 1-800-255-1139. You'll see that we're the cure for the common <u>health</u> plan.

Selection 4   Recorded messages

Answers to "Listen for specific information" exercise are underlined.
Announcer: Some managed care companies would rather give you a <u>recording</u> than give you <u>service</u>.
Well, when you call TakeCare Colorado, you'll <u>get</u> <u>through</u> the first time. You'll <u>speak</u> to
a real human being, one who has the <u>answers</u> you're <u>looking</u> for.

Selection 5   Distant headquarters

Answers to "Listen for specific information" exercise are underlined.
Announcer: Most managed care companies keep their <u>distance</u> by being headquartered halfway
across the <u>country</u>. Well, meet one that's located right here—TakeCare Colorado. Our
local roots mean we can <u>answer</u> questions and make <u>decisions</u> quickly. Plus we know
more about your <u>family</u> and your <u>needs</u>. After all, we <u>live</u> and <u>work</u> in Colorado too.

Selection 6   I have a question

[Sound effects: phone ringing, being picked up]
Operator: Complicated Health Plan.

Man: Hi. I'd like some informa—

Operator: Do you have your number, sir?

Man: Well, not handy, no.

Operator: I'm sorry, I can't help you without your number.

Man: Well, wait, it's uh…

Operator: Other people are waiting…

Man: Ah, 6, no—J—6034.

Operator: How may I help you, J6034?

Man: I just have a quest—

Operator: I see. You want to speak to Mrs. Smith in customer service.

Man: Oh, okay.

Operator: But she's on vacation for two weeks. How about Mr. Hubble?

Man: Fine.

Operator: He only speaks Botswanian. Is that all right?

Man: Is there anyone else I can talk to?

Operator: Yes, but…whoopsie…he's on a conference call with his analyst. Would you like to hold?

Man: By the way, what's your name?

Operator: Sorry, sir. It's against our policy to give out information. Have a nice day.

[dial tone]

Selection 7   Press "1" now

[Sound effects: phone ringing, being picked up]
Recording: Welcome to Complicated Health Plan. If you would like to speak to someone in medical management, press one now; for member services, press two now.

[sound of key]
Recording: To be put on hold for ten minutes, press one now.

[sound of key]
Recording: If you would like to listen to bland orchestrated pop songs, press one now.

[sound of key]
Recording: Please enter the square root of two hundred fifty-six now.

[sound of keys]
Recording: Hmm, lucky guess.

Recording: If you would like to order Chinese food while you're waiting, press three now.

[sound of key]
Recording: Please enter your weight now.

[sound of several keys]
Recording: Now in grams.

[sound of several keys]
Recording: Hunh! If you would like to be accidentally disconnected, press three now.

[phone being hung up, dial tone]

Selection 8   Small Businesses

[Tom Martino takes a call from Dee, who has a problem with her fish tank. They discuss how to deal with small businesses.

*Walmart is a large discount store chain.]
Dee: Hi.

Tom: Hi, what's going on, Dee?

Dee: Well, my husband had bought me—I'd been having problems with my fish tank—my husband for Christmas bought me a bunch of different things that I needed.

Tom: Oh, okay, like what?

Dee: Oh, like the underwater air filter, the outside filter...

Tom: Okay.

Dee: You know, stuff like that...I have a 55-gallon tank—I've been losing fish...

Tom: Okay.

Dee: So, I called the Fish Den to ask them for some help, because they've been there before when I thought my water was bad or something.

Tom: Yeah...

Dee: And I asked them for help, and he asked me what kind of air pump I had, and I told him that it was an Apollo. That's when he started getting really rude. He said, "Well, I don't know anything about that." And I said, "Well can you help me at all?" And he said—basically what he told me was...

Tom:	Hold on. You didn't buy the stuff from him, but you called him for help?
Dee:	Well, I didn't buy it, no, my hus-...it was a Christmas present.
Tom:	Did you know where your husband bought it?
Dee:	No, I know where he bought the air pump. He went out the next day because we'd put everything else together and my fish still were...
Tom:	Did you know...okay, you knew where he bought the air pump...did you buy anything from this fish place?
Dee:	I've boughten [sic] fish there before...
Tom:	But I mean did you ever purchase any of this stuff you were calling about?
Dee:	No.
Tom:	And, and okay, so then what?
Dee:	Well, then he basically told me because—and I understand, I didn't buy any of the stuff there, but they've been there to help me before, you know, they've checked my water; I bought my tank there—
Tom:	I understand: a professional courtesy.
Dee:	Right.
Tom:	Yeah.
Dee:	And he all but told me I was wasting his time and he hung up on me.
Tom:	Well, okay, there's [sic] two ways of looking at it.
Dee:	All right...
Tom:	Actually, three ways: One, the guy's a jerk, and he lost a customer. But number two, you can look at it this way: What right do you have buying the stuff somewhere else and wasting his time? Although that will never win him friends, I can understand how he feels because he's probably being driven out of... Where was it purchased? Just curiously, where was it purchased?
Dee:	Where was what?
Tom:	The air pump and stuff.
Dee:	Walmart.
Tom:	See, so he's probably so ticked off; he probably knows it comes from Walmart*. Did he mention it?
Dee:	Well, he said I went to a discount store, that he couldn't help me.
Tom:	So basically you're cutting off his fingers; he's thinking, "Man, look at this. Here's a woman...They go to discount stores; then they need help, and then they call us." Let me tell you something similar. Now I'm not justifying it; I'm not saying it's...well, I am justifying it, but I'm not saying it's right or wrong or indifferent. They have a right to feel the way they want. I personally feel, when they get that way, it becomes a spiral of death, I call it. Small companies get ticked off at big ones, so then they stop giving the service, even if you don't buy it there. And what the thing is, is if they win you over, next time you need something, you probably will go there. I don't know, maybe you won't.
Dee:	Well, if he would've just talked to me, and maybe made some suggestions on new valves or something like that...I probably more than likely would've went [sic] down there because I don't wanna buy a cheaper brand. And I probably would've went down there and seen what he had.
Tom:	But a lot of times when you do buy from neighborhood specialty stores, you buy consultation services as well. And I'll tell you, with computers, it happens alot. With computers what happens, you buy a mail order computer, you spend pennies on the dollar,

and then guess what, you call your local computer store and say, "I need help with this and this and this." And it ticks them off. Because they're thinking, "Hey! We're in business here, to make money, here you are cutting the life out of us and then coming to us for help." And that is a problem; I do understand it. Again, I would have a different approach.

Selection 9   How to treat a customer

[Tom Martino receives a call from another listener with a comment on Dee's conversation.

*King Soopers is a large supermarket; Target, K-Mart, and Walmart are large discount stores.]

Tom: KOA, on the hotline someone wants to comment...Steve wants to comment on the fish tank problem...

Steve: Yeah, Tom...I deal with a lot of independent retailers similar to it sounds like what this lady was calling that guy on. And the thing, I don't know, it sounded kinda like you were defending the Walmarts of the world and cutting down the independent...

Tom: Oh, I don't think so at all.

Steve: No?

Tom: I said I understand their feeling. You're cutting the life out of them by going somewhere else to shop, and then calling them for free advice. Then I said—then I said, on the other hand, I don't think you're gonna win a lot of friends that way, and if it was [sic] me, I'd handle it differently. I think I would probably try to win that customer over.

Steve: Well, it's just the fact that, y'know, she didn't say when she called 'em up, whether it was the day before Christmas, or the day after Christmas, or whatever, but y'know, a lot times, y'know, people wonder why small independent businesses go out of business, there's your classic example.

Tom: Oh, and I—believe me, I said I understand it. I think there are other ways to go about getting your business rather than getting mad at someone for shopping somewhere else. But I know why they do it. And I brought up the similar situation with computers, mail order computers. These people order computers through the mail, and then cry to their local retailer about...about problems!

Steve: Well, I think you do a great job for the consumer. It's just, there's times when I think that...have you ever owned a shop?

Tom: No. No.

Steve: You would be amazed at the some of the stories you hear...

Tom: Oh, I probably would.

Steve: I happened to be helping a person...helping one of my customers—a lady came in—she had owned a pair of boots for 4 years, and never worn 'em before, and wanted to know if she could bring 'em back.

Tom: [laughs] Hey...Let me tell you something. You're right, I never owned a shop, but you know, I've probably heard more experiences than any individual...

Steve: Without a doubt.

Tom: ...than any individual shop owner. Hey, how about the people who bring back the bone to King Soopers*: "I didn't like the roast," and they'll get a new one, like without even batting an eye, they get a new one!

Steve: Yeah, and the thing that people don't understand is, okay, sure, they may get a new one, but what does King Soopers have to do? They have to jack their prices up to take care of all these people.

Tom: You know, that's true, and I think their theory is, there aren't that many nuts around that they can handle it. And I think with a small business it's a little different because just one nut can cost you a lot of money. And the problem is…is knowing how to identify nuts, and knowing how to identify people with true concerns. Some of the things I do with my customer service work—I…there are formulas, there are actual formulas, or actual secrets to knowing who a nut is, and there are also secrets to know how to handle certain people so they will actually geometrically increase your business. I'm talking about…you can tick one person off, and lose thousands and thousands of dollars. It's up to you to know how to identify the person that can cost you business. Not everyone costs you business. Believe me, I know some people, when they tell me they don't like a place, I go there on purpose, because the person telling me has no credibility. But there are ways to identify them. And you're right; it's a tough world—it really is tough. A small business right now, when you have to compete with Target*, and K-Mart* and Walmart*, it's tough, and…

Steve: Have you ever written that up in booklet form for when you do some of your seminars?

Tom: No, no, I never write it up. What I do is we have handouts at the seminars but I never write it up. And you know, I feel that that's a service to consumers when I do that for businesses, because what I'm trying to do is show businesses how to treat consumers. I don't mean this to be a commercial for myself, but if you just listen to this show on a daily basis, you get that all free. I mean, because I do talk about some of the things that are absolutely ridiculous that businesses do. I have had businesses on this show over the last several years that have gone out of business completely over an argument with a consumer that started on this show for $100. They have completely lost their b—their entire business for a hundred dollars. Why? Because they were fighting an invisible war—one of principle. One that they thought they had to win. One that they realized that I should've…I tried to tell them: even if you win, you lose. There are times to give in.

Selection 10   Accommodate all the customers

*[Tom Martino comments on how stores can cater to families. *McDonald's refers to the world-wide hamburger restaurants, which are now installing large indoor playgrounds in some restaurants.]*

Tom: One of the dumbest things I've ever seen in my life is a company or a store where they need to have people come in as a family, or they have no choice…kids are running around, they're not busy, they don't have a place for the kids; they don't have anything for kids to do. See what McDonald's did with these playgrounds? Did you see that? I mean, y'know, going to McDonald's, kids bring their parents there—it's not the other way around. Now if a dealership had any smarts at all, they would have a little play section, maybe some toys so the kids could be kept busy while the salesman's trying to hammer mom and dad. I know it, you don't like when I use that word "hammer" but I'm not…I'm just saying basically when the salespeople are talking with mom and dad, it would be nice.

 # Chapter 10   Principles for Smart Consumers

Selection 11   Send it back

[Warren Byrne takes a call from Chuck about poor food and service in a restaurant called Morton's:]

Chuck: …We had gone there…I wanted to get a nice steak and I know they're known for steak. She'd ordered the fish of the day, and I had ordered the steak, the New York steak and…

Warren:	Mm-hmm...
Chuck:	...when they came out, my steak came out I ordered it medium...
Warren:	Uh-huh.
Chuck:	...and you know I expect a steak restaurant they know to cook, you know, the difference between rare, medium, and well done...
Warren:	Okay...
Chuck:	...the steak came out, incinerated. I mean, over-well-done, you couldn't even almost eat it.
Warren:	That's unusual. Most restaurants, most steak houses, will err on the side of making it too rare on the premise that you can always go back and cook it a little longer.
Chuck:	And then, my wife's fish, when it came out, it wasn't even cooked at all. It went into the center area there, and it was still cold on the inside.
Warren:	Hmm. Was the restaurant crowded at the time?
Chuck:	Excuse me?
Warren:	Was it crowded?
Chuck:	It was empty.
Warren:	It was empty?
Chuck:	Absolutely empty!
Warren:	What night of the week we talkin'?
Chuck:	Sunday night.

Selection 12   Give it a second chance

[The conversation continues from Selection 11:]

Warren:	Okay, let me, let me—let me give you a little bit of a clue, okay? A little bit of a hint: Don't go out to eat on Sunday night.
Chuck:	I guess I learned that!
Warren:	Well, what...and this is not a universal truth okay, but it...it works most of the time. Somewhere along the line, they've gotta give their chef a night off. So they pick the slowest night of the week which quite often is guess which one?
Chuck:	Sunday.
Warren:	...or Monday...or something like that. And so the odds of getting a good meal on a night like that are pretty slim. Now, on the flip side of that, you usually get better service because there are fewer people in the restaurant. So you take your choice...
Chuck:	The service that night was...horrible also.
Warren:	You lost out on both ends!
Chuck:	Yeah, I mean like I kind of had a bad feeling when I got in and sat down, we waited and waited and two other tables were seated by us...
Warren:	Yeah.
Chuck:	...and they got shown the menu the way they bring that card up and show all the steaks...
Warren:	Right.
Chuck:	...all about the lobster for the night, and finally I noticed our waiter, he was chatting with another table—I guess it was a friend of his. It just wasn't a good night.
Warren:	Now let me ask you a question. What did you do about all of this?

Chuck: What I did is, after they served us our meal—couldn't even find anyone to complain to, so finally I asked for the maitre d'. The maitre d' did come over, and I showed him the steak, and he says, "Let me buy" —he first offered to make a new steak for me.

Warren: Okay.

Chuck: ...but what had happened was that it was already ten minutes after they had served me the steak, so by then I had kinda lost my appetite.

Warren: Okay.

Chuck: And then he offered to pay for the steak, which they did.

Warren: Okay.

Chuck: And then, with my wife's fish, they sent it back. But when they brought it back, that was incinerated.

Warren: So what did they do about that? Or did you mention that?

Chuck: We mentioned that too. And they did pick up the steak and the fish.

Warren: Well, so it sounds like even though they botched the thing, they tried their best to make amends to you.

Chuck: They did. You know it just, I feel when you're spending that much money they probably should've offered either the whole meal free, 'cause we still had to pay for the salads and the potatoes, and the little app-...

Warren: I agree with you that they probably should've picked it all up. However, when you're thinking on your feet like that, sometimes you don't make the exact right decisions. I would urge you to give Morton's another try. Well certainly, after your call, it will probably generate a call or two either agreeing with you or disagreeing with you. But I think basically...Morton's has been there a long time now. It's been at least 5 or 6 years that Morton's has been there, and they've got a good reputation. So for now, I'm going to believe that yours was a Sunday night occurrence.

Chuck: Yeah, I guess so. Well, maybe I'll give it one more time.

Warren: All right.

Selection 13   You have to pay for a true estimate

[Tom Martino makes a comment on car repair estimates:]

Tom: [music] Hi, this is Tom Martino, the Troubleshooter on news radio, 85 KOA.

You know, speaking of car repairs, let's talk about one thing quickly: diagnostics. I get a lot of complaints sometimes from people who say, "You know, it was just a loose wire," or "It was just a one dollar electronic part," or "It was just a little tiny screw loose. It only took the guy two minutes to fix it." But what they don't realize, in some cases it takes 8 hours to find it. Finding a problem is the main part of what a mechanic does—finding the problem. If you go to a mechanic and you ask them for an estimate, and they want to give you a free estimate, they can do it. But usually, it's a "guess-timate" because until they actually get looking at it, they won't know what is wrong with it. Therefore, a true estimate, I mean a true...or a true diagnostic procedure takes time and money. You should be prepared to pay it, even if you don't want the service done. And they must also tell you—not tell you—but they must get your signature and then they must put the car back the way it was if you decide not to have the work done. But they are allowed to charge for that. And I will tell you, you can't expect mechanics to do free things because it's a small part, because it just doesn't work that way.

Selection 14   Save your receipt

[Tom Martino takes a call from Lynn, who has a problem after she bought a used appliance:]

Tom: Meanwhile, let's talk with Lynn. And Lynn wants to talk about a refrigerator. Lynn, what's happening?

Lynn: Well, this is sort of a long story here, but I'll make it short.

Tom: Make it short, and then I'll ask the questions!

Lynn: Okay. In 1989 in February, I bought a used refrigerator with a one-year warranty...

Tom: Okay.

Lynn: And it wasn't exactly the refrigerator I wanted, but I had to have one at the time. So, I made a deal, in writing, with the company I bought it from, that I could trade it in for a different one.

Tom: You did?

Lynn: ...if they found a different one...

Tom: And this was a used refrigerator?

Lynn: Right.

Tom: Right.

Lynn: But I wanted one with ice in the door and...

Tom: What exactly did that agreement say, that said, the one that said that you could trade it in?

Lynn: Okay. What it said was that they agreed to find me another refrigerator with ice in the door, and that I could trade straight across the one I had for the one they found within one year.

Tom: Okay, good. So what happened? What went wrong?

Lynn: Well, six months after I got this original refrigerator, the compressor went out on it.

Tom: Okay.

Lynn: So they came, and they picked it up for repairs, which—that was no problem, but I never heard back from them. So after about two weeks I called them back, and was told that the owner was on vacation and I'd have to call back again. So I called again another week later, and then was told that they had lost my refrigerator; they didn't know where it was.

Tom: Do you have any receipts to show that they took it?

Lynn: Yes.

Tom: Good!

Lynn: I do.

Tom: But they lost it...

Lynn: But they said they lost it. What I think they did was sold it to somebody else...

Tom: So what's the name of this place?

Lynn: M&N Services.

Tom: M as in Mary, N as in Nancy?

Lynn: Uh-huh.

Tom: M and N.

Lynn: Right.

Tom: Services?

Lynn: Yeah. Now, one other thing, the...right after they took the first one, I told them I wasn't in a real big hurry to find, to get the second one, because I was moving and I didn't need it right that minute.

Tom: Well...

Lynn: But that was, you know, that's been three years ago almost.

Tom: And how long did you, how...how many times have you been in touch with them?

Lynn: Oh, at least once a month for the last two years.

Tom: Once a month. And what have you been doing for a refrigerator?

Lynn: Ha ha. I've got one of those little two-cubic-foot bar refrigerators with no freezer in it.

Tom: Come on, really?

Lynn: Yup.

Tom: And this place, is it the same ownership, the same business?

Lynn: Yeah. I talked to them a month ago and told them that I was desperate, and I told them I wanted my money back, and he refuses to give me my money back.

Tom: Well, he's gonna have to do something for you.

Lynn: But, and then he said that he was still looking, and he would, as soon as he found one he let me...

Tom: Oh that's such a bunch of...

Lynn: And that was about a month ago...

Tom: If what you're telling me is true, that's a bunch of garbage. John, let's call M&N Services and find out what the heck's going on! That's almost impossible to believe!

Selection 15   Talk to the owner when necessary

[Continued from Selection 14:]

Tom: Now, Lynn said that in '89, in February of '89, she bought a refrigerator, and she had in writing that she could trade it in for one year on another refrigerator with a [sic] ice-maker in the door. And what happened was, before the year was out, the original refrigerator, the compressor went out, and then you said, well, we'll get you another refrigerator. She says, basically, since February of '89, she's been waiting for you to get her another refrigerator. And that's really what she said. Now, basically, what's the story, Doyle? I want to hear your side of the story.

Doyle: Okay. Did she tell you that number one, she's got electrical problems out there in her home? And that also she is building a cabin in the mountains or somewhere?

Tom: Well what does that have to do with you getting her a refrigerator, Doyle?

Doyle: The...hey, in order for her to straighten out her problem with the present refrigerator, she's gonna have to get that electrical end of it straightened up. Now I have the refrigerator here, but not ice and water in the door like she asked.

Tom: I see. Now, what do you mean her present refrigerator? Does she have a refrigerator?

Doyle: She has a refrigerator out there, sure. And she has...

Tom: Does she have a refrigerator from your store?

Doyle: She has one. Well, I guess 'cause she bought one from me and see, the problem wasn't with the refrigerator, it was with her...electrical outlets.

Tom: Now Lynn, Lynn, let me ask you something. You told me, Lynn...

Lynn:	Yeah.
Tom:	You told me that the refrigerator that you bought from him went out.
Lynn:	It did!
Tom:	And then he took it back to replace it.
Lynn:	That's right!
Tom:	And has never replaced it.
Lynn:	That's right. They lost it is what they said…
Tom:	I understand. So you have no refrigerator from that store…
Lynn:	No, I do not have a refrigerator.
Doyle:	I don't recall taking her refrigerator. To my knowledge, the refrigerator that she originally bought from me was still out there.
Lynn:	No, it is not!
Doyle:	Okay. Do you have your…Do you have your electrical end of it straightened out out there?
Tom:	Doyle, here's the point, basically, okay?
Doyle:	Okay.
Tom:	If she had a refrigerator go bad…
Doyle:	Okay…
Tom:	Okay? And you took it back and she has a receipt, she says, showing that you picked it up, and she's paid you for that refrigerator, and you were gonna either trade it or replace it, it doesn't matter what's going on in her house, it doesn't even matter if she has a house, the point is…
Doyle:	No problem. If she wants a refrigerator, come down, show me the receipt, I'll be glad to give her one. No problem! Have her bring that receipt over to my place of business and I'll settle up with her.
Tom:	Well, see, Lynn, I want you to do that. Doyle at M&N Services sounds reasonable. I want you to go over there; don't let any grass grow, do it. Then let me know what happens, okay? Because I believe he either owes you a refrigerator with ice and water in the door as promised, or the value of that original refrigerator with a one-year exchange privilege, or a refund. Now, you know, I think at this point a refund would probably be the easiest thing in the world since it's pretty apparent after three years, that if he can't find a refrigerator with ice and water in the door, that he's not gonna find one soon. John, he told you that that was the main problem.
Tom:	He couldn't find one with ice and water in it.
John:	That's correct, Tom.
Tom:	Well, we are going to see how Doyle handles this as a business. And we appreciate him talking to us.

Selection 16   Avoid buying used appliances

[*Follow-up to Selections 14 and 15, Tom Martino comments on the problem of buying used appliances:*]

Tom: I'll tell you what. We get a lot of complaints about used appliances in general. It's very difficult to check them out; it's very difficult. In many cases businesses that sell them to you aren't even around to service them, or to honor warranties. And in some cases, we've had companies deny warranties, saying that they abused the thing. Now, just recently, I mean just before the break, we heard this guy saying she had electrical problems, so he was gonna probably try to blame electrical problems on the compressor. That's fine; he can....he can do what he wants. In fact, he didn't even know that she had given back the refrigerator. This is a problem, folks, and she's been calling him for 2 years. This is a problem that can develop: I don't think it would happen like that with new appliances. Some—unfortunately—some people don't have a choice. Here's something you may want to consider. If you're buying used appliances, consider buying from individuals, and having it checked out—yeah, pay a service call beforehand and see how that works.

Unit 5
DATING, MARRIAGE, AND DIVORCE

Selection 1   Introduction to the main speaker

[music intro. Main speaker: Andrea Van Steenhouse.]

Andrea: I'm Andrea Van Steenhouse. 623-8585 is the number. On this Tuesday afternoon, maybe what we ought to be talking about is recovering from yesterday. A lot of people not very happy about some of the ways that things were turning out for them, and for good reason.

Some of the things that were happening had to do with friendships, or even love relationships where someone had betrayed another person. And someone called here last week asking about loyalty, and, in fact, what loyalty...a component of loyalty is indeed betrayal. That when you expect, that if this is someone close to you, that they won't be going behind your back and talking about things, going behind your back and doing things, and I suppose the ultimate betrayal is that of your spouse having an affair.

But we talked about more than that yesterday. Some of the ways in which people proved themselves not to be trusted, and we really heard more about how that had happened for people than we were able to resolve what you do about it. And perhaps we can talk today about whether or not things are worth repairing. "Some things are worth repairing; other things—life's too short." And that's a great way, I think, to look at it, except that if you put in the wrong column, it's a bigger mistake as far as I'm concerned not to repair something that ought to be repaired than it is to be repairing something that should've been let go. I think if you're gonna make a mistake, you'd make a mistake over-repairing rather than under-repairing.

But one of the things I'd like to talk about with you this afternoon is how you might repair a relationship, and if you indeed want to. Some of the things that might be going wrong that ought to be red flags for you. One of the things we talk about a lot on this show is, "How come we ignored those red flags?" And I'm gonna put that up there, the two R's for today, repair and red flags. Is there something—I'm asking you—that you would like to have paid more attention to, now that it's progressed down the line. Is there something that you think maybe you could have known that you ignored? Because we all ignore things. We ignore signs; we just do, 'cause we want it to work out. That's okay, no problem, especially when people are in love.

We're also talking about some of the red flags that people wish they would've saw [sic]. They say, "I wish I would've seen this coming. I wish I would've seen that red flag," and then they make themselves feel worse. And I suppose what I'm suggesting to you is, well, yes, it would've been nice if you could've known that. It'd kind of be nice if you could know a lot of things, notice a lot of things so that you would never make any mistakes. But sometimes a red flag doesn't look like a red flag when it's happening. It only looks like a red flag after you're smart enough after it's happened. Other times we talk about things, and we say, "Y'know, something went off; my alarm…"—y'know, and we talk a lot on this show about the alarm system—so throw one off at me, when it happened, "and I knew it was a problem, and I knew I wanted to take care of it except I didn't." Well, that doesn't mean you can't do something about it now. But we'll talk a bit about red flags, and if you even overreact to the red flags.

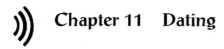

Chapter 11   Dating

Selection 2   An age difference

[Sherry talks to Andrea about a relationship with an 11-year age difference:]

Sherry: Hi, this is Sherry.

Andrea: Mm-hmm.

Sherry: And I have a question. I'm 22 years old and I am recently dating somebody that's 11 years older than me. And the relationship on the whole is good, but the fact that we are 11 years different in age—he's always reminding me of that, always saying, "You know, you're so smart for only being 22 years old." And I'm always constantly reminded of the age difference, but yet then he says, "Y'know, well, age doesn't matter to me," but yet it's constantly something that's an issue—that when there's a problem, he says, "Well, you're only 22; you wouldn't know."

Andrea: Yeah. So one could conclude that he's somewhat conflicted about the fact that you're a lot younger.

Sherry: Right.

Andrea: Does that—what you used as your first example was kind of a back-handed compliment. It doesn't sound like they're all back-handed. It sounds like he's somewhat demeaning to you.

Sherry: Right.

Andrea: And I wonder what…if it's so distressing to him, what's he doing with somebody so much younger?

Sherry: Right.

Andrea: What would be your guess?

Sherry: I honestly don't…I don't know other than I think…I think he's kind of….has a problem with the age, but yet I can sit down and have a conversation with him and keep up with him, and I think that's when he comes in and says, "You are so smart for only being 22 years old." And it's difficult for me; it's almost like my credibility of…y'know, I have a lot of credit for being only 22 years old, but yet how could I know so much at being 22. Kinda of like, y'know, he gives me credit, but yet…

Selection 3   Big Daddy

[The conversation from Selection 2 continues:]

Andrea: See, I would be worried, if I were you that somehow he picked somebody who in a stereotypical way appears to be less mature so that he could be either "Big Daddy" or be kind of controlling, and it's not quite that easy because you know more and say more than perhaps a typical 22-year-old, although maybe you are typical and maybe a lot of time...a lot of the time when you look at someone choosing someone younger who then gets kinda paternal—I mean that's kinda paternal to have somebody saying to you, "Gee, what a big girl to know all that at 22."

Sherry: Right. Right.

Andrea: They pick somebody for a reason, so they can feel like big daddy.

Sherry: Right.

Andrea: And I'll tell you what, people get sick of that in a hurry.

Sherry: Oh, I know.

Andrea: I mean, you must be tired of hearing that. And I would think that it would be time to say to him, y'know, "Knock it off. If it's so distressing to you to be with someone who is a lot younger...and yeah, there are things I don't know; there are things that I haven't done; that's a consequence of our age difference. If it's not okay with you, move..." And I don't mean say it to him in that way, but pretty soon it's gonna be kinda nauseating to you.

Sherry: Right, and it's already come to that point and...but yet he's still the person that says, "Y'know, I enjoy being with you; y'know, you're the only person I can sit down and talk to these sort of things intellectually," but yet I think he's struggling with the fact that —listen, y'know, we're 11 years older—or he's 11 years older. And y'know, I'll hear things like, "Gosh, you're not even as old as my baby brother."

Andrea: Well, but don't you wonder why he doesn't have a relationship where he can talk with someone closer to his own age?

Sherry: Umm...

Andrea: If you're the only woman he could talk to, that would worry me. Let me give you a general rule of thumb. When you're dating someone, and they behave in one way and speak in another, believe behavior.

Sherry: Okay.

Andrea: I don't care what he tells you. If his behavior continues to say to you there's a problem with it, believe behavior. And you might care about him enough to do something about it, but when you have two choices, I believe how people behave.

Selection 4   Breaking up

[Sandra asks Andrea how to get over breaking up a relationship:]

Andrea: Let's start off here with Sandra.

Sandra: Hi, there.

Andrea: Hi, what can I do for ya?

Sandra: I have a question about breaking up with my boyfriend. This guy was a guy that I went out with for about a year, and he was my first...first guy that I had ever fallen in love with, and we mutually decided to break up the relationship about 3 months ago. And I think it was a good decision because we had different values and things like that, but I'm trying to get over it. And If I hear a certain song, or if I'm on a certain street or something, I still think about him. And I was wondering what to do when these feelings come up, 'cause I'd like to get over it, and how I could get over it faster?

Selection 5   Getting over it

[The conversation continues from Selection 4:]

Andrea: Well first of all, three months is not a long time. And part of what you're faced with is that when you're close to someone, intimate with someone, it takes time. And all those memories that you're having are the reminders of the good things.

Sandra: Uh-huh.

Andrea: Now I'm sure there were bad things, but streets and songs don't remind you so much of the bad things as they make you long for the good parts.

Sandra: Exactly.

Andrea: And I'm assuming you haven't replaced him, which is not a bad idea since you're not a great risk yourself right now and your selection is probably thrown off. But I think to be able to say to yourself for the first 6 months after you break up with somebody, you're kinda vulnerable, and you remember good times and you reminisce, and you're lonely, and it's sad, and you see things, and see people, and are reminded of the times. And even though you're not—might not be doubting your decision, I think what you have to do is understand that that's how it works; that's how it feels when you've been close to someone, and you're not close to them anymore. But how do you get over it more quickly? Part of it is allowing time for that so that you have to tolerate the sadness. Most people who feel sad, they want to get away from it, so they pick another guy...

Sandra: Uh-huh.

Andrea: ...it doesn't get handled. It just gets stuffed for awhile, and then the next time you break up, you get a double dose: what you didn't deal with the first time, and then what you're gonna deal with the second time. So part of it, Sandra, is helping yourself build a tolerance for the sadness. On top of that, you need to get on with your life.

Sandra: Yeah.

Andrea: You simply need to get on with your life and not running away kinds of doing things, but spending times with people who make you feel good about yourself, doing some of the things that you might not have had time to do if you were wrapped up in a relationship with someone. But you have at least another three months ahead of you where you walk down the street and you feel sad because of the good times that you used to have with somebody, no matter how settled you are about that decision.

))) Chapter 12   Marriage

Selection 6   Another expensive wedding

[Andrea Van Steenhouse talks to Joan, whose daughter wants a second elaborate wedding, and wants her mother to pay for it:]

Joan: I have a daughter that had—was married and had a very elaborate wedding. And she is now engaged to be married again and has called and asked me if I won't change my mind and have another wedding. And my question—my answer was—"No, I haven't changed my mind, but I will do something, but I don't want to give this wedding."

Andrea: Yeah.

Joan: Y'know, I'll either give a brunch the next day or whatever. And she's invited me to go to the caterer, but I'm...she's angry with me, and the reason I know she's angry is because my daughter gradu-...the other—her sister graduated college on Sunday, and she didn't show up until I called over there. And her sister doesn't know that I called.

Andrea: Okay. Let me ask you a couple questions. How old is...

Joan: ...she's thirty.

Andrea: She's 30, and she was married at what age?

Joan: About...let's see...they...it's...21.

Andrea: And then she was married for how long?

Joan: Five years, no children.

Andrea: And then they got divorced...

Joan: Mm-hmm.

Andrea: And then she's met another man?

Joan: Right.

Andrea: And is it a financial issue for you?

Joan: That, and I just don't wanna do it again.

Andrea: Okay, and she thinks you ought to.

Joan: Well, she just keeps asking.

Andrea: Yeah. Why doesn't she provide herself a wedding?

Joan: Well that's what I told her.

Andrea: At 30, is she not able to do that?

Joan: Yes, they're very much able to do that. They just don't want to spend their money.

Andrea: Well, no doubt. So what would you like to ask me?

Joan: Well, I guess she's asked me and his mother to go to the caterer Thursday night. I don't ('scuse me) and I don't really know whether I wanna do that. I don't know if I even wanna get involved with the plans for the wedding. Or should I be involved even though I...

Andrea: Well why are you going to the caterer?

Joan: Pardon?

Andrea: Why would you be going to the caterer?

Joan: Well, that's a good question. I don't know why she wants me to go.

Selection 7   What to say

[The conversation from selection 6 continues:]

Andrea: Y'know, Joan, I think you need a pretty basic conversation with her that, "I'd like to give you a wedding gift of a thousand dollars or a brunch for 10, or however many people for a thousand dollars; that's the part I wanna play in this wedding. Y'know, I did a wedding once, and I don't want to do it again. What do you want from me?"

Joan: Is that wrong of me?

Andrea: No, it's not wrong of you. One wedding is enough.

Joan: I mean, I said I would give half the rehearsal dinner with his folks, or...

Andrea: Well, that's fine. What you wanna do is what's fine.

Joan: Okay.

Andrea: ...and she sounds pretty immature to me at 30 to be mad that you won't give her another big wedding.

Joan: Right.

Andrea: That's her choice. She'd like to get married again; that's wonderful. She's 30 years old. I'm assuming she's at some place in her life where she knows how much things cost, and that it's like somebody saying, "I went to college 4 years; I'd like to go another 4 years." And you say, "Well, actually I put people through college once." There's no reason for you to provide another wedding, and I think what you need to do is have a basic conversation with her about what you'll do, and ask, "Why do you want me there? I feel uncomfortable about it." See what she has in mind; she just might want some advice on what to have in which case it would be wonderful. But if she's trying to suck you into paying for it, let her know up front what your limits are.

Selection 8   The parents' choices

[Andrea comments further on the situation in selections 6 and 7. Music intro:]

Andrea: I'm Andrea Van Steenhouse. Well, I wanted to comment a little bit more on Joan's question. And I suppose what I want to say is that a parent gets to decide how much money they contribute to their grown child. Once someone turns 18, they're an adult, and you have choices about whether you want to send them to college. You have choices about what else you want to subsidize; you have choices about what kind of wedding you'd like to be involved in. You don't owe them any of that, but many people feel that that's important, and that, "Yes, I do want to put my child through college," and "Yes, I do want to provide a wedding." But to come back for a second big wedding is...I suppose I would have to say kind of unrealistic on the part of your daughter. What is she thinking? She ought to be embarrassed to be asking you for another wedding. And she ought to be saying to you, "Mom, I know you did this once before, and I'm sorry that didn't work, and now I want...I want to have another big wedding. And I can't afford all of it. Would you help me out?" But for her to be angry with you because you don't want to provide another lavish wedding suggests that she's misplacing some of her anger, and I'm assuming there are other things that she's angry about, and that it's getting focused here.

So I suppose what I wanna suggest further, Joan, is that you not engage in any kind of a battle with her, that "Gee, y'know, I'm really prepared to do this, and beyond that, I'm just not available. I'd like to be a part of this, and I'd like it to be easy, and I worry that because I can't meet your needs the way you'd like me to, that somehow this is gonna create a conflict for us, and I really don't want that to happen." You can't prevent it, but she's just naive to th—; either she doesn't have any friends who've been married twice, or she doesn't read the paper, or she doesn't pay attention to the world, or you raised her in such a way that she feels entitled to whatever she asks for. So if you're looking for an outside opinion, what I'm saying to you is no, she's not entitled to a second wedding; she wasn't even entitled to the first wedding. That was a choice. That was a gift from you. And if you think about it, as a gift, and she's coming back to you and demanding another big gift. Maybe that will clear your vision, clear your mind so that you know what to say to her.

Selection 9   A new daughter-in-law

[Andrea takes a call from Pat, who is having a problem with her new daughter-in-law.]

Pat: Yes, Andrea. I've got a new daughter-in-law that we have a major problem with. My son was married for four and a half years, and he got a divorce, and four days later he married someone else. And we've never met this person, and she came out to my daughter's wedding and was uncomfortable being around my ex-daughter-in-law and family.

Andrea: Now, how old is your son?

Pat: My son is 26.

Andrea: So he was married four and a half years. Did they have children?

Pat: No.

Andrea: No kids. And he got divorced. Did you know that divorce was coming?

Pat: Yes.

Andrea: Okay. And then four days later he gets married.

Pat: Right.

Andrea: Did you know that marriage was coming?

Pat: No.

Andrea: Okay.

Pat: But he was living with this person, so we knew…

Andrea: You mean while he was getting divorced?

Pat: Yes, while he was still getting divorced.

Andrea: Okay. Well, that's a bad sign, but continue.

Pat: And we had known his ex-wife even before he married her, like four or five years, so she was really a member of our family. She had lived at our house at times; y'know, she was a part of our family, and she's like my grandson's godmother, so we thought she should be a part of this daughter's wedding. And my daughter wanted her to be there. Well, the new daughter-in-law got so upset that my daughter-in-law and my son didn't even attend the wedding.

Andrea: Well, you know what?

Pat: And it was six months ago and I haven't spoke [sic] to her since. I spoke with my son and he wants to resolve it, and I…

Andrea: What's to resolve?

Pat: Well, I wanna have some sort of relationship with her, and I can't figure out how.

Andrea: Well, let's kind of go through this step by step.

Pat: Okay.

Andrea: Your daughter, who got married, has total control over who she invites to the wedding…

Pat: That's what I thought.

Andrea: …And each person invited to the wedding has total control over whether or not they want to come. So your daughter, who in my estimation is chief—she and her prospective husband—and everybody else gets to adjust. Now she chose to invite both. And they all have the option of coming or not coming. So your new daughter-in-law is so uncomfortable that she doesn't come. That's her choice. Now, beyond that…

Pat: My son also didn't come.

Andrea: Well, that's his choice. And they have the right to choose that. Now, why isn't she talking to you? Why do you have no relationship with her as a result of what she did about your daughter's invitation list.

Pat: After she got home, she decided to write us a letter and tell us what poor parents we had been to our son…this person who we'd only seen for three days. And my son doesn't feel that way. At the time…

Andrea: Did he see the letter?

Pat: Yes, which surprised us.

Andrea: What did he have to say?

Pat: He said that when he was upset with himself and feeling guilty, he did say some of those things to her.

Selection 10   Rise to the occasion

[The conversation from selection 9 continues:]

Andrea: Okay. So—I'm gonna say this, and I don't want it to sound the wrong way, but your son has married a nitwit.

Pat: I figured that out.

Andrea: Okay, so now you have a nitwit daughter-in-law except she's married to your son, and you want a relationship with them. You get to rise to the occasion. And what that means is, she's angry. I mean, feature this, Pat; she's mad at you for being the kind of parent you were to her husband. That's none of her business. Now if he's crazy, and you abused him, then I could understand how your bad parenting would have some kind of an impact on her. But what you're telling me is that, yeah, he, like every child who has parents, complained.

Pat: That's basically what it is.

Andrea: So now what you get to do is say to him, "Tell us what to do. We'd like a relationship with you." Because my guess is, if you stay out of it, if you say to him, "We love you. We'd like to welcome her into our lives. You guys chose what you wanted to do. I'm gonna try to just set that letter aside, but truly if you have problems with me," you say to your son, "I'd like you to come to me. How can we have a relationship?" Ask him for direction. But she will bury herself unless your son is really disturbed and needs to be married to someone who's off balance, which is a different problem. So for now, I'm saying to you: take the high road. Ask your son what to do. "We'd like a relationship with you; what we've done hasn't worked very well. Do you have any suggestions?"

Pat: Well, I have voiced that to him, and…

Andrea: What does he say?

Pat: …I've told him that I'd like to speak with her, y'know and he would like…I mean I've got a beautiful Mother's Day card from 'em and a real good phone call…

Andrea: Why don't you act like nothing happened?

Pat: That's what I've been trying to do.

Andrea: Nothing really happened. She wrote a stupid letter. And he missed a wedding, and he'll regret it someday.

Pat: Oh, he's told the sister already he's (sorry) he did it.

Andrea: So why don't you take the high road and act like nothing happened? There's nothing for you to do except ask your son, "Tell us how this can work. You know her, and we don't. Tell us how to be." No big, long, drawn-out sink-hole conversation, Pat.

Pat: Okay.

Andrea: Do you understand you won't gain by that? Do what you can do to help her feel a part of the family, but don't get your hopes up.

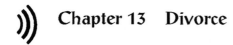

Chapter 13   Divorce

Selection 11   Surviving divorce

[Andrea comments on articles in <u>New Woman</u> magazine, June 1992 issue:]

Andrea: There was an interesting, a very interesting article...One of the ones however that I thought was as close to four columns of writing on one page pulling together a response to someone...The woman wrote in to Harriet Lerner, who has a column in that magazine, about her husband had left her for a man.

"After 24 years of marriage, her husband suddenly packed his bags and left me, [sic]—left her," she says, "for a rich male lover." And she was writing and talking about still being enraged, humiliated, and miserable. She feels betrayed, her femininity destroyed, and I really liked how she responded to this woman. She started out talking about, yes that must've been particularly devastating, but started to ask her some questions. "What do you want to develop over the next five years? What actions are you taking to ensure that you can support yourself economically?" Whereas right after a divorce, sometimes you're just figuring out how to get through the day, there comes a time when you have to begin to ask yourself some questions.

And then she began to ask questions about the marriage. "How do each of you think your marriage changed over time? What role did you both play in blocking open conversation about problems and complaints?" She started to ask her about things that she probably saw coming but ignored. She also asked her some questions that would not only ask her to take responsibility for part of what happened, but to take an objective look at the contributions to the marital problems, so that she isn't just feeling like this victim. Also talking about not putting all your eggs in one basket, so that your marriage is all that you have, if something happens to that marriage, whether it's a divorce or a death, or just being an awful marriage that you've decided not to get out of, what do you have to return to when that relationship ends?

So it was a very—if you want to read something that kind of pulls it together about, "Well, this happened and that happened, and this is what goes on now; this is what goes on later, and this is what you need to take a look at so that you have some idea of what happened, what your contribution was," it was I thought just...she does a real good job writing about that stuff. I'm impressed over time with her writing.

Selection 12   What's wrong with this picture?

[Andrea talks about the idea of self-analyzing a situation or relationship that feels strange:]

Andrea: Taking a look at the—maybe the big picture for you if something seems amiss or crooked. Maybe it's not even amiss. Maybe you just don't have it placed in the picture correctly. The way you know something is amiss is that it feels weird, kind of like this weather feels weird. You look out the window and you say, "This color outside is strange," or you look at how you maybe walked into work today, and it feels strange. And you realize it's felt strange for a couple weeks. And so then what you do is you say to yourself, "Is it me?" because that's very often the case that it's...we bring it with us. Or it is, "What's going on? It's strange around." And I think you develop your skills of perception, and you feel a lot smarter about it. But a good question to ask yourself is, "What's wrong with this picture?" And sometimes what's wrong with the picture is that you are behind the times. You are not with it. You're seeing things the way they used to be and maybe they're not that way, but we'll talk about those kinds of things.

We'll also talk about the relationships in which a person feels safe only when they're with that person and someone is reassuring them, but when they're gone, it doesn't feel so hot anymore. We'll talk about why that happens. One of the reasons that it happens, a lot of people say, y'know that old saw that if you think your partner's fooling around, they are. Well, that's probably a fairly adequate old saw. I think it's true a lot of the time. But it's not the only rule of thumb. It's not the only way that you assess what's going on. And when you don't feel safe around someone, generally that means—or not around somebody—you don't feel safe with the relationship, that means that you don't trust them. Some people aren't to be trusted. On the other hand, some people don't trust anybody. It's smart to know which it is. Are you generally nontrusting, and then you've chosen someone who kinda keeps you on edge a little bit? If you have, you know actually that's fairly fixable. We'll talk about it a little bit, see what you can do, and changing your behavior can make a big difference. On the other hand, if you've really chosen someone who's not to be trusted but who's kind of "slick," maybe there's not much you can do at all. And again it's smart to know the difference.

Selection 13   An insecure marriage

[Cathy calls Andrea for help in figuring out why she feels insecure about trusting her husband:]

Cathy: Hello, Andrea. Thanks for taking my call. My question...well, let me give you a little history on this. My husband is president of a company and employs quite a few people, and they started a bowling league. He asked me if I wanted to bowl, and due to a [sic] auto accident, it's not fun for me to do it, because it hurts my shoulder. So I said, "No that's okay, I think I'll pass." So his team consists of another couple, himself, and one of his secretaries who is single. And I'm just really feeling insecure with this because I didn't think it would be a single person taking my place; I thought it might be another male employee or something like that. And I really wanna know what I should do about the situation.

Andrea: And what...who is the other...not who...but what relationship to him is the other couple?

Cathy: It's one of...the man is his employee, and it's the man's wife.

Andrea: And...who is the secretary?

Cathy: It's the secretary in his office.

Andrea: Yeah. Do you know her?

Cathy: No, I've never met her.

Andrea: Well, I think you ought to meet her. What does he say about her?

Cathy: She's just a secretary. And then he says if…well, put it this way, he's got twenty secretaries. And he says—y'know, just to give you an idea it's just not like one secretary in the whole office—he says, "You're invited to go bowling. If you wanna go watch, you can watch. I'm not keeping any secrets. I'd never have an affair with anybody at work; that would be stupid. Y'know, you should trust me on this," and that's what he says, but I'm just really insecure with it.

Selection 14 An unequal relationship

[The conversation continues from Selection 13:]

Andrea: Well, y'know, there are two sides to it. On one hand, there's a big picture issue of why is there a league. Is that about something he thinks he needs to do in his business, or is it something that he wants to do for fun? And then the question would be why is he choosing to do something fun that would automatically exclude you as a participant, an active participant? So that would be one question I would have. On the other hand, you sound like you're not entirely convinced you can trust him. And I wonder what evidence you have that he might not be trustworthy?

Cathy: I really don't have any evidence. It's just he's not real communicative with me. We were in marriage counselling a year ago together, and I guess it's just, if he would give me more information, I would probably feel more secure.

Andrea: Well, what were you in marriage counselling for?

Cathy: We were in marriage counselling because he worked all the time, and he would come home real late at night, and it was hard for me because we just had a newborn child, and…

Andrea: Well, has that been changed?

Cathy: Uh-huh. He still works real late, but it's not totally me by myself anymore. At least he does come home and do some things or…but it's late. I mean when he comes home, it's after 8:00. He goes to work about 7:30 every morning.

Andrea: Cathy, why would he take on then yet another outside activity without you?

Cathy: That's what I said.

Andrea: Yeah, and he said…? What was his answer?

Cathy: If you want to come bowling with me, you can come watch.

Andrea: This relationship doesn't sound very equal.

Cathy: It's not. [crying]

Andrea: Well, I don't think that you guys did what you needed to do in marriage counselling. And I don't think it's about some secretary bowling with him. That you're really talking about a marriage in which he's not there very much, and you're kinda getting the crumbs, and the less you get, the more insecure you get, and now he's instituted something else to keep you away that he happens to be doing with really to me an incidental woman. It doesn't matter who she is. It's not the bowling, it's not the woman. This relationship isn't equal; your needs aren't being met.

Cathy: Yeah.

Andrea: And when you say to him, "Gosh, this worries me; I can't really participate," he says, "Well, come and watch." He doesn't sound like your needs are very important to him…

Cathy: Yeah.

Andrea: …and I…y'know, I just…[sigh]

Cathy: It hurts.

Andrea: Well, I think whatever the problem was...again, I understand that you saw someone to try to deal with the fact that he wasn't home very much. And maybe he came home a little bit earlier, but it's like you missed the big point which is where is his commitment to the intimacy in this relationship. You don't sound like you feel primary.

Cathy: I'm not.

Andrea: And if you are not primary, then you are at risk. And he may not be able to give you that. And then the question for you is..."Hunh, what's this about for me, that I've set myself up with somebody that doesn't care about me?" It's probably a repetitive pattern, but for me, I don't think you guys are finished with the work you need to do on the marriage, and I think you would be better off saying to him, "You know what? At first I thought it was the bowling, and then I thought it was the secretary. But I'm really aware that this marriage is not a priority for you, and that scares me to death. Not that you'd get involved with some secretary, or that you'd work an hour later, but that I'm getting the distinct message this marriage is not a priority, and I would like to do some talking about that," because you're a relatively young woman.

You've got a long haul ahead of you with somebody who cares so little about your needs. And if he kind of blows you off, I don't know what he'll say to that, you better find somebody to help you beef up your communication skills and find your spine, because you're gonna have to take charge of what you need out of this marriage, and the longer you take to do that, the less secure and more quivery inside you're gonna feel, and that's an awful feeling to be that scared inside.

Unit 6
WORK

Selection 1   Burnout

[Irene Rawlings reads a definition of burnout in men and women from the foreword to Dr. Robinson's book, written by Gloria Steinem:]

Irene: "Burnout, the need to be needed, an inability to say no—all these are masks of overdoing it that are especially evident in women. Burnout, the need to be in control, an inability to let go—all of these are symptoms of overdoing it that are especially evident in men. But whatever its gender mask, the emotional burnout that comes from obsessive doing and denial of authentic feeling is serious self-abuse."

Chapter 14   Overdoing It

Selection 2   Introduction to the topic

[Irene Rawlings introduces her guest, Dr. Bryan Robinson, and the topic of selections 2-4, "overdoing it."]

Irene: In case you've just joined us, we're talking with Dr. Bryan Robinson; he is one of the most respected authorities in the U.S. on addictive behavior. And he's just written a book called

Overdoing It, and this is what we're talking about; we're talking about being overachievers. Getting three A's and a B is not disgraceful, getting 3 B's and an A is not disgraceful either, but sometimes we feel it is, and we go about solving that, and trying to be perfect.

Selection 3   Overdoing it

[*QPA stands for Quality Point Average, similar to G.P.A., which stands for Grade Point Average on a school or college transcript.]

Irene: Why is overdoing it such a problem, such a contemporary problem?

Bryan: Well, I think today more than ever we are getting rewarded for overdoing it. I think that it's been around for a long, long time. But with the boundaries between home and work becoming so blurred, we're even more likely to overdo it. For example, we told ourselves that the modern technology would free us up, and we'd have more leisure time...

Irene: It was supposed to, yeah.

Bryan: It was supposed to, but it hasn't done that. With fax machines and laptop computers, and cellular telephones, we can be working literally anytime, anywhere. And we're seeing more of that going on at home, outside the regular work hours, and we're seeing more home being brought to work with kids in the workplace, more moms coming to work, and sometimes moms even nursing in the workplace, dashing—people dashing at lunchtime to a therapist or to, you know, pick up dry cleaning, or pick up dinner, whatever. So the boundaries are really getting blurred. Plus a lot of people have interpreted the woman's movement, women especially as, "I should be able to do everything, and give everything a hundred percent," which is really...puts you into a negative cycle; it's kind of a pitfall.

Irene: But isn't this—working day and night—isn't this kind of a requirement to get ahead in today's world?

Bryan: I don't think it's a requirement, but I think that a lot of people have interpreted that as a requirement. Most people who are overdoers don't realize sometimes that they are overdoing it. They see their level of work or their standard as normal. I'll give you an example of a woman that I talk about in the book, who is 38, she's working on her Ph.D., she's married, and she's working on her Ph.D. full time, and her standard was to make an A in her first statistics course. Now, you have to take three statistics courses for your Ph.D. and she ended up making an A + . So immediately her standard went to A + . Her minimum was A + . So in the second course she made an A + , and the third course, she made an A– and was devastated. She went into a deep depression. She even went to the professor of the course and asked if she could take the final exam over again. Now I have to tell you that there's no difference in the QPA* average when it's computed between an A– and an A + . This was her standard, and her own sense of inadequacy that was chiming in here, causing her to feel as if she had failed.

Irene: I'm just shaking my head here. If you say that overdoing it can begin in childhood, perhaps it began in childhood with this woman when she brought home her report card with 3 A's and a B, the mother or father said...zoomed in on the B—as my mother did, although I'm not as obsessive as the person you described—and didn't say, "Wow, what a good job, you got 3 A's." She would say, "Why did you get the B?" So...

Bryan: That's a great example, because I use that same example in the book. That's exactly what my folks said; it was usually math I would make the B in. And what happens with us as kids is we tend to look at the world through the eyes of our parents. So that if your folks say, "Hey, what happened, why didn't you make an A here?" and they ignore the A's, then you learn to focus that way too. We even have a name for that; it's called "telescopic thinking." In the book, I talk about the whole mindset of an overdoer. We think differently from people who don't overdo it. We tend to look for our flaws more. We tend to look for reasons why we haven't done enough, and it's...it's as Gloria Steinem says, it's self-abusive in that we're always telling ourselves that nothing we do is enough.

But one of the things I have to help my clients see is the little voice, the inner dialog that they have with themselves that they're so unaware of that has become such a part of them. And once you identify the voice, you realize what you're saying to yourself, I mean it's amazing sometimes, your reaction. But you're absolutely right, this telescopic thinking for me as a recovering workaholic, mine was more in the workplace, for some people it's— their overdoing is grades, for some it's in the home, for some it's sports, it could be in any arena. But for me, it was like I had to have the bodybuild of Arnold Schwarzenegger, and the sex appeal of Paul Newman, and the sensitivity of Mother Theresa, and the wit of Carol Burnett. And if I've had a bad tennis game, I compared myself to Boris Becker, and even if I was high in four or five of those areas, I went around feeling like a failure because my tennis game was bad. So we take the flaws, we magnify them, and perceptually, that's who we tell ourselves we are, and we forget about all these other wonderful things about us.

Irene: Our parents push us to succeed; they feel they're doing something good for us. And perhaps they're really not, because the anecdote about the A's and the B's, a lot of friends of mine have the same anecdote from their childhood, and maybe it's just parents that were brought up or came up in the depression, and felt that education and success were so important.

Bryan: I think you're right, and I think these are well-intended parents; I think they want the best for their kids, and they think that that's the way to achieve it. I was speaking with a woman in Cleveland recently, actually on a radio show, and she said that as a teenager, she went to the state competition with an essay and won second place, and she was so excited, and she called home to tell her dad, and her dad said, "Why couldn't you have been number one?" And it just devastated her, that you know...'cause she was still all excited, and it still wasn't good enough to him. And she's still trying to prove to dad—she's 28 now—trying to prove that she's okay, that she can make it. So a lot of us carry, y'know, those childhood images with us.

Irene: I was just going to ask that...how does my being an overdoer affect my family? And don't they usually benefit from what it is that I'm doing? If I'm supermom and I'm holding down a job, bringing in money, home in time to bake cookies and listen to them, and read bedtime stories, and A, B, C, D—just all in a row—don't they benefit from this?

Bryan: It depends. We know from the research that it's the quality of the time that moms and dads both spend with their kids. And especially for single moms—y'know, when we talk about overdoing it, a lot of single moms are overdoing it, and you just don't have...some of this you can't change. If you're a single mom and you have kids, you have to work; that's a given. But within those givens, there are things that you can do to take care of yourself and your family. And it's the quality of the time you're spending with your kids: are you reading to them? Are you talking to them? Are you asking them how they're doing? Are you taking them to the park, and really being with them, or as most overdoers are doing, are you watching TV because you're so tired from the day that you just can't answer another question? Are you—is your mind at work? There's something called "brownouts" that I talk about in the book that overdoers suffer from.

Irene: Why don't you tell us a little bit about brownouts too.

Bryan: In one of the cases in the book, Stefanie talks about this with her kids. She's an overdoing mom; she has a full-time job, she cooks, cleans, shuffles kids off to Little League and so forth. And the children can ask her a question, and they may ask her three times, and she hasn't even heard it the first time because her mind is on the next thing that has to be done. So brownouts are episodes of forgetfulness that occur as a result of our being so tired that we can't attend to the present because we're focused on the future. It's also, if you've got a problem at work, or if you've got a lot of things going, you're trying to think of what the next two or three things on your list are that need attending to.

Irene:	I'd like to interject a personal note here. I think that I suffered from overdoing it when my kids were little. And there were a lot of things that they did, and they said, that I only vaguely remember now. And I'm sorry, because those are times that have gone and will never come again.
Bryan:	That's right.
Irene:	And I'm sorry I didn't. I mean, I was not a bad mother; I was a good mother, but I wasn't always all there.

Selection 4   What should overdoers do to change?

Irene:	Now, how do we go about slowing down and paying more attention to ourselves without feeling guilt, and more importantly, and still get everything done, or should we just pare things away?
Bryan:	Well, the first thing I always say to people is you've got to take care of yourself, put yourself first. And the response I almost always get, and I imagine some of the listeners are thinking this now, "Boy, that's selfish for me to put myself first, when I've got kids, and I've got a job; there's no time for me." So if you think of the analogy of being on an airplane: The first thing the flight attendant says in the case of an emergency and the oxygen mask falls, who do you put the mask on, Irene? The child on your left or yourself?
Irene:	The flight attendant tells you to put it on yourself. That's so you don't black out before it's time to put the mask on the child.
Bryan:	Absolutely. 'Cause if you're not aware, if you're not, y'know, okay, then how can you possibly take care of your child? It's the same thing with overdoers, if we're not taking care of ourselves, there's no way we can take care of other people. I mean, we can to a certain point, but you're gonna be psychologically unavailable eventually, and your kids are gonna know it; even though you're with them, they're gonna resent the fact that you're not emotionally there. You may be at their concert, but your mind's back at work. You may be fishing with your son—if you're a father or a mom, either one—and thinking about what's the next thing on the agenda. And kids know this; they pick up on it. Your partners also know it, and they start to resent it, and it's the source of a lot of conflict. So, the first point is to ask yourself what you can do for you. The more you give to yourself, the more you're gonna have to give to other people. And there are simple things like pamper yourself, do physical things for yourself like soak in a hot tub, take a walk, take a break. I'll hear the refrain that there's no time to do these things. There's always some time to do at least— introduce one new thing that you can do for yourself.
Irene:	Well, y'know, when you talk to economists who tell you how to make money for yourself, one of their old refrains is "pay yourself first."
Bryan:	That's right.
Irene:	If you're doing…otherwise there's no money left.
Bryan:	Absolutely.
Irene:	There really isn't. And so maybe people will understand this. I certainly understand it better when it's equated that way.
Bryan:	If we think of ourselves as a bank account for example, if I'm always withdrawing, I'm gonna go bankrupt. And a lot of us who are overdoing it go emotionally bankrupt because we're not depositing, and the way to "deposit" is, in addition to those physical things that I mentioned, is to send ourselves healthy messages. Become aware of are you beating yourself up, are you say, putting yourself down, calling yourself names? Are you thinking negatively, and saying, "Oh well, I couldn't possibly, y'know, do this job very well"? I tend

to see that overdoers—especially moms who have full-time jobs in the workplace as well are—really are caught in a negative cycle of thinking that nothing they ever do is good enough, that they have to give everything a hundred percent. And they're always feeling like a failure because they're telescoping themselves like we talked about before. So it's important to look at the things that you are doing that are positive; learn to say no, especially women who tend to overcare. There's a whole chapter in this book called "Overcaring." Women, because they've traditionally been the nurturers, tend to be the ones that even if they're not working in the workplace, they are caring, thinking of everybody else, all the time, and that's a type of overdoing.

Irene: That's the hardest thing to do is to say no to someone that you care about. Do women overdo differently than men?

Bryan: Well, I think traditionally women, because they've been the nurturers, they tend to be the overcarers whereas men tend to overdo it in the workplace. Men tend to use their work—that kind of takes them away from feeling, and so forth...and I'm making real stereotypes here, and I realize that, but...

Irene: But we've got such a short period of time; it's difficult to go into anything really, in real depth.

Bryan: Right. But then—and then women traditionally have been the caregivers, and they've, I think, been told—not by the woman's movement, by a certain segment of society, it's been blamed on the woman's movement as Gloria Steinem says—but okay, you can have a job in the workplace, but you've gotta continue to be the main nurturer. You know, you bring up the child, you change the diapers, you keep the house clean, you do the cooking, you take on this extra job, so...but you don't give anything up.

Irene: Where do you suppose we got that? My mother told me, after giving me the best education that a woman could get, she told me, "Don't work." And I looked at her, because she'd also given me the message that I could do anything, right? "Don't work," she said, "because a woman who works has two jobs: one outside the home, and one in the home." So I think a lot of us grew up hearing that.

Bryan: I think a lot of us...all of us grew up hearing that in one way or another, and I think it's part of our culture now. I think there's a myth of the superwoman, and a lot of it maybe comes from our male-dominated society that says, "Okay, you can have this, but in order to have it, you've gotta sacrifice; y'know, you've got to add this on, you can't give anything up." And Gloria Steinem says we'll never be equal until men are willing to be equal in the home, so that women can be equal in the workplace, and not have that burden put on them.

Irene: What happens to overdoers when it comes time to retire? Although we hate to think about that, we all know that we must retire at some point; sometimes it's mandatory by law.

Bryan: Yeah, well if I were still as I used to be seven years ago, I wouldn't make it to retirement. Many of us never make it to retirement because we die before. And I mean that literally. We burnout. The body is a...we're humans; we're not machines. And overdoers tend to treat themselves as if they're machines; they don't take care of themselves, they don't eat right, they don't rest, they don't exercise very often. And nobody can do that but me. Nobody can do that for Bryan Robinson. I'm the only one that can eat for myself, and I'm the only one that can rest. I'm the only one that can send myself healthy messages and really take good care of myself, so many of us never get there. Those of us that do, don't really retire, unless we get into some kind of recovery, personal recovery, where we see the problem, and we learn to balance our lives out. Then we continue just going nigh into nothing up until retirement.

Irene: A lot of people who are overdoers retire and then die. Like boink—the next year.

Bryan: That's right. That's right.

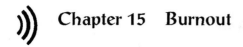 # Chapter 15   Burnout

Selection 5   What does an EMT do?

[In selections 5, 6, and 7, Andrea Van Steenhouse interviews Ann Shimkus, a paramedic, about her job and the burnout she experiences.]

[*EMT stands for Emergency Medical Technician]

Andrea: Let us start out this special kind of show today when we're talking with people who are there in times that we really hope we don't have, actually. Ann Shimkus, welcome to 85 KOA.

Ann: Thank you.

Andrea: You are a paramedic with Denver General Hospital. You've been in Denver a couple of years. You started back in '84 as an EMT*. What's your job—do you have a job description, an actual job description? What you do, and what you don't do, and what you don't do somebody else gets to do?

Ann: Yeah, being a paramedic, if you could think of an extension of the emergency room, bringing the equipment from the emergency room, and bringing it out into the field. We're the hands, eyes, ears of a doctor. We have resuscitative equipment, we have cardiac drugs, intubation, an EKG machine—it's all portable. So the sooner we can get that equipment and that care out to the person in need, whether or not they're ten minutes away from the closest hospital—I mean obviously here in the city, you're not that far away from any hospital. But if you work in a rural system, it's vital 'cause time is literally 'of the essence,' yeah.

Andrea: And is this something you thought about a long time ago? How did you—how did it turn out this is the kind of work that you do?

Ann: Yeah, I grew up in a small town in Pennsylvania, and I admit I got hooked by the sirens and just seeing that ambulance drive out. And I would always follow it to a degree, or just see, "Oh, it went up this street," and I would tell my mom, "Oh, it went up that street today." And I actually became interested in pursuing, y'know, going in Emergency Medical Technician school, and getting trained in this, and then graduate—I got to see more of it. Now I think I hate sirens. I mean, on my days off, I don't even want to see a bandaid. I mean, when I'm off, I'm off. I think it's evolved to the point where it's obviously more than excitement. It entails—you'll go through every emotion in this line of work.

Andrea: What kinds of people—if there is a such [sic] thing—get excited for one reason or another and begin the training, and find out they're not cut out for it? Have you heard from folks who've said, "Gee, I really thought that was me, and then I discovered X, Y, or Z about myself in training"?

Ann: Well, I think that's basically people who are really hooked on the excitement...and only think that that's part of it, and not everything works out perfectly. I mean you think you fit—that this superhero role, and you can be in it, and you realize that you can't. Y'know, that no matter what you do, you can't always, y'know, save that person.

Andrea: So it's really people's fantasies that get out of reality, y'know, out of whack and out of reality.

Ann: I think so. Exactly.

Andrea: When we come back, I'd like to hear about an average day. Do you work an 8-hour day?

Ann: We have a 10-hour day.

Andrea:	How many days a week?
Ann:	Four days a week.
Andrea:	Okay. What I'd like to hear when we come back is what's your day like? Are there days when not much happens? Are there days when lots happens? Can you predict to any extent—I suppose weekends and holidays and times like that—we'll talk about how you— you've already mentioned a little bit, you unplug when you leave—but a 10-hour day, 4 days a week, what an average day is like.

Selection 6   A typical day

[The interview continues from Selection 5:]

Andrea:	I'm Andrea Van Steenhouse. Our first guest is Ann Shimkus, who is a paramedic with Denver General Hospital. I'm reading on my blurb here that last year DGH saw over 45,000 emergency room visits. That's a lot of people coming in and out that door. Sixty percent auto accidents, 30% crime-related, and then 10% other. How about for you—what...is there such a thing as a typical day?
Ann:	A typical day...you can be guaranteed that there's alcohol involved.
Andrea:	Okay, no matter what you're gonna respond to.
Ann:	Well not, I would say the day—you refer to the day or the shift—absolutely certain that someone would be intoxicated.
Andrea:	Okay. Is that discouraging to you?
Ann:	It's discouraging when the innocent are involved. Y'know, I mean, you could tell people not to drink and drive until you're blue in the face, and y'know, so it's...
Andrea:	So one thing about a typical day is that somewhere along the line, one of the things that you're involved in will be alcohol-related.
Ann:	Absolutely, absolutely. I've been working the night shifts all through the summer, basically starting 9:00 at night till seven in the morning, and I would say 90% of those people are in some way, shape, or form intoxicated.
Andrea:	Wow, that's astounding.
Ann:	Yeah, it is, it really is.
Andrea:	Sorta stops you in your tracks, actually. Ninety percent! So you go—I mean do you just, you go to work, you show up?
Ann:	Go to work, show up...we have partners, and basically we live out of that ambulance for ten hours. We have designated areas where we sit in the city. And then we move around as more calls come in. But basically you'll find us in the park, you'll find us in a parking lot of stores, and you wonder, "Well, what do they do, just sitting around?" Well, we don't have places, fire houses, or y'know, someplace to sit. That's our office there basically. So it involves a lot of...you could be sitting, doing nothing for hours, and then you are go, go, go, go, go. So it's high, up down, up down...
Andrea:	So you're on call basically.
Ann:	Exactly.
Andrea:	And when a call comes in... how does it get to you? And how do they decide who gets it, and what's going on with that person? Does that matter?
Ann:	Well, we have E911 system, and basically the information will come up on a computer screen: where that caller is calling from, the address, the phone number. And our dispatchers are trained in emergency medical dispatching; they gain that information. Is

the party breathing? If they say no, then they can while they are giving that call out, they can give information as how to do CPR. So as I mentioned, we're all sitting in different areas of the city, so basically, if the call came south, then that car, that ambulance sitting in the southern area would receive that call. So that's how.

Andrea: And you're on your way.

Ann: Exactly, yeah.

Selection 7   Coping with burnout

*[The interview continues from Selection 5 and 6. *UPS stands for United Parcel Service, a quick delivery service for packages.]*

Andrea: I'm Andrea Van Steenhouse; we're talking with Ann Shimkus, who's a paramedic with Denver General, and I've got so many questions that we wanna try to keep on target here. I asked about burnout and about what it takes. You mentioned something during the break, and maybe that's important to talk about before we talk about what it takes, and what burnout is about. You said to me that you thought it was people's fantasy—it's like I really like seeing the UPS* truck come down the driveway; it always brings good stuff. I mean it's just…that's just the way it is. And it's not that way with an ambulance, even though, I guess I would've assumed like everyone else that if you're in trouble and you show up, that's great. And you're saying that's not always the case. Talk about that a little bit.

Ann: I'm saying that people think…well everyone wants to see an ambulance pull up in their driveway. Everyone…

Andrea: …If they need it.

Ann: Right. Everyone would welcome the sight of someone caring for them, someone, y'know, who's willing to help. And they don't. If you have an intoxicated party who's injured, he will be prepared to knock your block off. And he will fight with you physically and verbally because all he sees is that you're taking him away from his drink, you're taking him away from the bar, y'know, whether or not he fell off the stool or whatever…tripped. He is not competent to refuse treatment, and he has no idea, y'know, of the potential—the seriousness of the injury, and so you end up fighting with these people. Or someone who's overdosed, and say a friend calls 911 for them. They certainly, y'know, they made just an attempt on their life. They certainly don't want someone there taking them to the hospital, getting rid of this chemical, y'know, and saving their lives. So oftentimes, people think well, we have a cushy job, everyone likes us, well they don't. Y'know, it's…

Andrea: What does it take, as you look at…kind of "scan" you and your colleagues…is there anything you have in common that you think makes you or them the ones that would be in this job and not others?

Ann: I think the bottom line is we care about people…and that caring, there has to be a limit. Now I see myself at this point in my career, whereas before I cared a lot, or I would become emotionally involved. Now what my saving grace is to be emotionally distant. And I think that's what keeps people in it, to realize they can only do so much. We're not the…y'know, we don't walk on water. We cannot save everybody.

Andrea: What about burnout? How long can you do what you do without needing to move on?

Ann: Oh, not…not long. It's definitely a young person's career in my mind.

Andrea: Like young until when?

Ann: At the worst, I mean late 20's, early 30's. There are certainly people that do retire at Denver General, y'know, that have made it a career. But I mean I think the majority of places that I've worked, people will stay in this field for maybe 10 years; they'll move on to management, y'know, get into the office, or go on to teaching, just get off the streets. 'Cause it's not only emotionally taxing; it's very physically draining. I mean if you think about people, lifting people everyday. I mean, people don't conveniently have a heart attack on the first floor, y'know. You're carrying people, people that can't move for themselves. So it adds up.

Andrea: Is it a fair question to ask you how much longer for you, and where you're headed after this?

Ann: I would say I probably have another good 5 years, and then I'll really start to consider. I'm already starting to work towards another career only because right now I know that it will be down the road, and I don't want to start when I'm burned. Y'know, I still love what I'm doing now, and I guess I wanna to use that.

Andrea: Yeah, do it before you become a cynic. What about the things that surprise you, that—not the kinds of surprises that are unexpected and make you more stressed out, but the things that kind of in your mind say, "That was touching," or "That was humorous." The way someone handled something, the way someone—do you know what I'm saying? There are times when…the way humans respond whether it's who you're responding to, or someone with them that…I guess I think about in terms of radio. That whenever you think you've heard it all, then your next call is something that, you say, "Y'know, I didn't expect that." And it's in a good way, not in a bad way. And I wonder about those experiences for you.

Ann: Well, I mean, I think the best times when I'm working are those people that realize the job you have just done and are truly grateful, y'know, if that's what you're getting at. Just in touch with reality. I mean, oftentimes, people aren't. Y'know, whether they can't be because, y'know, their family member's sick or injured. But I mean if you have someone that has a good head on their shoulders, and y'know, just realizes that you did what you could, then that's…

Andrea: …that's a reward.

Ann: …that's what makes it. Yeah.

Chapter 16   The Work Force

Selection 8   How do I get into the workforce?

[Margie asks for Andrea Van Steenhouse's advice on how to get back in the workforce after staying home with her children for 6 years:]

Andrea: Margie, hi there, you're on 85 KOA.

Margie: Yes, my question was, how do you get back, or what's the best way to get back into the work force when you've been out of it for quite some time?

Andrea: Alright. How long have you been out of the workforce?

Margie: Oh, it's been six years since I've been home taking care of my three children, and my last one was six years ago.

Andrea: Yeah, and what did you do before you stopped?

Margie: I was a cashier, merchandising—fashion merchandising, and the last place I worked for was Payless shoe store.

Andrea: Yeah, and have you tried getting a job, and what's happening?

Margie: Yes, I've put some applications in and where I have worked, but y'know, then at the times they were hiring, but I have never gotten any calls or anything, so...

Andrea: Mm-hmm. Did you call them to say, "How's it going?" and "What do I need to do?"

Margie: I would check with them and stuff, but y'know, like I wasn't getting any calls, so I was thinking, y'know, that the amount of...that the experience that I put down was not current enough. I didn't put down everything I had done previous to five years. Normally, they want something that you've had, y'know, within the past five years, they don't ask for anything before that.

Andrea: Well, you may have to be a little more aggressive getting information out of these people. If you don't get a job, it's okay to call and say, "Gee, I kinda wanted to update my skills here, and I know I've been out of the work force in a while, and was applying for something that I'd done before, and in fact, I'd done it with you, and I wonder if you could give me any information about what it was that I didn't have that would be useful." Maybe there's something you need to do, or what you're looking for, "What skills you are looking for" so that you get some feedback, 'cause right now you are kinda blind. You don't know what they want; all you know is that you must not've had it because they didn't call you back. It could be as simple as the person who made a few more phone calls, went in in person again, asked more questions, might have worn them down so that they hired that person. It could be maybe they didn't hire anybody. So you don't know. You don't have enough information to judge what it is you're lacking.

    If you're applying for jobs that you've done before, we would assume that the experience you have is relevant, but you can't sit back and say, "Well, they didn't call me back; I must be doing it wrong. I must not have what they want. I must have been out of the work force too long." Do you know what I'm saying? You need to find out for sure, and generally if you were...if you say to people that you would really appreciate some information, that maybe you need to update your skills, or there are some things that have changed in the industry, and they could be really helpful to you to let you know what kinds of skills they're looking for—and it may be that you need to take a short course in something. But you have to ask that question.

Margie: Yeah.

Andrea: Because you and I could...let's say you and I decided that you hadn't had a job in a long time, and so that's what they wanted you to do, so you went to work for a temporary agency, okay? And you got some stuff under your belt only to find out that you were a perfectly acceptable candidate except they didn't have any jobs.

Margie: Mmm.

Andrea: So, you see what I'm saying? Why should we correct something until we know what the problem is? So the least you ought to do is call some of those places back, that you applied, and ask them if they could perhaps give you some information about what sorts of skills they look for, what was lacking in your application, in case you need to train yourself—to kind of get current for the market now. The other thing that I would strongly recommend if you're talking about clerical skills is that you go in to a temporary agency, and get somewhere in the workforce so you get the feel of what's going on right now.

Margie: The problem is I have kids, right? And I would have to work at a time when I know that I could be with them, and I can't be with them like say during school time and stuff like that, and during summer vacation it makes it hard because, y'know, you have to pay for someone to take care of them.

Andrea: Well, you gotta decide what's important to you right now. If you want a job...I know you want the flexibility that you just described to me; you may not have that luxury. If you want a job that's only on school days, only when your kids are in school, you need to apply to school.

Margie: Uh-huh.

Andrea: There's...nobody else works like that. Nobody else works from nine to three with days off—every other Friday for a teacher day and, y'know, a week in the middle of this, there just isn't a job like that. And it may be that you're not ready to go back to work yet. But the closest place to get that is at a temporary agency. You're available four hours a day, three days a week, and you say no when you don't wanna go in. In fact that's the only place that I know of that you're gonna have that kind of flexibility. And maybe you just wanna pick one day a week when you're willing to get a sitter, so that you can go to work, even if you wind up paying a sitter what you make. You need something on your resume, and you don't have it. And I know you'd like it to work easier; in this kind of a market, it doesn't work easier. Y'know, I think you're gonna be out of luck.

Selection 9   Get retrained

[Irene Rawlings interviews Kathy Ullyatt about a program that retrains women for computer jobs, and why:]

Irene: We're talking about the program which is called Women in Computer Science "W.I.C.S." We're talking with Kathy Ullyatt; she is the division director for the program. And she has said, and I'm quoting her here, "There is a difference between a job and a career. Most women who enter this program have jobs, and they're burned out, because they have jobs that are leading nowhere. The computer industry is career-oriented, which always entails more earning potential and a sense of pride." Have I misquoted you?

Kathy: No, that's about right, that's exactly...

Irene: Well, we need to know, I mean we need to tell women out there that they really can go out, they can join the WICS program if they're looking for a life change, and some of the women, y'know, have been working for many years. Others may be entering the work force for the first time...

Kathy: Exactly.

Irene: ...and they need...a need to be focused. Now what are the advantages of Women In Computer Science [WICS] over other computer science programs offered by universities?

Kathy: A couple of things I'd really like to emphasize: one is the level of support and help. It's not just coming to class on Tuesday nights, sitting through a three-hour lecture, going home, being on your own. There's an awful lot of support available and that makes women feel more comfortable when they're in the initial phases of getting into a techni-, highly technical and male-dominated field.

            Secondly is, an integral part of this program is help with finding a job at the end. One of the reasons our tuition is a little higher than some of the other programs in University College is that the extra tuition goes to the University Career Center. And that gives the women in the program full access to the Career Center, full access to on-campus interviewing, as well as a counselor that is assigned to the WICS program. And knowing that the students work (most of them work full time during the day and can't get to the career center from 8 to 4:30 when they're open), our counselor comes to the students, comes on the lab night, has personal interviews with the students, critiques resumés, and presents also several seminars. And the focus of the seminars is to prepare the women for the job search. We have seminars on skills analysis, writing a functional resumé, interviewing skills, etc. And then we do a lot of iterative critiquing of the resumés, so that they're ready. In April, we mail a resumé book to a targeted list of forty or so employers in the area. Last year, within 24 hours of that mailing, students were getting calls for interviews. In addition, being part of this program means you're part of a twelve-year tradition. I've got eleven years of graduates out in the work force; they're doing very well. They call me and tell me about jobs in their companies that are available.

Irene: That's known as networking.

Kathy: That's right.

Selection 10   People who need retraining

[The conversation from Selection 9 continues:]

Irene: We've kind of gone over the range, but could you tell us who generally takes this program? You have thirty students, you get to know them, I guess, fairly well.

Kathy: I do.

Irene: Who...who are these people?

Kathy: Basically they fall into I would say five categories. We still have the reentry woman, the woman who's been at home raising her kids, and has decided she needs to or wants to go back to work. I was in that category when I went through the program; I'm a graduate of the program.

Then we have people who have jobs. They're dead-end jobs, they're not using their intelligence, and they really want a career with a lot more earning potential.

We get people who have careers, their first careers, the things that they trained for—they're teachers, nurses, med techs, and they're totally burned out, and they're looking for some kind of transition into another industry.

We also get those who are seeing their industry dry up and shrink. I get a lot of people out of "The oil patch"—petroleum engineers and geophysicists who say, "Hey, I don't want to move to Houston; I'd like to stay in Denver."

Irene: CalHouston, Calgary, Hong Kong...

Kathy: Right. And so they're...they have decided that they want to transition into the computer industry. And then we also get some people who're really happy in their jobs, they're doing exactly what they want except because the computer is taking over, they need to gain more computer expertise in order to advance, and so they're planning on staying in their jobs.

Selection 11   Interviewing for a job

[Irene Rawlings interviews Debra Benton about how to interview for a new job:]

Irene: So we're gonna talk with Debra Benton. She majored in economics and in finance, and she landed out of college a sales job with an expense account, a salary, travel, everything you can imagine, and then she got fired. Now this book and everything in her life that came after that came from that one firing. So thanks so much for joining us, Debra, and thanks for writing the book, *Lions Don't Need to Roar*. Is there a formula for success? I mean, is there a...is it 'cause it's something that can be learned, or are you born with it?

Debra: You are born with it and you can relearn it. The problem is we unlearn it when we get educated and socialized. And we go to school, and we want to, y'know, move up. We get out of school, we get a job, we wanna be professional, and we end up looking boring and constipated trying to be taken seriously. And a lot that we had when we were young is what we need to succeed now but we've lost it.

Irene:	So how do we get it back? I mean, how are these skills learned? You are a consultant; you have your own company. As I say, it all came from this firing. You got fired and you…I'm sure you were stunned, y'know. "Why would someone fire me? I'm young, I'm attractive, I'm smart, I've…"
Debra:	…hardworking, honest.
Irene:	All that stuff, and suddenly you're out on the streets, and so you figure out why. You said you lacked the people skills.
Debra:	My boss said I lacked the people skills, which was a surprise, but nonetheless others, many listeners have had experiences in their work where there was said: "Y'know, there's just poor…" they were told, "There's just poor chemistry between you." Or "He leaves a bad taste in your mouth," or "…just, he's not dynamic enough," or "She just doesn't fit in." All those nebulous intangible reasons. And what it really is: someone is probably very competent, but they haven't learned how to show and project their competence. And being good and not projecting it is no better than not being good in my experience. And you can relearn these things but still be very genuine.
Irene:	What are some tricks to…to looking confident, even when you're not?
Debra:	Skills vs. tricks!
Irene:	Oh, sorry, sorry. Bad word, but…
Debra:	That's okay. But they can sound like tricks, because when we analyze them, they can. But really it is a skill when it becomes a habit. Walking into a room, you can walk in hurriedly, race towards the person you're gonna shake hands, sit down, put your hands in your lap, ready for the first question to be fired at you. Okay, or you can walk in, pause ever so slightly, non-verbally announce, "I'm here." Give him or her a split second to put down what they're doing, look up, maybe stand up, give you the attention due. As you approach them [sic], if you take a little longer, you don't dawdle of course, but just don't hurry like you're anxious and unxious and approach him, pause, perhaps shake hands, hold on a split second longer. Don't just do a flea flicker handshake like a politician, y'know, ready to go to the next person. Take a little more time. There are many things again as we dissect them, it can sound like seemingly insignificant, yet they create a picture, that before you open your mouth, you have…you have said about you what you want them to conclude, which is the start of controlling this conversation to how you want it to go.
Irene:	How important is a handshake?
Debra:	In our culture, we do "business on a handshake basis," right? I mean, million dollar deals are figuratively done in a handshake.
Irene:	Perhaps they are, I don't know anyone who does that, but nevertheless how important is it, actually?
Debra:	But it is part of the culture. It's the first time you get to…it's very important. It's the first time you get to touch. It enables them to hear your name, you hear their name; it sets the whole tone.
Irene:	What about names? I won't use the word "tricks" again. What are…what are some skills about remembering names? Someone once told me that what you are doing when you are introduced is so busily listening to make sure your name is being pronounced correctly that you often miss the other person's name. And certainly I've been in gatherings where five seconds later, I truly can't remember the name of the person I was just introduced to, and I feel so bad.
Debra:	Right. You and I and the listeners, we're intelligent people. We would remember the name—that's easy— if we heard it. But think about it: you're shaking hands, you're a little self-conscious, self-aware of how you're coming across. You are saying your name, like you just said, and you didn't even hear their name. It's not that you didn't remember it; you

didn't hear it. So obviously listen for it. If you slowed down, like I've suggested, and take a little more time, you'll likely hear it. Shortly thereafter, you could use it in the conversation. And if you fear forgetting it, you can write it down when you walk away from that conversation. But listening for it—hearing is the first step.

Irene: Is it shameful to say, "I'm sorry, I didn't get your name?"

Debra: Absolutely not. And another way is when you meet them again, you can just extend your hand and say, "Hello, Debra Benton..."

Irene: Give them your name...

Debra: Right, and that will invite... And again, honesty with a pleasant attitude is fine. Say, "You know, we met, and there were so many interesting people I met the other night, I can't remember everyone's name, I'm sorry, uh..." and kind of stop like that, and they'll say, "Well, Joe Blow."

Irene: Mm-hmm. Sure. What about people who just walk up and say, "Hi, you remember me, don't you?" You've had that happen to you.

Debra: Right. And I might say, "I do, and your face is so familiar, and my—I've just blocked your name."

Irene: ...and then that...that really...

Debra: ...which is true, which is honest, versus skipping around and acting like, "oh yes, oh yes" and like you know it, and...

Irene: And then of course your mind is going a mile a minute, you're not paying any attention to any clues that might be offered in the conversation, 'cause your mind is racing back through all the gatherings, all the office parties, all—whatever you've done in the last year, I mean you're sort of going nuts.

Unit 7
RENTING AN APARTMENT

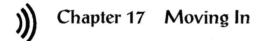

Chapter 17   Moving In

Selection 1   Signing a lease

[Greg calls Tom Martino about a landlord who tries to raise the rent after the lease was signed:]

Tom: Alright, Greg, what's going on?

Greg: Yeah, me and two of my friends, we moved into this place; we signed a lease for six months.

Tom: Okay...

Greg: ...for $625 a month.

Tom: Alright.

Greg: Okay, we've been living there for about a month.

Tom:	Now, you all signed the lease, Greg?
Greg:	Yes.
Tom:	Okay.
Greg:	See, let me tell you about that first. First, we…it was just gonna be two of us signing the lease.
Tom:	Uh-huh.
Greg:	And that's what she thought.
Tom:	Yeah…
Greg:	But we all three signed the lease. We had a friend that wanted to move out—move in with us.
Tom:	Okay, now you all signed for all of the lease.
Greg:	Yeah.
Tom:	It wasn't divided in thirds. In other words, you each signed for $625 a month.
Greg:	Well, no, we're splitting up the rent.
Tom:	I know that. You are splitting up the rent among yourselves.
Greg:	Yes.
Tom:	But as far as the landlord's concerned, each one of you signed a lease which said $625.
Greg:	Oh, yeah. Yes.
Tom:	You didn't sign one that said a third of that.
Greg:	No.
Tom:	Okay, go ahead, Greg.
Greg:	Okay, we've been living there about a month, and now she wants to raise our rent to 680.
Tom:	Well, how can she do that if you have a lease?
Greg:	Yeah! That's what I was wondering. Does she have that right to do that?
Tom:	Only if it's written in the lease. Dan Kaplis, again on my panel of experts, and he's here for today helping me out, Dan…
Dan:	How long was the lease for?
Greg:	Six months.
Tom:	I mean, she can't do it; she can, I mean she can try, but did you say to her, "Hey, we got a lease?"
Greg:	Well, actually that's why I'm calling you; I wanted to make sure I had that right to say that.
Tom:	Well, we…now mind you, we don't have the lease in front of us…
Greg:	Yeah.
Tom:	So does it say anything in there about the right to raise rent?
Greg:	Yeah, I…not that I remember. But…
Tom:	Do you have a copy of that lease?
Greg:	That's another thing. I told her to send me a copy, but …
Tom:	GREG!
Greg:	I know…
Tom:	GREGGGG!!! Come on, man!
Greg:	I know…

Tom:	You signed something and didn't keep a copy?
Greg:	I know, well we only had one…
Tom:	How many pages was that lease?
Greg:	It was one page.
Tom:	Okay, so she can't…
Dan:	I doubt it, Tom. I've never seen a standard lease like that that had a right to raise rent until the lease expired.
Tom:	Sure, sure.
Dan:	So, chances are it doesn't have that provision.
Tom:	Greg, did she say anything about why she's raising the rent?
Greg:	She said because three people are living there.
Tom:	But three people signed the lease.
Greg:	Yes, I know.
Tom:	Well, how many people does it say will live there?
Greg:	Three.
Tom:	In the lease.
Greg:	Yes.
Tom:	This woman is full of it.
Greg:	Okay.
Tom:	…and I don't mean water. Listen, Greg, if you want some help, you let me know.
Greg:	Okay.
Tom:	But just, just…just hang in there, because that sounds like…it sounds ridiculous, absolutely ridiculous.

Selection 2   What are the tenant's rights?

[Tom Martino takes a call from Brent, who says his landlord hasn't taken care of his requests. Barrie is an attorney.]

Tom:	Brent, what's happening?
Brent:	Oh, nothing much here. How ya doin'?
Tom:	So let's talk about your problem.
Brent:	Okay, well we're renting out this house over here, and I've made several requests to have…since we lived here in August—we moved in towards the end of August—and we've had squirrels living up in the attic, and I made several requests to have 'em removed.
Tom:	Yeah?
Brent:	It seems like the company is just ignoring us, and…
Tom:	Now remember we talked about this, and I held it over because I wanted to not rush you. But the point is this. You're renting a home, and unless those squirrels create some kind of a health or safety hazard…We all have this idea that when we rent a place, we have certain rights. The only rights we have are the rights set forth in the lease.
Brent:	Mm-hmm.
Tom:	Okay…and an additional right you may not find in the lease, which is peaceful enjoyment of the premises—private and peaceful. In other words, if you don't have a roof or walls,

you could argue that that's not habitable. However, when it comes to health and safety, if there was [sic] a health and safety hazard—let's say there was a health and safety hazard—that still doesn't mean that the landlord has to fix it. All that it means is that you're allowed to move. When it comes to squirrels being just a nuisance, I don't think you could even argue that they're a health and safety hazard. What do you think?

Brent: Okay, well they have eaten like a hole in the roof...

Tom: Yeah.

Brent: They came and fixed the fasset [sic] and soffit in two areas, y'know.

Tom: What does your lease say about pests? pest control?

Brent: Let me see here...

Tom: I think what you're gonna find. Let me just make a long story short here, Brent, let me just make a long story short.

Brent: Mm-hmm.

Tom: I don't think you're gonna find anything in the lease that will address this problem.

Brent: Yeah.

Tom: If your landlord doesn't want to fix it, I doubt that you can make them fix it.

Brent: Okay.

Tom: I think that, however, I don't know...is this serious enough, Barrie, that he could say it violates the lease?

Barrie: I think it could be a health hazard. Do you have children in the house with you, Brent?

Brent: No.

Barrie: Well...

Brent: Sure don't.

Barrie: I...even for an adult.

Tom: Brent, I gotta tell you something. It's gonna be hard on this one because it's a nuisance. But you see, as I said before, there are no laws that address habitability in this state.

Brent: Okay.

Tom: And I don't think you can make your landlord fix it. I don't think...you see, we can't call up and say, "Fix this."

Brent: Oh yeah, I understand that. I just—it just seemed like they're ignoring me all the time.

Tom: Well, they probably are. Do you have a lease?

Brent: Mm-hmm. Yeah.

Barrie: How long is it?

Brent: It's a year's lease.

Tom: Okay, you could probably, y'know, try asking them to let you out of it, or say that you're going to sue them for a release from the lease, because you can't tolerate it anymore.

Brent: Well, yeah, I mean, also 'cause it's not just the squirrels. It's, y'know, our house is easily accessible without the use of keys, and I asked—I requested dead bolts, and they says, [sic] "Well, you can buy 'em and bolt them in."

Tom: That's right. Exactly. See, Brent, that's the point. That's the point, and I don't mean to cut you off, I'm sorry, but the bottom line here is there's not a lot of help for tenants when it comes to opinions, like dead bolts is an opinion. Even though you think it's necessary, they don't. Squirrels being a nuisance, a noisy neighborhood, crime-ridden areas, these are all opinions. There's no habitability that protects you.

Selection 3   The cat and the bird cage

[Susan calls Tom Martino and Kerry, a legal expert, with a question about an unusual accident involving her cat and her neighbor's bird cage:]

Tom: Susan, how are you doing?

Susan: I'm doing fine. I have a little bit of a bizarre situation here. A neighbor claimed that my cat on a warm day in September went into her apartment, knocked over her bird cage. The bird cage fell to the floor and cracked, and in falling, the little water cup with water spilled onto her portable phone that was on the floor, and shorted it out.

Tom: Sounds like one of these games that kids play: you knock one thing down, it causes a chain reaction.

Susan: Well, she's claiming now that it shorted out her phone, and that it's now $130 total for the cage and the phone.

[sound of screaming cat]

Tom: Well, hold on now, Susan, you're telling me now...By the way, this is a question here: are we responsible, just for argument's sake, are we responsible, Kerry, for the actions of our animals?

Susan: The canine patrol man—policeman—said, yes, I am.

Kerry: I tell you what, I wouldn't be as interested in what the canine person says.

Tom: But we are, we are though.

Kerry: What we are responsible for, Tom, is negligence. Our own negligence if that negligence results in our animals doing damage. Whether it's the dog that bites somebody or the cat that causes this problem. If you can show that because you let your cat out, and your cat did this and that, yes, you have a responsibility to control your...

Tom: But what if she left her window open, the neighbor?

Susan: The neighbor chased the...there are three other tabby cats right in the complex where I live.

Tom: So first of all, she can't even prove it was yours.

Susan: Exactly.

Tom: So not only would she have to prove it was yours, she'd have to prove that your cat...how'd your cat enter the apartment?

Susan: She had the door open, which the police officer says, she has the privilege of doing that.

Tom: First of all, this police officer shouldn't be practicing law, but that's alright. Second of all, let's take it, let's just end it right here. You know why? Because how could she possibly prove it was your cat and not another one? Does your cat have any special identifying mark? Could she pick your cat out of a lineup?

Kerry: A feline lineup!

Tom: Could she...

Susan: Now wait a second. On his report, he claimed that the cat...what had happened was she called the canine officer, and he came here fifty minutes later. My cat was in the yard, he picked it up and put it into the what-do-you-call-it, the car, y'know, the truck that they have. And they said it was a spayed tabby cat, which mine was.

Tom: Now how the...hold on, hold on...

Susan: There was a time lapse there of...

Tom: So your cat happens to wander into the yard and gets framed!

Susan:	That's right. That's exactly what it boils down to.
Tom:	But we don't know, it could've been your cat, but we don't know that.
Susan:	Yes, it could've been; yes, it could've been.
Kerry:	There's one easy way around it...
Tom:	First of all, well hold it. That officer can't make sure. But by the way, let's...we'll take this up, we'll discuss this a little more, but first stay tuned for the latest...[fade]

Selection 4   Can she prove it?

[The conversation from Selection 3 continues:]

Tom:	Now, hold on a sec. The point is first, she cannot prove it was your cat; that's first. Even though there's a report, that animal control officer did not arrive on the scene until forty minutes later. Did the woman keep the cat captive for all that time?
Susan:	No, no, she didn't. She said that the cat ran out of the apartment and then he caught it fifty minutes later in her yard. And how does he know he caught the same cat?
Susan:	He doesn't know that. He doesn't know that. He said, "Yes, that's the cat."
Tom:	So maybe your...well, what does your cat have to say about it?
Susan:	[laughing] Oh, my cat has nothing to say about it.
Tom:	I mean, you didn't ask your cat at all what's going on? Is your cat, seriously, is your cat a bad cat?
Susan:	It's a lovable cat.
Tom:	I know, but you know, I have a cat, I have 2 cats, and if one of 'em—one of 'em, if they said he did it, I'd believe. But if they said the other one did it, I'd say, "No way." So y'know, you know the personality of your cat. How is your cat? Is your cat a bad kitty?
Susan:	No, she's a very mild-tempered cat, but the thing is, this thing is going to go to trial.
Tom:	She's suing you in small claims court.
Susan:	Well, it's municipal court, the summons says, and it's on February third, and I...
Tom:	Oh, hold on, the animal control officer is taking you to court. He gave you a summons for having a cat out of control.
Susan:	Yeah, they say it's "animal damaging property."
Tom:	I understand that, so really it's the city doing this, where they can actually order you to reimburse your neighbor. But even the city has to be able to prove it was your cat. So I mean, Kerry, shed some light on it.
Kerry:	That is the lineup...Okay, one other thing now, from a civil standpoint, the neighbor who's claiming the $130 worth of damages. If Susan wants to, she can...Susan, do you have homeowners' or renter's insurance on your property?
Susan:	I don't know if I had it at the time.
Kerry:	Well double-check that because if you do, simply turn it over to your insurance company and forget about it. Now if you don't have that, then you have something else. But y'know, here you're talking about the animal control people taking you to court, so what they have to prove...
Tom:	It's the same as if your dog bit someone. You'd get the same summons.
Kerry:	Right, but they still have to prove that it was your cat.
Tom:	Of course!

Kerry: That you're responsible for that animal.

Tom: Y'know what I would do to be funny? Y'know what I would do? I would take a picture of my cat and the other tabbies.

Susan: I have.

Tom: Well hold on...and the other tabbies in the neighborhood, and I'd go to court, and I'd say, I'd ask the animal control officer, "Could you please pick out the cat that did it?"

Kerry: Mm-hmm.

Susan: Exactly.

Tom: Because there's three of them. Or ask the neighbor. Now do they all look essentially the same?

Susan: They're pretty close, but I can't, unfortunately I can't. The others must be indoors for the winter, because I...I haven't seen the other ones. I only have one picture of one besides my own...there are two more around that I can't get pictures of.

Tom: In addition to...

Susan: Pardon?

Tom: In addition to the civil matter, the 130 bucks, you could be ordered to pay reimbursement; could she also be fined, though, Kerry?

Kerry: Oh yeah, I mean there are fines, but most times, what this city wants is just to get you to clean up your act: be more responsible for your animal. That's what they really want. That's why they have these things, not because people want to punish you for having this animal or that. They simply want to make better pet owners.

Susan: Well, the thing is though, I had inquired about whether there is, I mean there's a leash law here for dogs, but there isn't for cats, and every cat comes into our yard...

Tom: In other words, you weren't doing anything against the law, but still, if your cat is destructive, they have to...they can hold you responsible.

Kerry: Well, I'm concerned about this, Tom, and I don't claim to be an expert in this area of animal control, but think about it now, the animal did not do damage in a public area. The animal did damage inside someone's apartment. Now what business is it of the municipality if kitty does damage in somebody else's apartment. I don't know that that's a crime having been committed against the public.

Tom: You know, there are attorneys, by the way, that specialize in animal control issues, believe it or not. By the way, if anyone wants to comment on this, call the hotline at 629-0402, 629-0402 if you're an attorney, or you're an expert. We'd like to hear from you. Meanwhile, we're gonna take some other calls until we get some ideas, but the bottom line here, I would say is they still have to prove their case; so you have to prepare some kind of a defense.

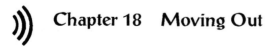

Chapter 18   Moving Out

Selection 5   Notify the manager

[Maria calls Tom Martino with a problem concerning her apartment manager, who says Maria did not give proper notice about moving out:]

Maria: Okay, I live in Brooks Towers on 15th and Curtis in downtown.

Tom: Yes.

Maria: And lease is gonna be up this December first. And on the contract it states that they need written notice thirty days prior, which is fine; I did that. I gave them a written letter, signed by both myself and Sandra Lopez, who are both on the lease. And now they're telling me they do not have that letter. I have a copy of it, and Sandra went down there and showed it to them today, and Karen, the manager of the building, was very rude, and basically was just telling us we were liars, that this is not, y'know, a valid letter, that we did not give it to her, that she's never lost anything in eighteen years and y'know, so she's just basically reneging on...y'know, I did my part of the contract. The fact that she lost it is not my fault.

Tom: You're right, it isn't your fault. Unfortunately, the burden may be on you to prove that you did it. But you have two of you who say you did.

Maria: Exactly.

Tom: You have a copy of the letter...

Maria: Exactly. And not only that, the following week, I believe, it was November third on a Tuesday, my little sister went downstairs as usual every month to drop off the rent, and when she spoke to the girl who she was giving the rent to, she verbally notified them that we were moving out of the apartment December first, and she, the woman who gave her the receipt for the rent, nodded and said, "That's fine." And then Stefanie told her, "Y'know, Sandra may decide to stay in the building, do you have a brochure?" and...so she could get the prices in the building, which she gave her, and she even offered to give her keys so she could look at the different...

Selection 6   Write the owner directly

[The conversation continues from Selection 5:]

Tom: Okay, Maria, what is the consequence from you not paying...for you supposedly not writing that letter?

Maria: $350 bucks—my deposit, I'm gonna be out of. And this is completely not my...

Tom: Now hold on here. Hold on. I know that, and I'm gonna tell you something, Maria. If they try to keep your 350 bucks, you can sue them for triple the amount.

Maria: Oh, good!

Tom: Okay. Now, you have to prove your case.

Maria: Okay.

Tom: But you got your sister, you got your roommate, you got a copy of the letter. It seems unlikely that you'd go through all of these lengths to try to cheat them.

Maria: Oh yeah, you know and on top of that, I was speaking with Karen this morning to try to fix the situation up, and she ended up hanging up on me; I mean the woman will not even work with me. And she's, y'know...

Tom: Well, here's another thing I would do. It's Brooks Towers?

Maria: Yes.

Tom: Okay, what I would do is I would go to...do you know who the owner is?

Maria: No, I'm not quite sure.

Tom: Well, I would write directly to the owner...

Maria: Okay.

Tom:	…and I would say, "Look, this is gonna cost you almost a thousand dollars if I have to take it to court." Now under the terms of your lease, they have a certain amount of time to return it. How long do they have? Sixty days?
Maria:	A certain amount—I'm sorry, the certain amount of time to return what?
Tom:	Your deposit.
Maria:	I'm not quite sure. That part I have not read.
Tom:	Okay, it's about sixty days.
Maria:	Probably.
Tom:	And if you don't hear anything within sixty days, then you can sue for triple the amount. But what you need to do is when you leave the building, you need to write another letter saying, "This is a follow-up to my original letter dated such-and-such. I expect to get my deposit back within sixty days or I plan on suing for triple the amount of damages. Your ascertation [sic] that I did not send the first letter is ridiculous. I have witnesses. I have a copy of the letter," and…y'know, and just say, "I intend to pursue this." We will help you pursue it, but we can't do it until we know that they're gonna keep your deposit. That's the bottom line. When we know they're gonna keep your deposit, then we do it.

Selection 7 Breaking the lease

[Nancy calls Tom Martino and Barrie Sullivan about how to break a lease on her mother's apartment before the lease has expired:]

Answers are underlined for the exercise "Keys to better comprehension: Recognizing confusing words.

Tom:	We're talking about consumer problems, complaints, questions, all kinds of things near and dear to our hearts. Let's go, okay? Nancy, your turn. You're on the air, and I'm here, Tom Martino, with Barrie Sullivan, our attorney for the day. Go ahead.
Nancy:	Yes, thanks for calling me back. I talked to you about ten days ago about a lease problem, my <u>elderly</u> mother wanting to move.
Tom:	And I said what we would like to do is get an attorney on, to get a second opinion, and I told you we'd call you when we had one. Okay, <u>recap</u> this for Barrie.
Nancy:	Okay, I have an elderly, very frail mother who lives out of state in Wisconsin. She would like to move here, in fact arrives tomorrow to look at <u>retirement</u> homes. And she really is at a point where she needs a place that <u>affords</u> more care. However, she has a lease that she unfortunately signed this spring, a year's lease on an apartment. Actually, Tom, since I talked to you, I finally got a copy of her lease, and I'm afraid it's a lost <u>cause</u>.
Tom:	Well, I asked you at the time we talked last, I said look, yes it's true, if she has a year's lease, she probably will <u>lose</u> some money, or they will try to come after her for the <u>remainder</u> of the lease. But I also said—look what's the deposit? Five…what did you say the deposit was?
Nancy:	I'm not sure; I think it's one month's rent, which is like 875.
Tom:	Okay, so let's say she lost $875, her deposit money. I said the <u>likelihood</u> of them coming after her in this state for the <u>default</u> on the rest of the lease is <u>unlikely</u>. Now, I'm not saying they wouldn't do it, but it's…go ahead.
Nancy:	Since I talked to you though, I do have this <u>lease</u> in my hand right now. And the last—this guy has thought of everything—the last paragraph reads: "…in the event of poor health, such as the <u>lessee</u> being judged mentally incompetent, upon doctor's orders advising lessee to enter a nursing home, etc…" and goes on, it said,

"…the lessee has the option to invoke a 90-day <u>termination</u> notice if it occurs during the months of April <u>through</u> September."

So he has that actually in the lease that, no, she wouldn't be held to the <u>full</u> year but she would be held…

Tom: …to 90 days. That might be the cheapest way out—is to pay the three-months' rent.

Nancy: Well, I think that's probably what we'll have to do.

Selection 8   Negotiate a solution

[The conversation from Selection 7 continues:]

Barrie: Have you tried communication, and by that I mean, have you called…

Tom: The landlord…

Barrie: …the landlord and say, "Look, here's the situation — we're going to give you the ninety-day termination. It would make it a lot easier if my mother could move out here in July, would you do your best to rent the premises? If they rent it in August, she doesn't have to stay there for the three months and…

Tom: Or if you ask the landlord if you can help rent it out again.

Nancy: Yeah, except that we're here, and…

Tom: Well, or your mom.

Barrie: But you could hire a management company to do it, or you could ask the landlord to rent it. Y'know, one of the problems is a lot of people are afraid to speak to a landlord and give them their intentions. Call up and say, "Here's what we're going to do, and here's why we need to do it." But rather than have my mother stay there, and also…

Tom: Yeah, during the ninety days we give you permission to show the apartment.

Barrie: "Would you please try to rent it; we'll make up the difference." They may be able to rent that thing July tenth.

Tom: In fact, they may want to rent it in the summer rather than waiting for winter. And if they can, why don't you say, "Look, we'll give you this 90-day notice, but we would love if you would show the apartment during this [sic] ninety days and as soon as you can get it rented, she'll move." You know, there are ways, as Barrie said, of using communication…

Nancy: Negotiate.

Tom: Oh, sure! And why would a landlord be upset with that? If he knows you're gonna leave in ninety days anyway, you're giving this landlord ninety-days' headstart to try to rent it out. You're telling this landlord, no matter when it is, if you decide you can rent this out in the middle of next month, we'll get out of here.

Nancy: Now legally, if if they would find a renter during that time, would she still be liable?

Tom: No. No, they're not allowed to collect double damages.

Nancy: Okay 'cause she's actually—notice of termination is specified, but it isn't…

Tom: No, no, listen, as Barrie recommended, let's say you give ninety-days' notice. Let's say, two months down the road, they find someone to rent it. They can't collect another month from you just for grins…just because you broke the contract. Remember there has to be more than a breach of contract; there has to be a loss associated with it. Let's say I had a one-year lease, and I moved out after two months. Now let's say that the landlord rented it out a month after I left. He cannot get me for that whole year's lease. He has to only get me for the one month that was vacant, or the difference in rent that it cost him if he had to rent it out cheaper because market conditions changed or something like that. But he would have to prove damages.

Barrie: Here's another thought on the communication factor. You may want to call a landlord after your mother's here, and let's suppose you find a place next week. And you call 'em and you say, "Referring to this paragraph, my mother can give you the ninety days, but how about this? We'd like to move her out in early July, and get her out here. You have the balance of July, we will give you not only that...that month of rent for July, but we'll give you an extra $200, would you let us out of the rent? Will you declare the rent...the lease null and void? Will you terminate it?" They may well...they may have a waiting list of people wanting to move in there.

Tom: Yeah. So, so at least try the negotiation, and then if you like, call us back, and we'll talk to you some more about this. We, you know, this is not a done deal when we get finished talking to ya. John, hold on, yes... John you have something...

John: Yeah, I just wanted to say she better get something in writing too...

Tom: Yeah.

John: If she cancels the lease...

Tom: Yeah, obviously, anything in writing. Otherwise you know what can happen—we've seen it before...A collection notice shows up a year later from something that you walked out on. That's true. Get all of your releases in writing. Good, good point.

Selection 9   Getting an eviction notice

[Rick has a conversation with Dan, an attorney, about an eviction notice he received because he was late with his rent:]

Dan: What's going on, Rick?

Rick: Yes, Dan, I got a question about... I told my landlord that I was gonna be late with the rent.

Dan: Yep.

Rick: Okay, and she said, "No problem," I could get it in by Friday, that there would be a $20 late—a $40 late charge.

Dan: Okay, what happened?

Rick: And come Saturday, she signs a note that says, "Demand for payment or the possession of premises." So I'm wondering why...where do I stand with this?

Dan: Well, Rick, she gave you till Friday; did you get her the rent by Friday?

Rick: No, but see, I went down Friday and told her I couldn't get the rent; I was waiting for a check, and she says, "Well, there'll be a late charge," and then Saturday she hung this thing on my door, so am I gonna get evicted now?

Dan: Well, Rick, partner, she's within her rights on this, because she made a deal, she stuck to it. By Saturday, she was within her rights to do this. Now normally, normally, you can avoid eviction 'cause landlords usually rather than undergoing the legal expense and trouble of evicting a tenant will work with you if you make good on the rent. So number one, I think you just need to cough up the cash now and make good on the rent. If you can't, then yeah, I think she's gonna bounce you, and she'd be within her rights. What do you think, Kerry?

Kerry: Oh absolutely, yeah.

Dan: Yeah.

Kerry: I mean especially where she did give you until Friday. Friday passed and what she's telling you is, you don't ask for a favor and then toss it back at me and say, "I need more time." Now what...

Rick:	Okay. Let me say again here then, now on my lease I have three days past rent due, okay, and then they start, then there's a late charge…
Dan:	Right.
Rick:	And then on my lease agreement, it says nothing about…they'll throw me out if I'm late, they just say I have a late charge.
Dan:	No, you see, the difference here is there's a difference between a late charge and eviction.
Rick:	Uh-huh.
Dan:	What he's saying is your rent is due on day one. If you don't pay it for three days, you're gonna pay a penalty.
Rick:	Right.
Dan:	…If you pay it. But if you don't pay it, and that three days passes, then you're subject to eviction.
Rick:	Okay, then, now I'm probably gonna pay the rent tomorrow, okay? But also on my lease agreement it says a $20 late charge, but on my thing here it says there's a $40 late charge. Can they raise my…late charge?
Dan:	No, no. She's stuck with the terms of the lease. Now most leases provide for other costs, reasonable attorney fees, etc. if they have to evict. So if you're gonna stay, pay her as quickly as possible and get a written agreement that she's gonna way [sic] these other fee-… waive, rather, these other fees and costs, and just let you stay for payment of the rent and the late charge.

)) Unit 8
RELATIONSHIPS

)) Chapter 19   Gender Differences

Selection 1   Gender differences

[Irene Rawlings interviews Cris Evatt about her book which compiles research on the differences between men and women:]

Irene:	You say that women use both sides of their brain more than men.
Cris:	Yes, that's because ten years ago it was discovered that in the corpus colossum—this is the area that is like a highway between the right and left half of the brain—in this corpus colossum, there are areas that are larger in women, so this facilitates communicating between the two halves better, whereas men tend to be in the right brain, and then "boom" they're over in the left brain.
Irene:	So…and women are kinda going back and forth.
Cris:	Women can be in both sides at once more easily.
Irene:	Now who is more jealous generally speaking: men or women?

Cris: Well, women are jealous more frequently. Both sexes of course get jealous, and when it comes to becoming really abusive, men are, y'know, a lot of men in prison are there because they have a jealous rage. But I would say women because women focus on their relationships as their primary thing.

Irene: Why do women tend to worry three times more than men?

Cris: There's a real unknown reason for this, and that is because it has to do with stress. Women have a more moderate response to stress. They have less heart rate—less increase in heart rate, blood pressure and adrenaline when they're under stress. So it's more comfortable for them to worry. Whereas when men worry, since they have a stronger response to stress, they tend to retreat.

Irene: Yeah, and have a heart attack or something like that.

Cris: Exactly.

Irene: Why do women more than men try to change people? They seem to—y'know, hope springs eternal in the female breast. Someone said that; maybe it was Shakespeare, I don't know. But why are we such hope addicts? We're addicted to hope.

Cris: Yes, we think we can change people. It's a form of nurturing for one thing; it's also that we focus so much on other people and what they're doing and we forget ourselves so we tend to want to improve them rather than ourselves oftentimes. It's just a real common thing, and this is men's number one complaint against women, is that we try to change them, and men want to be accepted, not controlled.

Irene: You also say that women smile more than men, and men are more facially neutral.

Cris: Yes, that's true. That's because women want to be liked and they fear they won't be, so they're always smiling to get approval and to please others. And it's also physiological. We are more animated—women are more animated on the outside—and men have more going on internally. So there's an internal animation, if you will, going on inside men.

Irene: Now are sports really modified forms of the hunting behavior, and is that why men really love sport?

Cris: Yes, it is. Sports consists of chasing, aiming, throwing, and making a killing—killing a prey. And if you look at most of the sports—all of sports, they contain all or some of those elements. For example, basketball: you're chasing, aiming and throwing. And the killing of the prey would be the making of the basket. Even something like running track would be the chasing part, and the time, the winning time would be the killing of the prey.

Irene: Football—goodness sakes!

Cris: Well, that's pretty obvious with football how that relates to hunting. Also, it is said that sports really became popular after we became farmers because men didn't have much to do with their hunting skills after that.

Irene: Let's talk about this: Why do men take up more space when they're sitting than women do...besides the fact that they might be bigger people?

Cris: Bigger people, yes. Men take up more space; they need more space too, like when they are talking to each other—there's more space between them than there is between two women. It's just that men are trying to get more for themselves. It's competing with other men; they try to take up as much space as possible, so if they're sitting on the sofa, they spread their legs wide. They use their arms in a bigger way. Women sit in a more confined way. And it's just the difference, y'know, in men being more dominating, and women being there for them.

Irene: Researching this book, *He and She: 60 Significant Differences between Men and Women*, did you come up with a theory as to why men tell more jokes and more stories than women?

Cris: Yes. They do that to get attention. Men…another overall thing going on is that men's traits are self-oriented or self-centered if you will, and women's traits are other-oriented. So telling jokes and stories is a way of being on center stage and drawing attention to the self.

Irene: That would be. I can never remember the punchline, so that's why I don't ever tell jokes. What is the real reason as far as you could tell from researching your book, *He and She*, what is the real reason—and forget the excuses—why many men are reluctant to commit to a relationship?

Cris: Men…the real reason is it goes back to the stress, the fact that men have a stronger response to stress than women, and need more physical distance. It's…men feel smothered when they're in relationships, whereas women need them more; they feel rejected if they don't have a relationship. So men risk feeling engulfed, and that's why they put off marriage. Y'know, when there's a little 2-year-old, a women is a reactor. She goes shopping, she reacts. The man goes shopping, and he retreats; it's too much [sic] stimuli. So the bottom line is that women are always seeking outside stimuli, and men are always running away from it.

Irene: Hmm, I'd never thought of that: why respect is so important. It's a big deal to men—getting…having the respect of other men. Why is this so important?

Cris: Yes, respect is as important as power and money for men. It's other men thinking that they're doing a good job; it's like a yardstick for performing well. So respect is really big, whereas in the woman's world, women don't worry so much about respect as they do about disrespect.

Irene: Oh. But women tend to have more intimate friends than men do, don't they?

Cris: Oh, absolutely. Women have far more friends, and that's because when we talk together, we talk about personal things: we talk about relationships, how we're feeling, our health. We talk about intimate things. Even if we meet somebody at the bus stop, y'know, we'll tell 'em our personal history. Whereas a male is more discreet, and he's competitive with other males, so he doesn't want that other male to know everything about him. There's another reason why males don't become intimate, and that's because their subject matter mostly revolves around things, around objects, and you can't get real close, as close to somebody when you're talking about how to fix things, how to make them, sports, business, politics, etc. So women's relationships are closer, and women have many more friends.

Irene: Well, you also say men, and this kind of goes back to the joke telling, that men tend to dominate public conversations, and retreat in private ones, whereas women do the opposite.

Cris: Right, that has to do with that intimacy again. In a public conversation where men dominate, you're talking about facts and information usually. And this is a very—this is something that's done at a distance from others. You're not intimate when you're talking about—you're talking in a classroom or a public meeting. So men raise their hands; women kinda sit back. Women like intimate one-to-one type conversations where they can talk personally, so they talk more at home, and men talk more out in public.

Irene: What are some ways that men show affection, one to another?

Cris: Oh, men slap each other on the back, they tease each other, they do each other—they do favors for one another. They're just—they have a lot of—affection is done by doing side-by-side activities. Like they'll go fishing together and not speak to each other maybe for several hours, but they feel a closeness, not talking. This is one thing women need to understand is that even though our relationships are more intimate, men's are more intimate than we think they are. 'Cause when they're doing things together—like if you see a group of boys…teenagers skateboarding together—there's a feeling of intimacy there that is not apparent to women.

Irene: Who brags more: men or women? And who nags more: men or women? Brag, nag, yeah.

Cris: Men brag more; they tell others things that make them look good whereas women tell their personal things, personal problems, which to men—men think this makes them look bad, y'know. So men are always bragging about performance, how well they do. As far as nagging goes, of course women get the award for nagging.

Irene: That's traditional. But is it still true—I mean, y'know when you watch the movies from the 50's, or read—still true?

Cris: That's still true, yes. It's true partly because men ignore a lot of women's requests. If they would do more of the things right away, quickly, then there would be less nagging.

Irene: I hope the men out there are listening to that. I really do. Y'know, in doing your research for your book, *He and She: 60 Significant Differences between Men and Women*, what was the biggest difference that you found between men and women?

Cris: Well, the biggest difference is the one I mentioned earlier, that men's traits seem to be self-focused. In other words, in varying degrees, like an extreme male would be 90% focused on himself and 10% focused on others. And a moderate male would be say 70% focused on self, 30 on others, and then it goes—it's like a scale. And then women start down at the other end. Y'know, they are like the average—we're talking about men and women as a group. Many, many women out there are 90% focused on others and their relationships, and only 10% aware of themselves and their own interests and what they want to do in life. And then there are some moderate women who are focused outward on people 70%, and on themselves 30, and then it goes down to zero where both sexes are balanced. And balanced human beings are either male or female, and a balanced human being focuses equally on self and others.

Irene: Well, you do say that generally women or girls are more person-centered, and boys or men are more thing-centered.

Cris: Yes, it's incredible, and they have studies that show that infant girls show less interest in objects and more interest in faces, whereas infant boys are the opposite. They show more interest in objects and less in people, so…so the girls from the beginning have a greater interest in people.

Irene: Thanks so much for talking with us.

Cris: Well, thank you. And there's one lesson that women must learn and that's to focus more on themselves and their interests, and men need to focus more outward on people and relationships.

 # Chapter 20   The Science of Romance

Selection 2   Set an objective

[In selections 2 through 6, Irene Rawlings interviews Jay Arthur about what he calls "The Science of Romance," namely his process for finding a wife:]

Irene: Hi! It's Irene Rawlings and I'm talking with Lowell Jay Arthur. Jay Arthur has just written a book called *Attracting Romance*, and aren't we all interested in romance in our lives?

Jay: We hope so.

Irene: Well, we are, we are. I mean, it's sort of, it's kind of the butter on the bread. It's…y'know, maybe you don't need it to live, but it makes life a lot more pleasant.

Jay: It makes it great, is what it does.

Irene: Great, all right. And your book will tell us the secrets to successful relationships. You do say that the same methods that can make me successful in business can help me in my romantic life. You say that romance can be or is a science. It's very sensible and it actually, saying that romance is a science is really not quite right, but what he does say is that some of the same logical methods that help to make you a successful person in business or volunteer work, or whatever it is you do can help you in your romantic life. It really is fairly logical: Do the things you like to do, and you probably will run across the person you wanna spend some time with.

Jay: Absolutely.

Irene: You say that romance can be or is a science.

Jay: I think it is.

Irene: Alright, talk to us about that.

Jay: Alright. One of things I discovered through my own adventures in singledom and actually getting married...

Irene: And you were single for quite a long time, were you not?

Jay: Yeah, fifteen years.

Irene: Oh, okay.

Jay: So at least out of college it was fifteen years. And so what I really started to notice as I looked back on how I attracted my marriage was I set a definite objective. There was something I wanted. Y'know, I really wanted to be married; I made that decision. And then I started figuring out what kind of person I wanted in my life, and what I wanted my life to be like with that person.

Irene: I mean, did you sort of sit down and say, "I want to picture my life fifteen years from now, and what do I look like, and who is around me?"

Jay: I did some of that, and I also started to envision what it would be like to be married, and what it would be like to be with this other person. And then I...

Irene: Twenty-four hours a day!

Jay: Yeah, really, I mean, and that's a lot of time. You have to get real clear about somebody you want to spend that much time with. A lot of divorces end up where people discover that they really only liked a couple of hours a day that they'd spent with that person.

Selection 3   What do you want?

[The interview continues from Selection 2:]

Answers are underlined for the exercise, "Keys to better comprehension: Understanding connecting words."

Irene: Let's talk more about the science of romance. We've been talking about relationships, <u>and</u> people need to commit, <u>so that</u> we're talking about being in the right place at the right time almost, you know, you have to...you decided you were going to commit to a long-term relationship; you wanted to be married in your late 30's. A lot of people don't. <u>But</u> you did, <u>and so</u> whoever came along had all the right characteristics, <u>and</u> just also happened to be in the right place at the right time. Right?

Jay: That's right.

Irene: All right, <u>so</u> what's so scientific about that?

Jay: Well, actually, not a whole lot, except that one of the things that I think is scientific about it is a lot of people I talk to can tell me a lot about what they don't want in a relationship, and so they focus all of their attention on what they don't want. "I don't want…"

Irene: …No smelly socks, no cap off the toothpaste, no dirty clothes all over the place, someone who…

Jay: No drinking, no smoking, no something, y'know. They've got this list of "don't wants." But what they haven't…and all that brings up is a picture of what they don't want, and so they have this vivid representation of what they don't want. And your unconscious doesn't know any better. It says, "Oh, there's a picture." He or she must want that, and so off it goes, and it starts offering your conscious mind pictures of the various people that it notices around you that are like that. And so you get what you don't want. And the science of this is you start to flip that around, you go, "Okay, if I don't want someone who smokes, what do I want? I want someone who's a nonsmoker. They smell a certain kind of way." And so you start to create a representation of the person you do want.

Irene: Should we make a list?

Jay: Absolutely. And the more robust and complete you can make it in terms of how they look, how they sound, how they feel. You want to start filling that in, what it's gonna smell like, what it's gonna taste like, I mean, and you really get this rich representation, you start embedding qualities in this person. What kind of a…what are they going to be like with my family, my kids? Y'know, what are they gonna be like with…

Irene: My parents.

Jay: My dogs.

Irene: My aunt, my old aunt that I adore, and everyone else thinks she's a crotchety old bag, yeah.

Jay: Yeah. What are they interested in? I dated somebody who was a sports fanatic, and she always wanted to go play baseball or do something like that. And unfortunately, I wasn't a big sports-crazy kind of a person.

Irene: So you wanted to do that like an eighth of your time, but not all the rest of the time.

Jay: Right. She filled up most of her spare time with that. And so what you wanna do is start to say, "What characteristics and qualities do I want in this person?" And you create this rich representation so it's sort of three-dimensional. It's almost to the point where you start to lick your lips, thinking about it. I mean, it's that good if you will.

Irene: Alright, I feel that way about pizza and watermelon. [laughs]

Selection 4   How to Start

[The interview continues from Selections 2 and 3:]

Irene: Where would you suggest—if I come up with a list of the things that I am interested in, not the things I don't want—the things I do want, and how I imagine my life to be from this point forward, y'know. Who I'm gonna be sharing it with, how we're gonna be sharing it, what we're gonna be doing of an autumn evening, or of a summer morning, what are we gonna be doing, what is it like? Having established that and knowing that I'm going to work from a positive point of view, what do I do next? What do I tomorrow morning when I wake up? This afternoon when I go home from work?

Jay: One of the real keys is repetition. That's how you keep sending that message to your unconscious. And typically a lot of the success literature says you should spend a little bit of time in the morning, and a little bit before you go to bed, just imagining, stepping into that future of what it's going to be like. And just really, as clearly as possible, experience it. Keep tweeking it and tuning it so it gets better. And what that will do is your unconscious will start to notice this, and then you'll just be walking along the street, and it's sort of like a lot of people experience when they start to buy a new car, or something, they'll start to see the kind of car they want. Your brain will offer that choice up to you. And so what you want to do is continue to repeat what this is gonna be like, and your brain will start to notice as you walk down the street: this person over here, that person over there. And unconsciously, you get pulled into the situations, the very situations you want.

Selection 5   Where to meet people

[The interview from Selections 2, 3, and 4 continues:]

Irene: Where are good places to meet people?

Jay: Where isn't?

Irene: Well, I don't know. I mean you shouldn't meet people in bars because they lie to you…

Jay: Well, that's a useful belief.

Irene: I don't know. They'll tell you that they're the head of General Motors, and they drive a Lamborghini, and they have a summer home on Capri and there in Aspen, and they're only just sort of here for a couple days with a friend.

Where do we go to meet people?

Jay: My observation is you wanna pick things that you love to do, so that number one, you're gonna love being there. If you don't enjoy bars, don't go. I spent a lot of time in bars and I wasn't very happy there. And I'd've been a lot better off doing other things that I was really interested in. Y'know, maybe I like spending more time in libraries. Maybe I should've spent more time in libraries 'cause I'll meet people that are interested in learning things. So I think the key thing is I have people write down a list of ten or twenty things that they love to do, and then schedule them into their life and go do those things. So, number one, they're gonna enjoy it; they're gonna be having fun while they're there, and they are more likely to attract people that are similar, have very similar interests to them.

Selection 6   What it takes to make it work

[The interview from Selections 2, 3, 4, and 5 concludes:]

Irene: How much time does a relationship take?

Jay: As much or as little as you want to put into it, I think.

Irene: Yeah, probably. Are there relationships that require no work, because they just happen, because you are just so absolutely compatible that you might finish each other's sentences.

Jay: Typically.

Irene: Yeah right, and/or are there other relationships where one of the partners, who wants it to work—maybe more than the other partner wants it to work—works at it 24 hours a day? I mean we're talking about perfume under the armpits, we're talking about getting dressed before…y'know, and all the makeup on, we're talking about perfect breakfast…we're talking about whatever it is that it takes to keep this other person. Yes? No?

Jay: I think people do create those kind of relationships. And if that's what they want, I mean, that's fine. But typically, I think a lot of people were programmed to be that way. Y'know, well, my parents always taught me to be this way. I mean, that's where we learn a lot of this junk, is from our parents. And if that's what you want, and you're happy in it, I'd say that was probably okay. But I don't think that that's really the way life is supposed to be. It's supposed to be a balance. And I find that most relationships that are really good, start easy; they work easily. I mean there are still things you have to clear up occasionally, and you have to have some conflict negotiation skills, some way to manage that, and you have to be able to deal with those sort of things. But by and large, your relationship is just gonna work; it's gonna flow. I mean, I'll come home and my wife will say, "Well what do you think about dinner?" and I'll say, "Well, I was thinking about eating at a certain place." And she said, "Well, I was thinking about that too."

Irene: Isn't that nice.

Jay: And it's like mentally you're aligned; it's just you're going together. And when I think one person is putting all the energy in, and the other person's not putting anything out, then there's an imbalance, and over time that imbalance will eat that relationship away.

Irene: Well, it will cause a certain amount of resentment, I should think in the person who is putting all the energy into it.

 # Chapter 21   Getting Love Right

Selection 7   Introduction to the main speaker

[In selections 7 through 11, Irene Rawlings interviews Terence Gorski on the techniques he teaches for good communication and healthy relationships:]

Irene: We're talking with Terence Gorski. He is a nationally and internationally acclaimed speaker who conducts lectures and workshops. He is in the relationship field now; he got into that as a little bit of an accident because he was in basically relapse prevention.

Terence: Prevention...

Irene: And you discovered that bad relationships were often a cause for people to relapse from a drug or cigarette or...or drinking habit that they'd had. A bad relationship, and bang, they were at it again. And so then you decided to go into relationships.

Selection 8   Healthy relationships: need vs. choice

[The interview continues from Selection 7:]

Terence: When you're looking at partners, it's important to do...y'know, when we're getting in touch with selecting a partner, the first thing when I work with somebody, I want them to get them in touch with their romantic ideal. I have 'em take a sheet of paper, fold it in half, fold it in half again, have four squares, and just in general:

"If you could have your ideal partner, what would they look like physically?"

Then, "What would their personality be like?"

And then, "What would their social situation be like? Would they be successful or a failure, lots of friends, not very many friends?"

Then the fourth square is the most important one:

"What would this person be able to do for you that you believe you can't do for yourself?"

Irene: In a healthy relationship, what is...is there a right answer to that? I mean, I always believed that if you are in a healthy relationship, there is almost nothing this person can do for you that you can't do for yourself.

Terence: That's correct. Because people who are in healthy relationships are not bonded together by need. They're bonded together by choice. They choose to be with each other, and they realize that if the relationship ends, it may be sad, and it may be difficult, and it may be inconvenient, but they're gonna be able to get on with their life, and have their life the way they want it, whether or not this particular individual partner is going to be there for them.

Irene: I was just thinking that, y'know, if you're a whole person, and you're leading a life which is satisfying in all ways except that you'd like to share it with someone, perhaps someone that has your same interests, and y'know, you'd like to share your life and do what it is that you like to do when you get someone who's compatible, and it ends up being a nice situation.

Terence: And that's a healthy relationship. But the other version of this, the unhealthy relationship is when I look inside of myself and I don't like what I see. There's a big gaping hole inside of me, and I'm lonely and empty and unsatisfied and unhappy. And then I pull out this romantic ideal and say, "If I could find someone like this, I would be magically fixed."

Irene: Life would be worth living.

Terence: And life would be worth living. So I go out on the quest to find the perfect partner who's going to magically fix me and make everything better. And I invest my energy into finding this partner, rather than investing the energy into taking care of whatever it is about me that makes me feel incomplete and not worthwhile.

Selection 9   Helpful/non-helpful ways of communicating

[The interview from Selections 7 and 8 continues:]

Irene: What you're saying basically is...is you can solve your own problems if you work at them. You can solve the relationship problems by working together, but you cannot solve your partner's problems. That's what you're saying.

Terence: That's right. If you have a character defect or a personality glitch or some kind of problem that's interfering with the relationship, the only thing I can do is I can say, "This is what I see is going on with you, and this is how it's affecting me." And then I can make a request for you to change it and be supportive. Other than that, it's your choice: Do you want to change, or don't you? So you choose. Same thing: you to me.

Irene: And you obviously can't make someone change.

Terence: That's right. You can't.

Irene: Is there a right way and a wrong way of asking someone to either do something or stop doing something that you either need to have done, or you don't want to ever have done again?

Terence: Oh, yes. There are correct—there are helpful and non-helpful ways of communicating. Most people who get involved in intimate relationships seem to think communication is something that just spontaneously happens. And the biggest mistake that couples make first of all is they insist upon their right to verbally dump on their partner at will. They basically fail to afford them the respect that they would give a grocery store clerk. So the first rule of communication is when there are important or serious things to be communicated, communicate by appointment only. Come up to your partner and make an appointment. Say, "I've got something really serious to talk to you about. Is this a good time, or can we clear a time where there's no distractions, where we can both be involved in this without our mind being on other things?"

Irene: Okay, as soon as someone says that to me, I get...I need to know right away, because I get very worried about what this something might be.

Terence: Well, so then you're gonna clear a space as soon as you possibly can to talk about it hopefully.

Irene: Right away. Right away.

Terence: See, but sometimes that's not possible. Something comes up and you have an important appointment, or a show you have to do, and you say, "No, I can't do it right now, I would love to, but the earliest time I can do it, how about here." And you negotiate a time and a space where you have at least twenty to thirty minutes or longer where you can deal with it, depending on how serious it is.

Irene: With no distractions.

Terence: With no distractions, correct. And that's very important because most people get involved in talking about extremely critical issues in their relationship at a moment where the phone's ringing, and the kids are raising havoc, and they're at work on the telephone, and you just can't deal with it at that point.

Selection 10   How to get a relationship back on track

[The interview from Selections 7, 8, and 9 continues:]

Irene: Now, if you're in a relationship right now, and it's not terribly fulfilling, and you're not communicating well with your partner, are there some basic steps you can take to begin to enhance this current relationship and get it on some kind of a track, assuming that you're committed to this relationship and you do want it to work? Otherwise you could, I guess, you could go on to…

Terence: Sure, the first step is you have to go through, and you have to start with yourself.

Irene: Alright.

Terence: You have to go through and you have to say,

"What am I looking for in this relationship?"

"What do I want my partner to give me that they're not giving me?"

"What do I want them to do for me that I can't do for myself?"

And it often starts out when I work with couples and they come in and they're having relationship problems, the first thing I have them do is what I call, "The problem list," which is just "Let's dump out every single problem you can think of in the relationship and write it down on a list. We often take file cards and write one problem per card. Then we take and we divide them into three problems. Which is his problem? Which is her problem? Which is a problem that they share together? And let's classify these. Now very often this process alone starts the couple on the road to working it out, because the whole problem is I've been trying to fix your problem while you're trying to fix mine, and I'm ignoring mine and ours. So we get that sorted out. Then we take and say,

"Now, all right, what are you, what are each of you willing to do to address your problems?"

"Are you willing to get into counseling, get into therapy, set up a plan to do this?" and now,

"And how are you going to support each other in that process? How are you gonna make, invite the other person to support them in the problem solving that they need to do?"

And now let's take a look at the "us" problems. And now then we move into the second step of the process, which is communication training. The number one skill that couples need if they wanna have a healthy, intimate relationship is the skill of communicating. You have to be a healthy, intimate communicator.

Irene: Why don't you briefly tell us about that 'cause we're almost out of time.

Terence: Okay, the process is a very simple one where first of all you make an appointment to talk. And then the person who has the issue has to learn how to introspect and say,

"The issue I want to talk to you about is..."

"What I'm thinking about this issue is..."

"How I'm feeling about this issue is..." and

"What I have an urge to do about it is..."

and they put it out on the table. Then the person who is listening, their job at that point is to be a pure listener; they are—their job then is to give feedback and say,

"This is what I'm hearing:"

"What I'm hearing you say is the issue is this..."

"What I'm hearing you say is your thinking about the issue is this..."

"How you feel about the issue is this..."

"What you want to do about it is that..."

"Do I have it right?"

And if they got it right, the partner says yes. If they don't, they say, "No, you misunderstood this part of it." Then the roles switch. And the person who is—see there are two roles in a communication: there is the person who is the talker, and there is the listener. You have to have self-disclosure skills and active listening skills. Then the roles switch, and the person who was listening says:

"Well, my reaction to the idea is..."

"Y'know, you're bringing up this issue; here's my understanding of the issue."

"Here's what I'm thinking about it."

"Here's how I'm feeling about it."

"Here's what I want to do about it. Now do you hear what I'm saying?"

And then the other person becomes the active listener and gives feedback, and then you have a productive—what is called an intimate dialog.

Irene: It sounds very important.

Terence: Yes.

Irene: Communication and honesty.

Terence: That's correct.

Irene: Probably two of the most important things in a relationship.

Selection 11 The Law of Neurotic Attraction

[The interview from Selections 7 through 10 concludes:]

Terence: So the way you begin developing a philosophy to learn how to get love right is you begin looking at yourself. Because there's a real crazy law which is called the Law of Neurotic Attraction.

Irene: Ooh, yeah. I've heard of that. Actually I participated in that. Alright.

Terence: We all have. And the Law of Neurotic Attraction is very simple. It simply states that you tend to attract and feel attracted to somebody who is at about the same level of psychological growth as you are at, y'know, two or three degrees above or below. And that if you meet someone who is a lot more "integrated" than you are, you're going to be intimidated and not get along with them very well.

If you meet someone who's significantly less integrated than you are, you're gonna have a great deal of difficulty cause you're gonna keep stumbling upon the snags in their personality that you've already grown beyond. So within a certain range, you're gonna be attracted to people who are at a very similar level of development that you are.

Unit 9
FAMILIES

Chapter 22   Parenting

Selection 1   Healthy arguing?

[Andrea Van Steenhouse comments:]
Andrea: Let me respond to this last fax, and we may wanna talk about it more another time, but I wanted to make my first pass through this: Someone writes in asking about he and his wife have been married 13 years. "Healthy arguing" has been something that they have been able to handle all this time and that—this came in last week—they were arguing, and it just kind of went over the mark. She got so frustrated with him, finally struck him in the face with her hand, he wasn't hurt, but emotionally was devastated. He retaliated by pushing her to the bed—in the process bloodied her nose. Well, that's bad enough; to make it worse, there were kids watching, relatively young kids. And what he's wanting to know: what do they do to repair what happened; what do you say to the kids?

Selection 2   The perfect opportunity

[Andrea continues with her comments from Selection 1:]
Andrea: If they've seen you guys argue, you have the perfect opportunity to talk to them about you guys made a mistake, that usually you're able to handle things, and that things get so awful you wanna hit somebody, sometimes you have to just walk away. I think you talk about what that means, what that means about conflict resolution. Then you two need to look at it, maybe you need to look at it before you talk to them—what happened in this argument? What was the trigger that made this one so frustrating that you couldn't resolve it in the way that some of your other arguing has allowed you to resolve? It may be that although you talk about being a couple that "constructive and healthy arguing" has been a good tool for you, it may be that your marriage has more conflict than you can handle. It might be that you might have to resolve some of these things so that you argue less—healthy arguing, yes—but maybe not quite so much of it. The instruction to the kids is talk about sometimes this happens; it doesn't say anything about them; it doesn't say anything about how much you care about each other, but you and mom are going to take a look at it, because you're concerned because you know and they know it's inappropriate to hit. [music to end]

Selection 3   Conflicting roles

[Andrea Van Steenhouse comments on women who have a job as well as a family:]

Andrea: When you have conflicting roles in your life, it makes it really hard. One of the studies they'd done suggested that people who have to choose between a job and a family have a lot more problems than those who have—see themselves as having fewer conflicts. Now there are some people who have a job and a family who don't see it as a conflict. But when you do, your role may put you into a quandary. You're a wife; you're a mother; you might be a community activist; you might have a paid job outside the home, and something has to give. And one of the things that's smart to do is kind of to organize how you look at it. And we'll talk about how you do that. Okay, so you got conflicting roles, you feel torn in different directions; you can't do well at anything because you're sort of doing everything that you can for each one of them. We'll talk about how to pull that together so that it looks like you're managing those roles. And if you can't manage them, then maybe you wanna get out of one of them. But if you can't, then you're stuck. We'll talk about some of the techniques for managing that.

Selection 4   Working mothers: another perspective

[Irene Rawlings interviews Beth Saavedra, author of Meditations for New Mothers. *Beth has a different perspective on mothers who also work.]*

Beth: It's a big challenge for mothers today, because oftentimes mothers feels like it's an either/or proposition that they have to work or have a child. And the reality is more and more women are choosing to do both, and also not be superwomen, so it's a tricky…it's a tricky line to balance. But I do have a quote that says, "To choose to have a child is to choose forever to have your heart walk outside of your body." Which means, just as we've been talking about, that you are constantly attached to your child, no matter how old they get, but you will learn to walk those lines. And you will learn to create balance and harmony in your life, and you'll realize that not everything you do is going to send your child to a therapist. And that's wonderful.

Irene: Yes, yes. I've just always felt that if you loved them hard enough, and that you had…your heart kind of in the right place, which obviously is outside your own body, that there was very little that…that you could do wrong. I mean you…

Beth: Yes, I think that's true. I think if you build a solid foundation with your child, especially in the early years, and…

Irene: How early are we talking "early years"? I mean, by what point is the child's personality formed already?

Beth: Well, you know there's a lot of information on that that definitely is conflicting. But there are new studies coming out that are just fascinating about how important, extremely important it is for a child to be with his/her mother until they're close to four years old. Now, that doesn't mean consistently. I'm not advocating that a mother stay home full time if she's not so inclined. But there's definite research that's coming out saying that, y'know, a mother's role is more important in some regards than we had thought, and that the bonding process lasts quite a bit longer. In fact, children go into shock oftentimes if they are separated too early. And that's why I think a lot of us are fighting for parental leave and family leave, that allows both mother and father to have time with their children hopefully within the first two years, not just the first few months.

People need concrete support, and especially nowadays. I did write another meditation about people needing the support of community because nowadays we oftentimes don't have our parents close by, or brothers and sisters live in another state or even in another country. And so especially when you come home for the first few months or the first few years, you may feel extremely isolated if you can't hook up with a co-op, a baby sitting co-op, or a mothers' group...

And this is just a wonderful way to remind mothers that we have what Mary Catherine Bateson calls peripheral vision: the ability to be attentive to multiple demands and to think about more than one thing at a time. And I think that's a very valuable trait that mothers do have. And sometimes we think of ourselves as being scattered and airheads because of it, and that's been oftentimes how we've been portrayed, but this is a wonderful, wonderful trait that mothers develop especially in the first few years.

Irene: Well, we have eyes in the backs of our heads, right?

Beth: Exactly.

Irene: But we are also able to keep lots of balloons in the air, which means that what we do is, you get up in the morning and you say, "I need to do this and this and this, and I need to go to work, and what's for dinner besides."

Beth: Exactly.

Irene: You get it all in order before you leave the house in the morning.

Beth: Right, and you can take your needs into account as well as the needs of many other individuals, which is extremely important in this day and age. I mean we no longer can afford ecologically to have a one-track mind. We can no longer afford it in the family, in the work place, and I think that's something that women very much have to offer, especially mothers.

Irene: I think that the "me" generation is over.

Selection 5   A Dad on the road

[Andrea Van Steenhouse comments on a solution to a previous call about a woman who is having problems with a small child because the husband is frequently out of town:]

Andrea: I got a really nifty fax from someone who heard the call from the woman whose husband is out of town, and she's having trouble with her 3-year-old. And if you remember, the 3-year-old was really missing dad, and was just basically going nuts. These were her comments, and I hope that woman is listening, or perhaps someone else that might've had a similar ordeal. Instead of getting upset when he cried for his dad, she says she commiserated with her son about how they both missed daddy and looked forward to his return. And I'll tell you, nothing cures that kind of whining than to whine with them. And I don't mean it negatively, but when you say, "Oh, gee, me too. Isn't this awful?" You are not the enemy anymore and something changes. It may not be exactly the direction you want, but things change when you do that. Secondly, she said, "I let him know I was excited about all the special time we could spend alone together and did things with him that his dad doesn't particularly like to do: trips to the library, bike rides, art projects, walks, etc." She really felt like in the stretches that dad was gone, that was a really productive way for her to handle that. Her 3-year-old seemed to respond. So if that's something that you're wrestling with, or if that person is still listening, you might wanna try some of those suggestions.

Selection 6   A Dad in the air

[Andrea Van Steenhouse takes a call from another traveling father who has a solution to help his son adjust to his absence:]

Jack: I just heard you talking about a person with a 3-year-old that missed his dad while he was on a trip, and I didn't hear the original call, but I fly for an airline, and I'm out of town three or four—sometimes five days a week. And what we....we have a 17-year-old now, but I think really is a well-adjusted, super kid. But when he was about two or so, we put up a map of the U.S. up on the wall in his bedroom. And we discussed about where I was gonna go, and then we marked the towns with pins, and then my wife would discuss with him while I was gone where I was. And it worked great, I mean.

Andrea: That's a great idea. Kids love those pins.

Jack: Not only that, but he knows more about geography than geography teachers.

Andrea: You bet, you bet.

Jack: I mean it, in the U.S.

Andrea: Well, and they like knowing...that's funny you should mention it. We ended up in a store...into Eatons in Vancouver, and grownups were standing in line to get pins to put a pin in where they were from. All over the world, people wanted to put a pin in their town. I mean it's sort of the reverse of it, but certainly two or three isn't too young to start that. I just hope that this dad doesn't go to Topeka every week. It might make it kind of hard if he went to the same place every week.

Jack: Actually it isn't. You can still make a game out of it. You can talk about the towns that he's gonna pass through, and I used to bring home, as he got older, I would bring home some of the, y'know, the "Welcome to Des Moines" things that the Chamber of Commerce puts out....

Andrea: That's a great idea.

Jack: And we even let him plan one of the trips. We did a long weekend in Boston and let him plan all the activities while we were in Boston. And you have to have a little bit of patience if you do the fifth tour of Old Ironsides, but...

Andrea: What a resourceful way to go about this! Good for you guys.

Jack: It's worked great.

Andrea: I appreciate that comment and it's interesting when you take it as something that might be kind of fun instead of as a drag. What a great suggestion to make a game out of it. But the burden is on the parent at home with the child, but I tell you what: if you have the choice of listening to him cry and whine and throw temper tantrums, and figuring out a way how to have a game out of it, I would certainly vote for the latter.

 ## Chapter 23   Stepfamilies

Selection 7   Stepfamilies

[In Selections 7 through 10, Irene Rawlings interviews Judith Bond about stepfamilies from a social worker's point of view:]

Irene: Our guest today is Judith Bond. She is a licensed clinical social worker at the Aurora Community Mental Health Center. And we're talking to her because she is presenting a seminar; The Adolescent Issues Series Seminar at Presbyterian/St. Luke's Hospital will feature something called "The Stepfamily Challenge." And she tells us that by the year 2000, there will be more stepfamilies than any other kind of family. And this is...her seminar is geared to this. Thanks so much for joining us, Judith—really appreciate it. Why don't you tell us what your seminar will feature? What will you talk about? You know, we...stepfamilies are a little bit...y'know, "stepmother" is a scary word, isn't it? I mean...

Judith: ...for everybody.

Irene: I mean, for the mother and for the children. Because, y'know, there are always wicked stepmothers; I don't think there were ever any good stepmothers in any of the literature that we read, were there?

Judith: Not in any of the fairy tales that are in our culture. No, it's always the wicked stepmother or the abusive stepfather, or the poor stepchild.

Irene: Mm-hmm. Yeah.

Judith: So stepfamilies had a lot of negative cultural stereotypes that come along with them.

Some people are now using the term "blended family." But our society calls stepmothers "stepmothers," stepfathers "stepfathers," and stepchildren "stepchildren," and we have not come up with a new word that's going to give a better connotation.

Irene: Just a kinder word all around.

Judith: Right. So possibly what we're needing to do is start having good stepmothers in the literature and good stepfathers, and happy stepfamilies. We need more books showing stepfamily situations. We need more shows on TV.

Selection 8   Yours, mine, and ours

[Selection 7 continues:]

Irene: What kind of education should people have before they enter a stepfamily situation? You hear, for example, a mother will say, will have her child say, or her new spouse's child say, "You can't tell me that; you're not my mother." "You can't boss me; you're not my mother." I've heard that a lot from friends of mine who've gotten remarried, and I feel sure that the husband hears, y'know, from his kids, the opposite side, y'know, "You can't boss me; you're not my father." "You don't have anything to do...I'm gonna go home to my real father." What kind of education do people have to have to deal with situations like that which are really quite common?

Judith: I believe what our seminar offers is we talk about the differences between nuclear families—we go through all the stages of a nuclear family, which most of us know about. Y'know, two people come together, they have a honeymoon—they get married, they spend time together, they learn how they are going to interact together, and then they decide to have a child. And then they have nine months to prepare for that child. And then they start developing their parenting skills with that child. And the children come one by one.

Stepfamilies start out totally different: first of all, they have this fantasy when they meet each other that the person who is going to be the stepparent, or potentially a stepparent will look at the biological parent, and they automatically go, "Oh, isn't this person just wonderful?" And whether it's a mother or a father, it's like, "She's such a great mother," or "He's such a great father." And they walk in thinking that person is this great parent, and that somehow they're just gonna step in and be a partner with that person. The biological parent on the other hand is going, "I'm looking for a new mate. I'm looking for someone to replace—to be a new mom to my children, a new mother." But what they are doing many times in their own mind the fantasy is they are recreating the nuclear family. "We are going to become a family again, just like we had before." That is a fantasy; that is not gonna happen.

Irene: I don't guess it ever happens, does it? There are...

Judith: No. It can't happen. Possibly in—I mean there might be a 1% chance if a former spouse died, but even there you've got issues, because what happens many times with a stepfamily where the former spouse is dead is they have glorified and put a halo on the dead parent—or the dead mom or dead dad. And the children have said, y'know, in their minds this parent can do no wrong, and even though there may have been lots of problems in the family, lots of problems in the marriage or some problems, there are no problems once that parent dies, or that spouse dies.

Irene: You know that happened to me when I was a kid. My dad died when I was six; my mother kind of...she was in her 40's, and she had dates. Y'know, gentlemen came to take her to dinner. I mean, it wasn't a date like a date, but she did put perfume on her wrists, and y'know, she was ready to go out.

Judith: You knew it was a date.

Irene: Yes, and it really...I brought out pictures of my father and put little paper garlands around them, and all this kind of thing. And many years later, I was consumed with guilt thinking that because I had done all this as a kid, that she had never gotten remarried. She then told me, well if she'd wanted to get married—remarried—she would've got remarried despite what I was doing. But I wonder how many kids do put obstacles in their parents' way when the parent is looking for a new relationship or a new—to put a new family together.

Judith: I believe most children do, whether it's conscious or unconscious. I do not believe there is a child...that's not true, that's not true. I believe <u>most</u> children want their parents to be reunited. And so when they see one parent starting to date again, that's starting to destroy that fantasy. And they may genuinely like this person a lot; and they may even accept this person as long as they're just a date to their parent. But once the family comes together, there can be problems. I mean, there could be problems before the marriage; there could be problems after the marriage. But I believe there will eventually be problems, because the children are gonna lose some status the minute that their parent remarries.

One of the things that most people don't realize for children, when their parent remarries, is that the children become members of a third family. Most people think it's a second family; it's not. Their first family is their nuclear parent family: mom and dad together. Their second family happens after the parents divorce and they have two single parent families. That's their second family. And what happens many times during that second family is generational boundaries kind of break down; they fade. And where a mom or a father may have had more closeness with their spouse when they were married, they start to develop that spouse [sic: closeness] with children. They also start setting up rules with the kids together; they include the kids in the rules. They let the kids help make decisions about money matters, about TV, about what they're gonna eat, where they're gonna go on vacation. It's a very natural thing to happen in a single parent family. It is not a natural thing to happen with two adults and a family.

Irene: And then also the non-custodial parent often tends to spoil the children, y'know, when you have two single households, where you live and where you hang out and where you stand in front of the refrigerator too long and the parent yells at you to shut the refrigerator. That's one household. The other household is the one where you visit, and there, a lot of things are possible that are not possible in other places. So you do get a little bit spoiled by the non-custodial parent who—whether he or she wants to—spends a little more time, a little more money, y'know, the gifts may be a little more elaborate, the vacations may be a little further away...maybe not to Telluride, but to Mexico or to China or Paris, or something like that. And then...then the parents remarry, and then there are other concerns, other families...

Judith: Yes...yes.

Irene: And then the money, even the non-custodial parent then has a family to worry about, and the money just doesn't flow, the attention doesn't flow quite as much as it used to.

Judith: And I believe that can happen in joint-custody families too where both parents, I mean, are sharing custody. There can be some subtle rivalry, some subtle competition about who's